HAMISH MACINNES

THE FOX OF GLENCOE

First published in 2021 by Scottish Mountaineering Press.

Second edition published in 2026 by Scottish Mountaineering Press.

Copyright © Hamish MacInnes and individual authors 2021.

All photos © Hamish MacInnes Collection unless otherwise stated.

The authors and contributors have asserted their rights under the Copyright, Design and Patents Act 1988 to be identified as the authors of this work.

All material in this book has been edited or rewritten. Some sections have previously been published in significantly different form elsewhere.

A catalogue record of this book is available from the British Library.

ISBN: 978-1-907233-63-0

All rights reserved. No part of this publication may be reproduced, stored in or introduced into a retrieval system, or transmitted in any form or by any means (electronic, mechanical, photocopying, recording or otherwise), without the prior written permission of the publisher.

Every effort has been made to obtain the necessary permissions with reference to copyright material. We apologise for any omission in this respect and will be pleased to make the appropriate acknowledgements in any future edition.

Designed by Gino Di Meo Studio.
Production by Rob Lovell

Printed in the UK by CPI UK limited.

HAMISH MACINNES

THE FOX OF GLENCOE   EDITED BY DEZIREE WILSON

Scottish
Mountaineering
Press

CONTENTS

The Fox of Glencoe
By Sir Chris Bonington
Page 7

Knowing Hamish
By Sir Michael Palin
Page 9

01. A Brief Sojourn
to the Matterhorn
Page 14

02. Misadventures on the
Charmoz-Grépon and a Drainpipe
Page 20

03. Murder in the Marmolada
Page 25

04. A Sermon on the Pulpit
Page 30

05. Uncommon Men
Page 34

06. Goddess Mother of
the World
Page 40

07. A Festive Encounter with
Mount Rudolf's West Face
Page 46

08. A Contested First
Ascent of Couloir Peak
Page 51

09. A Long Climb in the Antipodes
Page 54

10. Perambulations on Mount Cook
Page 60

11. Retreat from Rakaposhi
Page 68

Recollections from Rakaposhi
By Mike Banks
Page 76

12. The Kingdom of Hunza
Page 78

13. In the Footsteps of the Masters
Page 82

14. Thirteen Days on Shkhelda Ridge with Four Days of Food
Page 90

A Shepherd's Tale
By Walter Elliot
Page 102

15. The Great Herdsman of Etive
Page 106

16. The Glencoe School of Winter Climbing
Page 110

The MacInnes Stretcher
Page 116

17. A Mini, a Train and a Corpse
Page 118

Observations on a Rescue
By John Cleare
Page 125

18. The Cuillin Ridge in Winter
Page 128

19. Stacks of Fun
Page 144

20. The Evolution of the Terrordactyl
Page 150

21. A First Ascent in the Frosty Caucasus
Page 156

22. The Lost World
Page 174

23. Hobbling Around on the Eiger
Page 194

24. Not All That Glitters
Page 206

25. Among my Souvenirs
Page 216

26. The Drongs
Page 220

27. A Cabin by the Sea
Page 226

28. Chicken in a Basket
Page 246

29. Jaguars in Glen Coe
Page 251

30. Kilts, Claymores and Cameras
Page 254

31. Y-Fronts Rescue
Page 260

32. Across the Divide
Page 266

33. Journey's End
Page 268

Editor's Note
Page 275

Publisher's Note
Page 277

THE FOX OF GLENCOE
By Sir Chris Bonington CVO, CBE, DL

Hamish was my oldest and closest friend. I first met him when I was staying in Lagangarbh, a climbers' hut at the head of Glen Coe. I was 16 and had only been climbing for a year, so I was very lucky to fall in with Hamish, who was about five years older than me and already a very talented mountaineer.

Because I was the only person around, Hamish introduced me to winter climbing, and together we made the first winter ascent of Raven's Gully on Buachaille Etive Mòr, a major testpiece at the time. Over the years, we shared many experiences in the mountains, and he joined me on some of my biggest and most important Himalayan expeditions. He looked after all the oxygen equipment and designed specialist box tents for our failed attempt on the South West Face of Everest in 1972, and he accompanied me again as Deputy Leader in 1975, when our team finally succeeded in reaching the summit.

'The Fox of Glencoe', an affectionate reference to Hamish's cunning as a mountaineer and rescuer, was a very appropriate nickname. He was such an original, a complete individualist, steering his own course through life, never bothering about what others might think of him. Multi-talented and at times eccentric, he was a truly amazing man who contributed so much to our sport in so many ways.

KNOWING HAMISH
By Sir Michael Palin KCMG, CBE, FRGS

Looking back, I realise now that, long before I met him, a Hamish-like figure occupied a unique place in my life. Lean, taciturn, fearless and resourceful, he was a combination of the adventurous qualities I admired so much, but that growing up in suburban Sheffield had offered me little chance to emulate.

Despite this, our paths would surely never have crossed had it not been for a quality my firm-faced heroes rarely displayed: a sense of fun. When I first saw Hamish in action, he was not saving lives in a snow-filled gully or hauling himself to the top of some previously unclimbed peak. He was on the slopes of Glen Coe, hurling dummy knights in armour off the Bridge of Death and into the Gorge of Eternal Peril as we filmed Monty Python and the Holy Grail. This was my introduction to the man and his manner.

Hamish and I bonded not so much over ice axes or expeditions, but as fellow appreciators of the unorthodox and eccentric. Here was a man who would take infinite care inching a wounded climber down a mountainside one minute, and the next drive a high-performance car at Formula One speeds along public roads.

Not long before his death, I was commiserating with Hamish over the passing of the days when he had sped through Glen Coe in an E-Type Jaguar when he gave me one of his quick and mischievous half-smiles and admitted that he had recently acquired a Ford Mustang of enormous power. Seeing my startled reaction, he quickly added, 'But I only drive it at night.' My eyes widened. 'At night?' I queried. 'Why at night?'
'No police around.'

Time spent with Hamish was never wasted. As he was describing some new design for a stretcher or something similar, he'd break off for an aside about Sean Connery or a suggestion that had just popped into his head. 'Have you ever climbed K2, Michael?' There was nothing he couldn't do, and nothing he thought I couldn't do.

He liked danger but never for its own sake; it had to be part of a constructive experience. Risk was assumed and evaluated but never allowed to stand in the way of a challenge. It was an essential part of life. The most hazardous, frightening and unforgettable climb I ever did was not in the Andes or the Himalayas but on the Aonach Eagach Ridge in Glen Coe. Hamish, knowing that my son was a keen climber, arranged and filmed it all and called in the helicopter to take us off the ridge just ahead of a rapidly approaching blizzard.

Hamish's horizons stretched much wider than those of most mortals. To be with him was to experience and be seduced by the infinite potential of life. Whatever it was, it was worth a go. He was as proud of designing an ice axe as he was of making his own 'birch wine' from the sap of silver birch trees. He wasn't sentimental—he'd seen too many people die in the mountains. Yet he cared mightily for the ducks that would gather outside his door at Tigh a' Voulin in Glencoe. He had a hard-nosed grip on reality but found an outlet as a prolific writer of fiction.

Even when he seemed at his most vulnerable, coping with the crisis that saw him confined to a forbidding psychiatric hospital near Inverness, he found his own unique way of dealing with it. I visited him there and noticed that he didn't sleep in the bed but rather in a sleeping bag on top of it. His way of dealing with incarceration was to treat it like an expedition, the same attitude that later saw him climb onto the roof of the hospital in protest. While most of the patients there could hardly move, Hamish was off up the mountain.

He defied the illness and recovered from his near-death experience in typical Hamish-like fashion. Not for him an armchair and slippers. Instead, he took to the task of downloading his vast collection of photographs as a way of, as he put it, 'recreating my memory'—using the past to build his future. And the thing about Hamish was that, despite his success in facing so many challenges, pride was not the point. For Hamish, pride was as fleeting as one of his swift smiles. Doing things, making things, climbing things and writing things was what kept him going. But there was one condition: it had to be done better than anyone had ever done it before.

I valued his friendship as much as any other in my life. Because it was unlike any other. Yes, that I hope would have fulfilled Hamish's criteria: a friendship unlike any other.

Anti-clockwise from below:

Hamish as a toddler
© Effie MacInnes Tod

Hamish with sisters Effie,
Christina and Flora
and brother Archibald
© Effie MacInnes Tod

Hamish aged 21, running rock climbing courses on the Isle of Skye for the Scottish Youth Hostel Association

01. A BRIEF SOJOURN TO THE MATTERHORN

In the summer of 1948, I was a young climber of 18 living in Greenock on the West Coast of Scotland, and I had an urge to see the wider—and higher—world. The aftermath of the Second World War had left its mark, and ration books and bread tokens reflected the austerity of the times. The allowance for overseas travellers was a measly £5, which limited my means but didn't dampen my enthusiasm.

My mode of travel was hitchhiking, and I set off wearing my Black Watch kilt, which had been kindly donated by a brother-in-law whose waistline had now expanded. As a regiment, The Black Watch had been renowned throughout the two world wars as 'The Ladies from Hell' and, rather naively, I thought my kilt would serve as a passport rather than a reminder of more hostile times.

My first port of call was Dover, and there was more hitching than hiking to get there. Happily, the very morning I arrived, jam came off the ration list. I was able to gorge myself with a jar of delicious raspberry jam as a birthday treat, but I had to stump up some of my precious bread coupons in the process.

As I waited on the docks for the ferry, my meagre holiday budget sunk in. How could I survive on my Matterhorn quest with only £5? As I pondered this, a well-kent voice from Greenock hailed me. It was W.H. Thompson, a garage owner, inventor and local politician. Salvation! A short time beforehand, I had attended one of his flamboyant meetings, where Councillor Thompson had sought to persuade a recalcitrant audience he meant business by wielding a fire axe whilst clad in an Air Raid Precautions (ARP) boiler suit topped with a steel helmet. His props included an Anderson air-raid shelter and a portable siren. It had been a convincing show.

Today, however, he was on the dockside in a pinstriped suit, having just returned from a business trip to France. I asked if he could lend me some francs, assuring him that my dad, a respected businessman, would pay him back. 'No problem,' he replied, for he understood the penury of non-business travellers like me. Clutching my newly acquired fortune in French currency—the equivalent of around £30 at the time—I boarded the ferry, resolved to vote for the re-election of councillor Thompson in his respective ward, with or without his props.

Landing in Calais, Lady Luck smiled on me again for, shortly after taking to the road, thumb raised hopefully, an Austin 16 1945 glided to a halt beside me. (I knew a fair bit about cars, having recently built a roadworthy vehicle from scratch.) The benevolent driver was a distinguished-looking gent with a ruddy face, nicotine-stained teeth and an Irish brogue.

'Now, would ye be after a lift, laddie?' he said.

'Yes,' I replied. 'I'm heading to Switzerland.'

'Well, now, jump in and mind the kilt. I'm going there—eventually.'

I could scarcely believe my luck. Eyeing a pile of sandwiches and a bottle of Irish whisky, I realised that my saviour was also a gourmet. It transpired that my new friend was a racehorse owner from Dublin, and he was on a mission to visit all the cathedrals in northern France. After some ten days pounding the stone floors of the august shrines, I learned enough about saints and martyrs to write a treatise—quite a confession for a nonbeliever.

I found the flatlands of France somewhat dull, but I perked up as we crossed the border into Switzerland and I could see snow-clad mountains. My generous companion—whose name I never learned—bade me *adieu* just south of Interlaken. He was, like so many of his kind, a good Samaritan.

After wangling free bed and breakfast at an opulent hotel on the summit of one of the high passes, I had a good night's sleep, despite the hard wooden boards of the communal sleeping platform.

At 5:00 am, I ate a hearty breakfast and took to the road again, heading for Visp. I was dusty and hungry but excited to be in the mountains once more. Passing through the quaint streets of the old town, a kind-hearted woman in a red headscarf pointed to a table and chair outside her log cabin and motioned me to sit. Even after all these years, I still remember the delicious bowl of salad and the glass of apfelsaft she brought me. *Berg heil!*

I hit the road again with a new spring in my step. I was almost there. Suddenly, the Matterhorn dominated the view. An elegant, celestial finger pointing to the heavens, it had a profound effect on me. Later, I associated

The East Face of the Matterhorn
© John Cleare

the scene with Oscar Wilde's *The Ballad of Reading Gaol*. It may seem like a strange comparison, but it pulled the same strings:

> *I never saw a man who looked*
> *With such a wistful eye*
> *Upon that little tent of blue*
> *Which prisoners call the sky,*
> *And at every wandering cloud that trailed*
> *Its ravelled fleeces by.*

In Zermatt, I found lodgings at the Hotel Bahnhof, where hosts Bernard Biner and his sister were sympathetic to my plight. I left my kilt and rucksack with them and made an early start in perfect weather with my well-worn climbing clothes and homemade anorak, clutching my modified ice axe, obtained from the Glasgow Barras market as a 'coal pick, guid for the cellar'.

Walking up the narrow streets, I felt I was in Valhalla, with the ghosts of those first ascensionists, Whymper, Taugwalder and Croz lurking in the shadows of the doorways. I took the trail branch beyond the town to the Matterhorn, whose countenance now seemed more forbidding. There were few fellow travellers, and I relished the solitude.

This was long before the advent of cable cars, and it was a hot slog up to the glacial lake of Schwarzsee at over 6,000 ft. I was relieved that I had left my ill-conceived Bergen rucksack back in the hotel in Zermatt and rejoiced in the crisp air, the distant clang of cowbells and the serenity of it all. Eventually, I reached the Hörnli Hut, which was nothing to write home about in those days, but I didn't stop; I had a strict schedule.

Finally on steeper ground, I realised I was near the edge of the North Face of the Matterhorn where the Solvay refuge hut clings precariously to the rock. I now had to keep a wary eye as the odd boulder bounced down the face, seeking a target.

I progressed carefully upwards on more treacherous terrain to the fixed ropes at The Shoulder; no ice, thank goodness! This had been the scene of great Victorian tragedy back in 1865, when, after a triumphant party led by Edward Whymper claimed the first ascent of the mountain, four of the climbers fell down the North Face to their deaths during the descent. The fatalities shook the mountaineering world, and even parliament raised questions. Whymper, who had unfairly shouldered most of the blame for the accident, saw his world collapse, and the memories of that day became his constant companions, haunting him everywhere he went:

> 'Every night, do you understand, I see my comrades of the Matterhorn slipping on their backs, their arms outstretched, one after the other, in perfect order at equal distances—Croz the guide, first, then Hadow, then Hudson, and lastly Douglas. Yes, I shall always see them...'

Later, he wrote:

> 'Climb if you will, but remember that courage and strength are naught without prudence, and a momentary negligence can destroy the happiness of a lifetime; do nothing in haste; look well to each step and think at the beginning what may be the end.'

Feeling somewhat melancholic, I climbed the exposed wire cable to reach the Swiss summit with a breeze from the Schönbiel side and the Swiss and Italian summit crosses glinting in the distance. I felt an aura of tranquillity in this lofty place, as I would find later in the Himalayas. There were plenty of ghosts up there with nailed boots and alpenstocks. I raised my Barras ice axe in salutation to the two crosses and made haste back to Zermatt, where I relaxed after conquering the grotty face of that magnificent heap of rubble in a single, sweaty day.

N.B. It has been widely reported that Hamish was only 16 when he travelled to the Alps to climb the Matterhorn. His own account of being, in fact, 18 is supported by his recollection of 'gorging' himself on jam as it had just come off the ration list—post Second World War rationing only began to lift after 1948.

The Nantillons Face
of the Charmoz-Grépon
© Dave Cuthbertson

02. MISADVENTURES ON THE CHARMOZ-GRÉPON AND A DRAINPIPE

Looking back through time, one tends to remember events in the mountains through rose-tinted snow goggles: the thrill of a wonderful panorama or a blood-red sunset, rather than monotonous hikes up moraines and glaciers, or indeed the many mishaps and misadventures that punctuate a lifetime of climbing.

As an eager and impecunious youth, I travelled to Chamonix to see for myself what all the fuss was about. I wasn't disappointed. As the bus wound its way up the valley, jagged granite spires pierced a cerulean sky for as far as my eye could see. Here was a lifetime's worth of climbing, and I was eager to start exploring. Upon arrival, I repaired to Snell Sports in the centre of the town, where Messieurs Snell imparted information to mountaineers, irrespective of making a sale. Coffee and conversation flowed freely, and there were plenty of animated discussions to be had about conditions, the latest climbing equipment and other important matters. I was looking for a guidebook in English, for I had a plan. As I browsed, an athletic-looking individual at the counter addressed me in English. I noticed that he had a mountain guide badge and a companion, an English client who was buying some Piz Buin and a pair of gloves.

'Are you going climbing?' he said.

'Yes,' I replied. 'I want to do the Charmoz-Grépon Traverse.'

'Alone?' he asked quizzically.

'Well, er, yes,' I replied.

A true Alpine classic, the Charmoz-Grépon had captured my imagination ever since I first heard of it, and I was intent on completing a solo ascent of this famous mountain journey.

My interrogator continued to study me with interest for a while, and as his client finished paying, he turned to me again.

'I may be able to help you. We're doing that climb tomorrow. You could solo behind us and you wouldn't need a guidebook.'

Amazed at his generosity, I gratefully accepted the offer, not realising that I was speaking to Lionel Terray, probably the greatest of all Chamonix guides. Much, much later, having spent 30 years as leader of the Glencoe Mountain Rescue Team, I mused on how it is sometimes preferable to keep an eye on someone when you know they are determined on a rash course of action rather than try to dissuade them.

The next day, we set off, chatting amiably until we reached the start of difficulties, whereupon guide and client roped up. I had a rope, too, casually coiled over my shoulder. I followed within earshot of the duo, feeling somewhat overwhelmed by the magnitude of the great face and the architecture of its immense walls and towers. With youthful confidence, I was eager to get to grips with the climb and didn't consider that I might have bitten off more than I could chew. Lionel belayed his client up an awkward-looking narrow fissure I later learned was the famous Mummery Crack, the hardest pitch on the route, named after the famous Victorian English mountaineer Albert F. Mummery. Lionel took a keen interest in how I fared on this tricky ground, amusedly referring to me as the 'guideless Aberdonian'. As we ascended, so the difficulties increased, and I surmised that I must have passed muster, for he left me to it.

The three of us moved efficiently over the terrain, and we reached the summit in blazing sunshine. Surrounded by lofty spires and pinnacles, we had lunch, and Lionel asked, 'Do you like our mountains then, Hamish?'

'Sure thing,' I replied, as I relished my simple meal of dried figs. 'They're a bit bigger than my crags back home in Scotland.'

After taking some time to savour our accomplishment and the view from our mountain eyrie, we made our way to the abseil point. Lionel threaded his rope through a tape sling, which was secured on a rock bollard, and he belayed his client from above. I planned to use my own rope, and I sunned myself on a rock while I waited my turn. The descent was a vertical wall of about 40 ft which terminated on a tiny ledge, and from here there was a drop of around 600 ft to the glacier below. I waited until Lionel reached the ledge and threaded my rope through the sling without a second thought. Just as I put my full weight on the sling, it snapped, and I found myself plunging earthwards. I struck the ledge below with great force, my legs jack-knifing up beneath me, my knees doubling up and impacting my eyes with a force that blinded me. I also managed to hit my head along the way.

Lionel heard my cry and scrambled up, dragging me in from the narrow ledge which had providently and abruptly cut short my rapid descent. Just then, he spotted his friend and fellow guide Raymond Lambert descending the face of the Grépon and called for his help. Raymond was accompanied by an aspirant guide, and he sent his prodigy down to get help.

With the assistance of the two guides, I somehow managed to climb down, facing inward, as I couldn't put weight on my heels. By gently rubbing my eyes, I could see vague outlines, but I was otherwise blind.

Since those early days as a rescuee, I have been in charge of hundreds of call-outs, many resulting in death. Without wishing to be morbid, I got used to seeing corpses, mutilated to an extent rarely witnessed except in the trenches, such as my father had seen at Passchendaele.

My accident occurred in a time of self-reliance, with no helicopters, mobile phones or instant forecasts, but I had been 'lucky', for two of the greatest Alpine mountaineers had been at hand.

In those days, Chamonix hospital was renowned as the place for broken bones and trauma. While I recuperated there, some of my scruffy climbing friends invaded the sanctity of the ward and promised to throw a party as soon as I was released. Thankfully, my head wound wasn't life-threatening and I left the hospital after a few days, albeit with the gait of a clumsy ballet dancer.

During the celebrations, my mental faculties, which had been improving since the accident, declined after excessive consumption of wine, and I was told later by a relatively sober pal that I had climbed up the drainpipe of a tall building. The pipe was made of rolled steel, so it appeared to be a safe way up to the gutter. Unfortunately, the clips holding it to the wall were not of comparable strength, and it had buckled underneath me, acting like a hinge. I had swung down and out for about 20 ft like a character in a Charlie Chaplin film, until the pipe had collapsed and I had fallen like a rag doll to the pavement, whereupon I was dragged face-down by my drunken friends straight back to Chamonix hospital.

I want to pay tribute to all who took part in getting me off the Charmoz-Grépon, especially Lionel and Raymond. I met Raymond again a few years later after his Everest expeditions, and I discovered he had suffered a fate worse than my own. He had been caught in a horrendous blizzard in the French Alps, and all his toes had to be amputated. Within a few months of this, however, he was climbing hard rock again.

'You know, Scotchman,' he told me wryly, 'I am climbing better than before—there is less leverage!'

Tragically, Lionel died while rock climbing in the Vercors, south of Grenoble, when he was only 44. Not many people knew that he fought for France with the French Resistance in the Second World War. He was a real hero. Vive la montagne.

The Charmoz is seen on the left, the Grépon on the right
© Dave Cuthbertson

03. MURDER IN THE MARMOLADA

If you take to the hills at a young age, you will inevitably serve as an apprentice or tea boy until you can prove that you are no longer an aspirant but a dependable young mountaineer. This is not a dull process, however, for as well as learning new skills, there are myriad places to explore and new horizons to be gleaned.

When I was still a teenager, I was taken under the wing of Derek Haworth, a keen mountaineer from a well-to-do family in Blackpool who had studied medicine at Edinburgh but failed his finals due to a fondness for climbing, fast motorbikes and women.

Derek was a knight of a latter age and one of the leading climbers at the time. His legacy of new routes both at home and in the Alps included Suicide Groove in Wales, Crack of Double Doom on Skye, Surgeon's Gully on Ben Nevis and the first British ascent of the Mittellegi Ridge on the Eiger—a remarkable feat at the time. He also had a four-valve Rudge motorbike, which he rode like a maniac as I perched precariously on the pillion in pursuit of new adventures.

Eager to explore the wider world, I persuaded Derek to ride out to the Marmolada in the Italian Dolomites, a veritable limestone fortress of rock faces, gullies and buttresses on a scale that can seem overwhelming to the uninitiated. It seemed like just the place for me to develop my newly acquired mountaineering skills.

After two full days of travelling at top speed on Derek's Rudge, we arrived in the gathering dusk and hiked up through Alpine meadows, where wild flowers waltzed gracefully in the gloaming. Toiling up toward the apron of the Marmolada wall, we crossed a newly mown pasture and spied a quaint barn. The carved wooden doors were open and, in the fading light, we could see that it was full of dry hay. With the thankfulness of travellers stumbling upon an oasis, we took off our rucksacks and stamped out two crude circular nests to bed down on, hoping for a few hours shut-eye before our attempt of the face. I unearthed a torch from my pack, and as the beam swung round, I saw a man's head protruding from the hay. The startled resident spoke no English, and we spoke no Italian, but we greeted each other with a nod.

I unpacked some dates and a couple of apples, and we ate a silent repast. As I settled down to sleep, I discovered a hayfork beneath me and counted myself lucky that I hadn't sat on it. Later, I realised that it could have come in handy.

We rose early the next day so as to avoid getting benighted on the route, but the sun was already stealing across the snow on the highest peaks. The low reflected light from the stars filtered through the open barn doors, eerily illuminating the head of our sleeping companion as we bade him a silent goodbye. I envied him his rest.

I don't recall much of the route, but we climbed unroped for as long as possible. Derek, like a diligent boy scout, was well prepared. A bibliophile, he had with him an original guidebook with a description of the face in German, which he translated for me. I went into relax mode, relying on my friend to do both thinking and route finding. After all, I was an apprentice.

Eventually, we tied on to Derek's new-fangled hawser-laid nylon rope, unique at the time in this war-ravaged country. Derek set a hard pace, and we climbed together up steeper rock without stopping, although, as a gesture to safety, he placed the occasional sling runner over a rock spike, which I recovered *en passant*—a risky technique that is still used today, though not recommended.

As we negotiated the harder sections, I recalled that an English governess named Beatrice Tomassen had, with two top Swiss guides, made the first female ascent of the south side of the mountain in 1901, and I mused on this remarkable feat and the rudimentary equipment they would have used.

Dusk was creeping in as we reached the summit, but back then there was no *téléphérique* down the gentler side of the mountain that is now popular with skiers. In proper darkness, we had to negotiate ice without crampons to reach a glassy wire rope hanging down the ridge, where today there is a chunky via ferrata handrail to grab hold of.

We stopped at a narrow ledge and agreed that we should bivvy before descending any further. Like all such pensions, it was spartan, and I reminisced about all that lovely warm hay in the barn.

The South Face of the
Marmolada in profile
© John Cleare

The following day, we descended to a snug, sun-drenched café in a small hamlet. Next to our table was a notice board, which functioned as the local newspaper. As we ordered coffee and croissants, Derek spotted a poster with the headline:

'WANTED FOR MURDER'

'That's the hay man!' he cried. Sure enough, on the poster was a large drawing of our scarecrow friend—or fiend!—from the barn. It seemed that he had murdered an English girl, and her parents were offering a reward for his capture, the equivalent of several thousand pounds.

After gulping down our cappuccinos, we repaired to the local police station, where, in a whitewashed room, we signed our statements and gave our addresses. Needless to say, we never got the reward. Well, it was Italy.

Later, I learned that Derek had had an accident with his Rudge motorbike when he was heading back to Calais. A large truck had hit him coming out of a siding, and both Derek and his bike were catapulted into a field over a high hedge. The truck didn't stop, and Derek lay unconscious with a compound fracture of his leg. Eventually, he came to but couldn't move and no one heard his calls for help.

Two days later, he was found, and by then the wound was septic. He was taken to hospital in Calais, where, in true post-war style, they wanted to operate without anaesthetic. Thankfully, they sent him over to Dover, and after several months of recovery, Derek wrote to tell me that he had some convalescence leave coming up. Could I suggest a suitable easy climbing venue? At that time, I was stationed in the Austrian Tirol, where I climbed with the local guides, a gregarious but hard bunch, some of whom were ex-Wehrmacht. Sometimes we drove down into the Sud-Tirol, and on a couple of these sorties I had admired a trio of pinnacles known as the Vajolet Towers. I invited Derek to join me on an exploration of these shapely limestone spires (which were later used in the opening scene of the film *Cliffhanger*) and, despite his newly acquired limp, he was as keen as ever.

Relishing being back in the otherworldly landscape of the Dolomites, we made light work of the first two towers, Torre Delago and Torre Stabeler, which were quite straightforward at around grade IV+. The third tower, Torre Winkler, had an appealing fissure imaginatively named Winkler Crack running up its centre. We moved quickly in the fading light, and as I neared the top, a stone dislodged and whistled down, hitting Derek squarely on the head. He wasn't having much luck!

Abseiling down to Derek's tiny belay shelf, I saw his scalp was a bloody mess. Despite this, he was conscious and rummaging in his pocket for a heliograph, which can be used for both signalling in an emergency and as a small domestic shaving mirror. He squinted up at a reflected view of his injury.

'Separate the hairs into strands across the scalp wound, Hamish, then tie them together using one of those locking slip knots,' he instructed calmly.

I did as I was told, and after completing the DIY job on Derek's scalp, we retreated to the Rifugio Vajolet mountain hut close to the feet of the towers, where I caused a certain amount of consternation when I assured the residents that my friend required no further treatment. This was substantiated by the patient himself, however, and we drank our amber apfelsafts and bade *adieu*.

When Derek later emigrated to Canada, he and his wife Tine became renowned in the medical profession, made a fortune in real estate and generously supported the Banff Mountain Film Festival. I was delighted to see him again years later when I was a guest speaker at the festival but, despite now being a seasoned climber, I still felt like the apprentice as I recalled wind-blown days on the pillion of his Rudge motorbike going flat out over high Alpine passes.

Hamish would visit the Alps for weeks at a time with nothing but a rucksack and his stripped down Manx

04. A SERMON ON THE PULPIT

I was lucky to spend my time in national service in the Austrian Tirol at a leave centre in the French Zone for the British Army of the Rhine troops. The village was called Ehrwald, and it was an idyllic place dwarfed by the massif of the Wetterstein, a magnificent-looking lump of friable limestone. Luckily for us, army routine was non-existent there, and I spent several days a week in the mountains with local guides and members of the rescue team, putting up new routes such as the East Wall of the Hinterer Drachenkopf. Several of these climbers had been high up in the Wehrmacht, but politics were never discussed as I conversed with them in the local patois. It was an education for me, especially in the use of pitons, which were hand-forged from high-quality steel and unobtainable in the West at that time but in plentiful supply in nearby Garmish.

    I spent more time at my friend Hans Spielman's home—the Hotel Spielman—than at my own hostelry, the Hotel Sonnenspitze. Hans was often busy running the hotel, and when I couldn't find another climbing partner, I would solo routes. On one such venture, I suffered frostbite after removing my gloves on the first winter ascent of The New World, an impressive rock formation several hundred feet high. The resident doctor at the Sonnenspitze spent a few days looking at my blackened fingers and suggested amputation, for this was before penicillin was widely available. I refused, and instead my fingers were swathed in paraffin gauze for several weeks. They eventually recovered when they were exposed to fresh air, but the consequences of my exploits didn't go unnoticed, and I struggled to persuade anyone to climb with me except Hans or his pals on weekends.

    In the winter of 1949, I had earned a few days' leave from the Ehrwald Centre and planned to fulfil a longstanding ambition to repeat one of Herman Buhl's winter climbs: the Predigtstuhl, or Pulpit, in the Wilder Kaiser mountains in the Austrian Tirol.

I had met Herman but never climbed with him, making do with reports of his achievements in a local newspaper, which Hans's sister Elli would translate in the family's private lounge while their father hovered in the background, sipping red wine and nodding knowingly. A mountain guide and pioneer of Alpine-style mountaineering in the Himalayas, Herman was a world-class mountaineer even by modern standards, and he regularly succeeded on the most improbable climbs.

With high pressure and a reasonable forecast, conditions seemed perfect for my attempt on the route, but there was the perennial problem of finding someone to climb with. The usual Austrian gang were all busy, but I met a guest in the Sonnenspitze, a physical training instructor on vacation by the name of Dave Stuart and, over an apfelsaft, I asked if he would be interested in doing a winter climb with me. I told him it had been climbed before but didn't mention Herman as, not yet being a climber, Dave probably wouldn't have heard of him.

Two days later, we set off up the Predigtstuhl, which was well named, for it was a celestial-looking place in its icy winter garb. I had already kitted out my new friend with ten-point crampons and a Stubai North Wall hammer—a short axe with a hammer head instead of an adze at the blunt end. With his robust physique, climbing boots, woollen mitts and anorak, Dave looked the part at least. We also had the luxury of two 150 ft nylon climbing ropes— rare items in a country still suffering from post-war deprivation.

After wading through the interminable powder, we were confronted with the seriousness of our quest. We wrestled with our crampons, roped up, and I showed Dave the fundamentals of belaying and the hazards of wearing his newly-acquired lethal footwear. There was ice everywhere, reminiscent of a hard Scottish winter route. I mused that crampons seemed to be the wrong footwear, and better progress might be made in stockinged feet, something I had put to good effect back home on occasion.

As Dave followed me up the first pitch, it was clear he was an instinctive climber, a natural in this vertical playground and well-versed in handling ropes from his time in the gym. We got to grips with the climb and progressed slowly upwards. After a particularly tricky section, I reached a spot where I could insert a piton. It seemed sound enough, and I shouted down to Dave that I would haul both the rucksacks up and tie them onto the free rope. After a struggle, I managed to bring them up to a point just below my belay, but they got jammed under an overhang. Dave had clipped the North Wall hammer to one of the rucksacks, and as I tried to haul it up, the karabiner caught under on the rock and opened. The hammer spiralled down to the belay below, where it hit Dave pick first on top of his bare head. I feared he was dead as I lowered him down to a sloping ledge and secured the rope so that he couldn't slide off into the abyss.

When I reached Dave, he was alive but incapable of assisting with our necessary retreat; small wonder: a weaker person would have most likely succumbed to that trauma. I created a veneer of security by hammering in a peg amid the tangle of ropes and slings. There was so much space beneath our feet that I could barely get any purchase on our shallow ledge.

Recalling that I had a military shell dressing in my first aid box, I rummaged in my rucksack. I fashioned the dressing over Dave's head, tying the two lugs of the bandage under his chin and knotting it. A balaclava fitted snugly over the bandage. Dave now resembled a Victorian lady mountaineer with her coiffure secured by a scarf. Well, except for all the blood.

Lower down, as the angle eased, the difficulties increased, for I no longer had the assistance of gravity and Dave was by now barely mobile. Amid the fading crepuscular shadows, I could see our trail marked by a series of faraway dots in the vast expanse of snow. I knew that there was a mountain hut nearby, but where? The shadows had merged into a black void. At last, I found the hut, and as expected, it was locked up for the winter. I gave silent apologies as I used my ice axe to force the door, but this was an emergency, and I had to get Dave into shelter immediately and summon assistance.

We waited in that hut for a long time before help arrived—long enough for me to contemplate my recklessness. I knew that it had been a mistake to take someone so inexperienced on such a technical climb, even though this was something I had done before when lacking a climbing partner, as had many of my colleagues. This is probably why I later took to solo climbing, especially when compiling climbing guides, resolving that if I couldn't do the majority of the climbs myself, I couldn't complete the book.

There was a happy ending to this tale, though. Dave made a remarkable recovery after treatment at the Sonnenspitze from the overworked doctor who had treated my fingers for frostbite. Raising a finger and shaking his head, the good doctor rebuked me: 'At least on our last professional encounter, Hamish, the damage was self-inflicted!'

Hamish 'MacPiton' using tactics he learned in Austria to peg his way up Porcupine Wall on The Cobbler © John Cunningham

05. UNCOMMON MEN

I confess to having been in a dilemma for many years about whether to write about the infamous Creagh Dhu Club. I am indebted to Chris Lyons for taking on the daunting task of recording his own account in longhand during his lunch breaks at John Brown's shipyard in Clydebank and sending it to me. A member of the illustrious club himself, Chris was an accomplished bard and scribe who captured the essence of an era long gone. This exclusive group, which enrolled only 132 members in its 45-year history, was unique in many ways and survived the aftermath of the Great Depression, the Second World War and post-war austerity.

I, too, have written of my Elysian years with these hard climbers, most of whom had trained as wrestlers. Although I had to dig deep into my memory of over four score years, the time I spent with the Creagh Dhu Club was probably the most memorable of my life, and I was lucky to have such excellent teachers to show me the ropes.

Many of the club's members toiled amid the grime and smog of the Glasgow shipyards six days a week. On rare days off, they would walk or hitch from the city to tackle some of the hardest routes in Scotland, telling yarns round campfires long into the night as damp clothes steamed, and I, youthful and eager, listened enthralled until the embers reflected the dawn light. These men, among the very best climbers in Scotland, were criticised for being both aggressive and reckless. They were neither, but the 'yerds' they worked in were harsh environments and if you didn't fight for your rights, you went under. Recklessness implies incompetence, and it was just the opposite. They were supremely physically fit, and I weight-trained with them when climbing was still a recreation for toffs. Many of my first ascents were with Creagh Dhu Club members, usually Bill Smith and John Cunningham, who were some of the leading climbers of their generation. As a rule, we never 'bagged' summits after climbing, for fear that we would be classed as Munroists. That was for jessies!

The club members were ardent poachers, and those who later emigrated regularly returned for poaching holidays. After an incident involving an irate and drunken gamekeeper who discharged his 12-bore shotgun and shattered the bus's rear window, it was agreed that no rifles were allowed on board when there was poached deer in the boot.

Realising that a bus was too public and restrictive for weekend transport, some club members bought motorbikes on which they would race each other down Loch Lomondside. There was some fierce competition from other motorcycle clubs, one of which had a TT champion in its ranks.

Meanwhile, other rock tigers were on the loose. The Ptarmigan Club's Jock Nimlin was a hammerhead crane driver in Clydebank, and from his lofty cab he could see the hills of Arrochar. At clocking-off time on a Saturday evening, he and his friends would take a tramcar to Milngavie and hike to Balmaha on Loch Lomondside. A friendly local had given them the use of his rowing boat, and they would make their way across the loch at dusk, then hitch a lift on the milk lorry to Tarbet and onwards to The Cobbler, the jewel in the crown of the Arrochar Alps. Jock pioneered many hard routes here, much to the chagrin of the competitive Creagh Dhu Club members. Ardgartan Wall, an easy classic slabby line put up by Jock way back in 1937, had been my first rock climb as a fit 15-year-old, and I was soon hooked on the glinting corrugated folds of The Cobbler's mica schist walls. Probably the most idyllic and memorable, though not the most difficult, was Whither Whether, which remains a classic to this day. As I meandered up perfect rock on tiny rugosities, I could feel the exposure seeping through the soles of my climbing boots.

The Creagh Dhu Club's climbing was severely curtailed during the Second World War, but as soon as the restrictions were lifted, some of them formed the vanguard of British post-war Alpinists. In the dark days of the Great Depression, it was almost impossible to obtain equipment and clothing, and ex-army surplus was not yet on the market. En masse, they repaired to their favourite outfitters, the Glasgow Barras market, where they each bought the necessary garb for their prospective Alpine adventures.

With protracted bargaining, the cost per person was under £1. Furthermore, six lucky members were each given a pair of brand new postman's trousers. Dressed in these narrow-legged breeks with bright scarlet flashings, they cut dashing figures and were nicknamed the 'foreskin fusiliers' by their less fortunate club mates. Some of the others made their own lighter anoraks with blackout material obtained from the Royal Navy.

The club's first Alpine expedition was a success, and others soon took on some of the most classic routes. There followed ever more difficult ascents, some of which had not been climbed for six years. An attempt was even made on the North Face of the Matterhorn, but it had to be abandoned due to dangerous rockfall.

The club established a base camp just outside Zermatt and gave it the ignominious title The City Dump, a reference to the camp's insalubrious appearance. They were always glad to return to this urban howff after their sorties in the local mountains, but soon became aware of resentment brewing among the local guides, who couldn't understand the broad Glaswegian patois and had to suffer the indignity of shepherding tourists around as these hardened interlopers bagged some of the most difficult ice routes in the area.

Moreover, the club members insisted that the numerous scrapes they were involved in were due to circumstances outwith their control. During one attempt of the North Face of Lyskam, several club members were reported missing in a severe electrical storm that was accompanied by heavy snowfall. When the remaining club members were approached by the Swiss Rescue Service and quoted £200 to recover the bodies of their pals, they replied, 'We'll take our friends down when the storm clears.'

The Swiss hadn't realised the toughness and tenacity of the shipyard workers, who had in fact survived the 16-hour storm and had cut their way across to a ridge offering an escape line. They were met en route back to Zermatt by the Creagh Dhu Club rescue party. 'We were really worried last night,' said one. 'We thought you were going to cost the club a fortune!'

Back at base, the boys were interrupted by the chief guide and a local gendarme, who had decided that the brash foreigners would be run out of town.

With painstaking care, the gendarme laid down the law: Nobody was allowed to work in Switzerland without a work permit. Nobody was allowed to act as a mountain guide until they were qualified. No qualified mountain guide could be employed in the district without the permission of the chief guide, and so on.

There was muttering from club members. 'Bloody closed shop,' said one. 'Infringement of human rights,' grumbled another.

Alex Muir, a hard man even by Creagh Dhu Club standards, addressed the gendarme and the chief guide: 'Gentlemen, Britain has become a poor nation because of the war, but in the future people like us will become your new clients.'

This struck a chord with the guide, but the gendarmes remained unimpressed.

Much beer had been imbibed by now, however, and the detente didn't last long. Willie Wilkes, recently back from fighting with Tito's communist revolutionaries in Europe, gate-crashed a formal do for some aspirant guides at a local hotel and was forcibly evicted by the hotel's owner. When Willie was propelled through the ornately carved doorway, war was declared, and both parties piled out onto a quaint street twinkling with fairy lights.

Soon, more drunken patrons of the aspirant guides' ball began to pour onto the street—minus their female companions. The Creagh Dhu Club took up position. Big Bill Bernard, a heavyweight wrestler, broke the menacing silence. 'Friends,' he grinned, 'I think we are about to play a starring role in an epic.'

'I don't fancy the look of those overhanging balconies,' ventured Chook, a handy two-fisted scrapper. The balconies, a few feet above street level, were full of sightseers anxious to see what was going on.

'Aye, it's a bad place to take a stand,' agreed Allen Muir, concerned at the number of potential witnesses to the forthcoming brawl. 'Let's force our way to the top of the hill, then turn to gain the advantage.'

The tactic paid off. There was general panic among the guides, and they were forced back toward the village centre. Then, Wilkes cut out from the wedge of the Creagh Dhu line and confronted the enemy. A big blond guide using his head as a battering ram carried Wilkes along with him. Meantime, our heroes regrouped, throwing some of the opposition aside before rejoining their mates. A club member called Sunshine managed to rescue a battered Wilkes from the clutches of the burly-looking guide. Sunshine's girlfriend was a black pudding bender and Sunshine himself had aspirations to become a Peruvian bullfighter, so the guide had little chance.

In the chaos that ensued, the Creagh Dhu Club, masters at fighting, put their wrestling talents to good use. Suddenly, as quickly as it started, the onslaught ended when one of the Swiss pulled a knife and was arrested by a gendarme.

Disinclined to let the evening's entertainment come to such an abrupt and relatively painless end, Chook pointed to a bewildered-looking guide and shouted to Bill Ross, a 17-stone copper from Glasgow, 'Hey, big yin, there's one you missed!'

'No, I didnae,' the officer of the law bellowed as he swung his mighty fist and knocked the victim into the air, whereupon he cartwheeled across the street, hit some low steps and rolled into a flower bed. The Creagh Dhu Club howled in delight, and young Chook raised Bill's hand victoriously. 'The best punch o' the night!' he cried.

Their elation turned to embarrassment when, out of nowhere, a dainty lady flew up to the triumphant copper and began beating his chest with her tiny fists.

'You great big fool, why do you hit my fiancé?' she cried from a height level with Bill's midriff. 'He is from Chamonix and he hates the Swiss guides. In the war, he fought alongside the Jocks as your ally... then you go and punch him!'

The Creagh Dhu Club outside Achintee Farm in 1942

Hamish on the Creagh Dhu Club's
two-man Everest expedition with
a borrowed tent

06. GODDESS MOTHER OF THE WORLD

Since Edmund Hillary and Tenzing Norgay first topped out on the highest point on our planet in 1953, many have perished in the quest to emulate their remarkable climb. Size certainly is everything where Everest is concerned and, at 29,032 ft (8,849 m), its celestial snows have an irresistible allure.

Despite the Sherpa name for the popular ascent from the South Col being 'Yak Route', it is no pushover. Above 8,000 m, in what is known as 'the death zone', the weather is frequently ferocious, the lack of oxygen can make you hallucinate and every step becomes an agonising effort in slow motion. Everest doesn't come easy or cheap, and today people pay tens of thousands of pounds for the privilege of accessing this infamous mountain.

In the early 1950s, I was one of many who fell under the mountain's spell, drawn to the challenges of those upper slopes straddling Nepal and Tibet where the bodies of Mallory and Irvine lay. I set off on my motorcycle from Greenock to visit mountaineer Bill Murray in Lochgoilhead, a small village on the West Coast of Scotland, for I had read that he was about to undertake a reconnaissance expedition to the hitherto restricted Nepalese side with, amongst others, Eric Shipton and Ed Hillary. I was keen to hear of their plans. This expedition would be key to unlocking the Everest problem, for they identified a possible line of ascent up the Western Cwm glacier to the South Col, followed by a relatively easy ridge to the summit.

In 1952, a Swiss team led by André Roche succeeded in forcing a route to the South Col, from where they made a dramatic but unsuccessful summit bid. I later attended a lecture given by André in Edinburgh's Usher Hall, and afterwards he told me about the large cache of expedition food and oxygen bottles they had left at the foot of the slopes leading to the South Col. 'A Scotsman's heaven,' he said, with a twinkle in his eye.

For me, the die was cast. This was a unique opportunity—free food and equipment on the doorstep of the mountain! What more could an impoverished mountaineer ask for?

I tried to persuade my Creagh Dhu Club pals to down tools in the Glasgow shipyards and accompany me on an extended holiday to Everest, but found no takers for my proposal. However, one member of the club, John Cunningham, had emigrated to New Zealand the previous year, and I wrote to see if he could be persuaded to give it a go.

Soon after, I found myself on the long sea voyage to Christchurch in New Zealand's South Island, where I met John and we concocted a plan. We had recently heard of a forthcoming British Everest expedition from the Nepalese side to be led by John Hunt, whose team included Ed Hillary, and we were spurred on by the competition.

However, planning was not a high priority for our newly-formed two-man Creagh Dhu Himalayan expedition team. I had purchased our equipment at the Glasgow Barras market, and a friend had donated an old tent—that was about it. We had a budget of £40 after we paid our one-way passage to India.

Before leaving the UK, I had been refused permission to enter Nepal for an Everest attempt, and the Royal Geographical Society didn't want to know two indigent climbers from north of Hadrian's Wall. We realised that stealth and subterfuge would be necessary if we were to achieve our objective. Only a handful of white men had previously approached Everest from the Nepalese side, and we were soon to discover that there were armed guards on the steep, narrow mountain trails leading to our destination following the recent invasion of Tibet by the Chinese.

Alas, by the time we arrived at Base Camp, Everest had already fallen to Hillary and Norgay. Having carried all our equipment on our backs from India and evaded the police posts en route, we trudged onwards despondent yet undeterred, but quickly realised that attempting the second ascent of the mountain would be futile, as all the cached Swiss food had been scoffed by Hunt's British expedition team.

We licked our wounds, consumed a naturally frozen sheep and some potatoes we had bought from a local Sherpa, made an attempt on nearby Pumori (23,494ft) but were beaten back by avalanches, and finally succeeded in making the first ascent of a rock spire called Pingero.

By now, we were penniless and, between us, seven stones lighter.

Hamish and John's expedition was largely self-powered, assisted by a few locals

We had both nearly starved to death, and the high altitude and deprivations took a terrible toll on my tooth fillings. Lying in a frigid canvas box in the eternal snows, where oxygen and sympathy were in scant supply, I had tried remedial doses of both whisky and cloves to no avail. Immersed in my misery, I had fleeting thoughts of St Apollonia, who had her teeth brutally removed by the Romans for refusing to renounce Christianity. Now there was a test of faith!

Even the lower Himalayan altitudes were fraught with dental pitfalls, for the locals added small bits of gravel to the rice, no doubt to swell weight and therefore profit. They had the sense to swill their own rice in a pot lid like a prospector's gold pan so that heavy metals and gravel gravitated to the bottom, but we were unseasoned greenhorns. Later, a permanently stooped drillmaster would rebore and refill my mouth over several jaw-breaking months.

Once Everest was conquered, every country wanted a footprint on the summit snows, and alternative routes were attempted. International expeditions collapsed in disagreement and patriotic fervour. Litter began to accumulate at the South Col, which turned into the highest scrapyard in the world, with discarded oxygen bottles and dead bodies abound. A loo was even carried to this windswept spot but relieving oneself risked frostbite despite the built-in fore and aft zips of modern down suits.

Everest is a mountain of extremes: acute lack of oxygen and ferocious weather, to say nothing of personal ambition. The inexperienced taking the normal route from the South Col will find few Samaritans up there should they fall by the wayside, for those stopping to assist risk succumbing themselves. There are no funeral arrangements in the death zone: you lie where you die. It pays to remember that the summit is the halfway point, and a good percentage of climbers who successfully reach the top never make it down.

Even though dozens of Sherpas have perished on those treacherous slopes over the years, the Everest hordes have provided employment to these hardy people. A renaissance is underway, as it was in the Alps in the late 1800s, when local porters in the high Alpine valleys eventually became guides and achieved new income and status. There is a booming economy in these once-remote mountain villages, but there are still human rights issues to address.

Many years after my youthful and ill-conceived attempt with John Cunningham, I was fortunate to accompany Chris Bonington on two expeditions to the mountain's relentlessly steep South West Face and was his deputy on the successful 1975 trip that saw Doug Scott and Dougal Haston become the first Britons to reach the summit. I was asked to design equipment for the trip and, working from an idea initiated by Don Whillans, I developed rectangular tents with adjustable front legs that enabled them to be pitched on any angle of slope, and a fabric cowl that deflected snow. These helped the team move up and down the mountain relatively safely, but we faced an onslaught of avalanches, one of which almost overwhelmed me, filling my lungs with freezing powder so that I felt as though I was drowning.

Chris deserves to be called Mr Everest for his long association with the mountain. Later, after his aborted North East Ridge expedition in 1982, when Pete Boardman and Joe Tasker died, Chris promised his long-suffering wife, Wendy, that he would give up on Everest. There were just too many sad memories, too many friends lost. But, as another friend of mine once said, 'Never Say Never Again'.

In 1985, Chris went back—with Wendy's blessing—for an attempt of the normal route from the South Col. After his onerous and selfless role over the years as an expedition leader, he joined up with a Norwegian expedition led by his friend, Arne Ness. Chris succeeded in reaching the summit at the age of 50, then the oldest person to have climbed the mountain. In doing so, he found peace up in the rarefied air where Tibetans say the gods live, and I think at last came to terms with an old adversary.

Descending crevassed terrain

07. A FESTIVE ENCOUNTER WITH MOUNT RUDOLF'S WEST FACE

As far as gold prospecting was concerned, I was a 'greenhorn' or 'new chump' as they are colloquially called in New Zealand, but two long-toothed local stalwarts, Donald the Dag and Thomas the Turd, had told me of particles of gold they had found in moss on a cliff at a place called Long Beach, 30 ft above the Callery River in the country's South Island. I decided to try my luck there with my pal Dave Dawe, a man of vast intellect who could trounce me at chess and outwit me in philosophical debate.

The name Long Beach suggests buckets, spades and sandcastles, but in fact it is a chaos of boulders where the gorge walls rise several thousands of feet above the river. It has an atmosphere of desolation, at least since the prospectors of old cleared it out. Some of those bearded pioneers had come down from the Klondike of North West Canada after the gold had run out there. The bush is so tenacious that it is sometimes necessary to use axes and secateurs to make progress, and some of my adventurous local friends described having to descend thousands of feet down a bush-infested face at treetop level, Tarzan-style, to avoid the high-angled tangle of supplejack and its allies far below. Meanwhile, New Zealand's home-grown sandfly, voracious and with no respect for privacy, is a worthy rival of the Scottish midge.

To cut a long story short, after thrashing our way through a misery of cliffs and supplejack bush, we didn't find much in the way of gold at Long Beach, but I spied a peak rising out of the expanse of the nearby Franz Josef Glacier snowfield like a tooth, with a west face steep enough to capture my imagination.

At that time, the chief guide at the nearby Franz Josef Hotel was a man called Harry Ayres, who was known for having taken Edmund Hillary under his wing and inducting him into the sport of mountaineering. Winter climbing was virtually unknown in New Zealand back then, but it is probably the best place in the world to find snow terrain comparable to the Himalayas, for it has a maze of glaciers and severe weather, despite its lower altitude. This was the perfect initiation for someone who would go on to make the first ascent of Mount Everest, and it is why Kiwis have been so successful on the world's highest mountains.

Anyway, Harry had heard of Dave's and my ignominious retreat from the Callery and, aware of our aspirations to pioneer winter climbing in the New Zealand Alps, he offered us work trail-cutting through the bush, which meant we had access to the mountain huts and other perks.

Delighted with this arrangement, we decided to spend our first free weekend crunching our way up the glacier to take a look at the peak that had caught my attention, which I found out had the rather festive name Mount Rudolf.

That year, the snow cover on the serrated Franz Josef Glacier presented a serious access obstacle, with concealed crevasses lying in wait like trapdoors for unsuspecting trespassers. Although I had climbed in the European Alps from a young age, I had limited knowledge of glaciers in those days. Many years after my apprenticeship on the mountains of New Zealand, I would become an expert on slow-moving ice and spend countless pre-dawn sorties on the treacherous Khumbu Icefall with Dougal Haston and Doug Scott during our attempt of the South West Face of Everest, a place where many climbers and Sherpas have lost their lives over the years.

Back then, it could sometimes take a whole day to gain the ice plateau of the Franz from the moraine, but we were young, fit and eager, and we emerged onto the great ice basin in only a few hours. On our left, the Almer Hut perched on a snowy plinth like a Christmas cake, and our objective, the West Face of Mount Rudolf, rose before us, plastered in ice and framed by a cerulean sky. A couple of squawking keas buzzed us, and I recalled an old kiwi superstition that they are reincarnated climbers. With some experience of the local mountains by now, I was not, however, fooled by the benign-looking panorama. This was New Zealand: it would not be beer and skittles.

After a battle to open the snow-plastered door of the hut, we flung our gear on the bunks, prepared some food and hit the sack, for all big New Zealand climbs start at a sparrow's—or kea's—fart.

At dawn, we waded through gaiter-high snow as the sun stole across the tops and Mount Rudolf glowed a fiery red like the nose of its Yuletide namesake. Soon we were in crevasse country, each slot inconveniently camouflaged by a white blanket of snow. We saw the tracks of a chamois and marvelled at how it had tested snow bridges with a little hoof. A bit further on, we came to an abrupt halt. A deep *rimaye*—a gap between the mountain and glacier—barred the way, and we became so absorbed in overcoming this obstacle that we didn't notice the telltale 'hogsbacks' overhead: smooth, lenticular clouds that signal high winds and impending poor weather.

Before venturing to New Zealand, I had been accustomed to hard winter climbs and suboptimal conditions in Scotland, and this stood me in good stead for the verglas-bedecked rock I now found myself teetering upon. We were climbing on double 150 ft ropes and the pitches were long and the runners few and far between. Whenever I encountered a decent patch of snow ice, I took a break from my enthusiastic hacking to place the odd ice peg and cut steps for Dave, for he had only ten downward-facing points on his crampons, whilst I had 12, with new-fangled horizontal front points that enabled me to drive them into the ice more effectively.

As we climbed higher, the weather deteriorated, and a ferocious westerly storm hit us horizontally with all the windchill it could muster. Dave, who was not accustomed to climbing in such appalling conditions, battled on valiantly, and we eventually topped out on an arbitrary-looking high point in a whiteout. With no time for any self-congratulation, we acknowledged the summit and grovelled our way toward the descent route.

In summer, this would have been a doddle, but in that storm and with a uniform coating of wet snow over verglas, it was perilous. I managed to whack a peg in and tied on the end of one of our ropes, but the shrieking wind made it impossible to throw the rope down, and I had to entrust Dave with sorting it out as he descended.

Somehow, in the confusion of attempting to untangle everything, Dave lost his gloves and, after fruitless attempts to gain purchase on the diamond-hard verglas, snapped the points off his crampons. We were now in a white hell, and to complicate matters further, it was getting dark.

Lowering Dave to a snow patch, I yelled down to him to untie from my belay rope and drive his axe in for security. I abseiled down on frozen double ropes, which now had all the pliability of steel cables and were nigh-on impossible to retrieve. This palaver had to be repeated again and again until we finally reached easier ground, resembling two cheerless snowmen.

Dave's hands were now frostbitten, and I realised it was imperative that we reach the Almer Hut, pronto. Stumbling in the white void, I spied its outline at last, but we had great trouble getting the door open, for we had forgotten to cover over the keyhole, and the wretched hut was now filled with powder. Still, it was vital shelter from the elements, and I immediately put the primus to work for a brew and, more importantly, hot water to treat Dave's frostbite.

We spent the next day recuperating in the hut and nursing Dave's hands with warm water. It would be some time before he would be slashing the Franz Josef bush again. The following day, he was well enough to leave the hut, and we set off on a slow and weary trek off the traitorous glacier, which now conspired to make the crevasses appear wider and the seracs more sinister than I remembered. At last, we made it down to the moraine and reached the haven of a small hut close to the hotel. We had made it, but I calculated the score to be Mount Rudolf: 2, Dave and me: 1. Although we had succeeded in making the first winter ascent of the West Face of Mount Rudolf, it had been a narrow escape. I reflected that it had been a serious mistake to ignore those hogsbacks. We should have foregone our attempt and humbly retreated.

08. A CONTESTED FIRST ASCENT OF COULOIR PEAK

Couloir Peak was one of my first solo ascents in New Zealand. I had visited the place earlier with some of the local Canterbury Club climbers to reconnoitre some unclimbed 2,000 ft faces, but deep snow curbed any ambitious plans at that time so I returned alone a short while later, for the great wall of the mountain was like a magnet. It wasn't a great sweep of immaculate granite like a Chamonix Aiguille—in fact, the rock looked fairly suspect—but with a bit of luck, a snap of frost might keep any wayward rock in situ.

As I crunched my way across névé in a still dawn with the Southern Cross suspended in the heavens above me, I mused that there is something to be said for the contemplative life of the sadhu: the silence and overpowering sense of, not quite tranquillity, but I suppose presence that is felt by devotees and ascetics of any calling. There was something meditative about the rhythmic rasp of my crampons biting into the pristine snow. Ahead, the mass of Couloir Peak looked like a heap of mani prayer stones outside a Buddhist gompa.

As I ascended onto trickier terrain, I shifted my focus from the philosophical to the corporeal. Tapering rock portals funnelled the snow into a gully that tilted upward like an unending treadmill. Everything was bonded, safe as houses. At one point, in the interests of security, I created a tension traverse using a Glasgow shipyard piton and my doubled rope: this was what it was all about!

As the sun rose, I gained the summit and was rewarded with a panorama that took in sun-drenched slopes all the way to the Cameron River. I sat awhile in abstracted reverie before tramping back to the tin box mountain hut, where, in keeping with tradition, I wrote an entry in the crumpled hut log:

'Up south face of Couloir Peak, left peg at rock crux, four hours, H. MacInnes.'

This seemingly innocent testimony led to consternation which took many years to resolve. In the following year's edition of the *Canterbury*

Mountaineering Club Journal, my claim was reported as a 'false ascent' by an 'irresponsible solo climber', amongst other things. Many years passed before a further entry appeared in the club journal, verifying that the piton I had used on my traverse had been found by a party making the second ascent of the route. I was duly acquitted.

Facing: The Linda Glacier

Below: The Sheila Face of Aoraki/Mount Cook
© Colin Monteath

Mount Sefton © Colin Monteath

09. A LONG CLIMB IN THE ANTIPODES

Alone amid a great cirque of peaks that form the central New Zealand Alps, I was camped out in a delightful glade, with a freshwater stream to fill my billy can and, at arm's length, a profusion of succulent, blood-red wild raspberries superimposed against the magnificent great white wall of Mount Sefton.

Beyond lay the ruin of the old Hermitage and the edifice of the new Hermitage: a haven for the ubiquitous tourist, but nevertheless a symbol of intrusion in this pristine landscape. Despite the tranquillity of my idyllic surroundings, I yearned for the scrape of sharp crampons on ice and the security of my all-metal Message ice hammer driven in above me.

It was an interminably steep slog up to the blank wall of Mount Sefton, and it didn't look any easier from close up. Fortunately, I had brought a rope and a selection of ice pegs made in John Brown's Shipyard back home in Glasgow. Gone was my fantasy of good névé; the reality was a sinister-looking slab of ice which I fancied might, with an ominous crack, disengage from the mountain like a pane of glass. With solo climbing, in particular, there comes a time when you wonder, *What the hell am I doing here?* This was one such occasion, but I realised it before I ventured too much further. There was no peg to abseil from, and my position was too precarious to attempt to drive one in, so I had to make do with just my front crampon points gently pressing into the slab and the pick of my ice axe hooked into the surface with the delicacy of a signwriter.

Some hours later, after an involved retreat that required me to keep my wits about me, I reached the safety of the steep grass and scree lower down the mountain, and I sat in the sunshine for a while. A spotlessly white Mount Sefton sneered at me. I lifted my snow goggles to look across toward the elegant white pyramid of Aoraki/Mount Cook. An intriguing rocky ridge ran down from the summit of the low peak of Cook to the Hooker Glacier some 10,000 ft below. It looked fairly tricksome and likely to involve at least a couple of bivouacs.

Such casual observations often set a chain of events in motion, and victory against one adversary can raise hopes of defeating another. The weather broke, and I retreated to a climbing hut just a few miles beyond the Hermitage, where I met a tall, bearded American called Peter Robinson. Peter was a geologist from The University of Otago in Dunedin, and I knew his professor, Noel Odell, from Everest yore. We immediately struck up a friendship and, between intermittent showers, we climbed many routes together on a nearby crag and planned some adventures on a grander scale. I suggested we inspect the long ridge I had spied after my failed attempt of Mount Sefton, and Peter was keen, so we set off early one morning with our swag for what I now knew was the unclimbed South West Ridge of Nazomi (9,716 ft).

By mid-afternoon, we arrived at the foot of the ridge at the edge of the Hooker Glacier, a grubby mass of ice that inches ponderously toward the Hermitage. We couldn't see much snow or ice on the rock above, so we decided to cache our crampons and ice axes just above the glacier and solo up the lower reaches of the climb on what looked like comparatively decent rock. To our right lay the Mona Glacier, desiccated by crevasses, and to the left was a plumb vertical amphitheatre overhung by an unnamed glacier spewing out from Nazomi. We noted with some trepidation that this glacier overlapped our route—so much for caching our gear! With celerity and little security, we scuttled beneath the dripping tongue of ice, where we were delighted to discover a source of ice-cold water from meltwater streams. After a stairway of ledges and slabs, we arrived at the second buttress, severed by a monstrous gully comprised of ribs of greywacke, which my geological friend assured me was pretty good rock for climbing. I was sceptical, given New Zealanders' fondness for giving their mountains affectionate names such as 'Rotten Tommy'.

No matter. I slithered up a slick icy groove before arriving at a point where the gully divides. The north branch was loose and alive with the sound of pebbles whizzing by. I cobbled together a belay, and Peter climbed through, tackling a right-angled corner and rib, then traversing leftwards to a cave at the top of the second buttress. From here, the ground eased off, and we savoured the simplicity of soloing for a while.

Cloud spilled over the divide like a drover's soggy plaid. Visibility came and went as if at the whim of a conjurer's cape—now you see me, now you don't!—but during a brief lifting of the clouds, we glimpsed a formidable-looking gendarme directly ahead. There appeared to be no way of bypassing this other than via an icy slab resembling an angled mirror. It was now gone 7:00 pm and dusk strode purposefully up the valleys. With my survival instincts in alert mode, I found a small niche in the rock, and Peter levelled a platform and rendered it with snow. It wasn't exactly five-star, but the view was something else, with the Southern Cross gleaming in the dusky sky and the mountains aglow, as if The Almighty had turned down the dimmer switch.

Dinner was a customary handful of dates, peanuts and other unidentifiables, and then we slid gratefully into our sleeping bags. Squinting out from time to time, I could see the twinkling lights of the Hermitage, but I concluded that ours was the superior pension and pulled the top of my bag over my head.

We awoke to a sky greenish in hue with the Morning Star like a headlamp overhead. High-altitude, lens-shaped clouds made us uneasy—these were 'hogsbacks' that foretell bad weather on this island sandwiched between the Tasman Sea and the Pacific Ocean. I shuffled like a penguin in my sleeping bag into Peter's annexe of the cave. We planned to be back come sundown, so we cached our sleeping bags and non-essential gear and set off for what we expected to be an easy day.

Confidence soon confronted reality. I teetered across a slab toward the disagreeable-looking gendarme, then traversed right to where the overhang was only a few feet high. At the top was a V-shaped groove coated with verglas: the crux of the climb. I hammered in a piton and stood in a sling to reach a belay ledge. Peter then laybacked a groove with zero protection, eventually surmounting the gendarme.

I continued up a short arête to a spectacular rocky tightrope of greenish quartz, whose undercut rock emphasised the exposure. It was over 100 ft long and so sharp in places that we were obliged to revert to an embarrassing, uncomfortable equestrian method known as *à cheval*. At the far end was a deep notch in which two large chockstones were deterred from crashing thousands of feet down to the glacier by two smaller stones of dubious integrity. We skittered nervously across to a terrace, then over further towers to the main pillar on the ridge.

By mid-afternoon, we arrived at the top of the tower, which we christened 'The Gnome', due to its ungainly profile. Conscious of the dark clouds scudding across the sky above us, we hurriedly descended the backside of our corpulent friend.

Rather than boring you with countless descriptions of rotten rock, ridges, chimneys and icy grooves, let us arrive, several abseils later, to a point above an unnamed glacier on our right.

The weather took a turn for the worse, as I had feared it would. We used our piton hammers to clear ice from holds as a capricious wind chilled us to the bone. This was no place for tired mountaineers. With cold, clumsy fingers, Peter dropped his hammer, which spun down the face tunefully, headed directly for the Mona Glacier. It paused on a narrow ledge, in preparation for its next leap, then bounced merrily onwards, stopping at the last kerb-width ledge before the precipice 130 ft below us. I belayed Peter as he descended to retrieve the wayward hammer. Then we traversed a gully where we were forced to excavate small holds from both ice and rotten rock with our tools. Then we battled an overhanging wall of greasy rock. Then another one. The kaleidoscopic (not so) merry-go-round continued for 18 pitches: delicate, hard climbing on friable rock cemented in place by a mean slick of verglas.

After our tribulations, the penultimate ridge to the summit of Nazomi was a doddle, but we were now shattered and fearful of further deterioration in the weather. With nothing left to climb, we hurried down, determined not to stop for a moment, for we were in need of a good bivouac and our sleeping bags. Abseil anchors were as rare as hen's teeth, and we had no tat with which to attach our abseil ropes. It took us over two hours to descend a couple of hundred feet.

Fortunately, the sun had made enough brief appearances to melt the ice on the south side and, as it dropped like a stone out of the sky, we fumbled our way toward our troglodyte haven. A handful of nuts and fruit and then into the sleeping bags. Bliss.

Waking early, we had a somewhat nauseating breakfast of tinned mackerel. Then we were back at the dangerous yo-yoing game that is abseiling. Knowing we were exhausted and dehydrated, we kept the rope on even as we reached easy ground—too many climbers have lost their lives after letting their guard down.

After navigating a 50-degree maze, we finally reached the Hooker Glacier and were reunited with our axes and crampons and a trickle of meltwater to quench our raging thirsts. Like low-powered automatons, we trudged onwards to the Unwin Hut, where we were welcomed by stair rods of rain and a storm in which we struggled to stay upright.

Peter decided it was time to get back to his lab and rock samples, and I planned to hole up for a few days before looking at a possible new route on Mount Cook.

Today, the South West Ridge of Nazomi is a popular route, and it is sometimes used as a final expedition test for New Zealand Alpine Guides. It is now called 'MacInnes Ridge', despite the fact that I didn't climb it solo.

Hamish and friends at the Maltebrun Hut

Aoraki/Mount Cook
© Colin Monteath

10. PERAMBULATIONS ON MOUNT COOK

Aoraki, or Cloud Piercer, is the old Māori name for Mount Cook, an elegant peak once described by the astute Dutch sailor and geographer Abel Tasman as 'A great uplifted high', before he veered south, then north again to pass those aptly named landmarks Cape Foulwind and Cape Farewell. The interconnected elements of sea and mountains have a lot in common, with inclement weather a constant danger for mariners and mountaineers alike.

I had been a solitary commuter on the upper regions of Mount Cook for some time and had made the second ascent of the eponymous Zurbriggen Ridge, not just to repeat the Swiss Guide's remarkable first ascent but to take emergency food to the summit, for I had aspirations of a solo ascent of the mountain's great East Face. I had succeeded in burying the grub in the summit snow, but not, alas, in climbing said face. My concern about impending rockfall turned out to be justified, for the whole thing later broke away in a ginormous avalanche, falling thousands of feet to the glacier below and almost overwhelming the popular Ball Shelter, which, luckily, was empty of tourists at the time.

The descent route from Zurbriggen Ridge was via the Linda Glacier below, and I came across a fathomless crevasse blocking my progress. It was probably about 10 ft wide—no bigger than dozens I had leapt over during my winter sorties on the Franz Joseph and Fox Glaciers, but with overhanging edges, which made it a bit awkward. I took a deep breath, double-checked that my crampons were on properly and stuffed my Dachstein mitts in my back pocket before taking a leap of faith across the divide. I dusted myself down and casually made my way back to the old Haast Hut, built in 1916 to commemorate the first fatalities on New Zealand's highest mountain.

Years later, in a coffee shop I frequented back home in Glencoe, I had an encounter with a young man who asked if I was Hamish MacInnes. I could tell from his accent that he was a Kiwi and felt an instant kinship with the lad.

'My dad is Oscar Coberger. He has the climbing shop at Arthur's Pass.'

I knew the shop well from my time exploring the Southern Alps. 'Ah, it's a small world,' I replied.

'You went down the Linda after going solo to the summit of Mount Cook.' It was a statement, rather than a question.

'Hmm,' I said, noncommittally, wondering what was coming next.

'That same day, my dad and I climbed Cook by another route, and on our descent we saw prints next to a big crevasse on the Linda. We found Dachstein mitts at the edge and assumed that someone had fallen in. Dad belayed me down into the crevasse, which looked bottomless, so I thought that whoever had tried to jump across must have fallen to his death.'

'Good God!' I said in astonishment, realising the trouble I'd inadvertently caused.

'It was only when we eventually got down to the Haast Hut and found your entry in the hut calendar book: "Up Zurbriggen's to summit, down Linda, H. MacInnes," that we realised that you were all right.'

He seemed happy enough to see me alive at least, and his recollection reminded me of other eventful solo explorations I had had on Mount Cook.

During my time spent in the Darran Range, a spine of peaks in New Zealand's South Island, I chanced upon my old friend John Hammond from Glencoe. The last time I had seen him was with Chris Bonington, when we had done the first winter ascent of Agag's Groove on Buachaille Etive Mòr, and we arranged to meet at the Hermitage Hotel in Mount Cook Village and plan a climb together.

When I arrived at the Unwin Hut close to the Hermitage a few days later, I discovered with dismay that John had fallen to his death on the mountain and the guides couldn't recover his body. Feeling a bit depressed, for I was losing too many friends, I trudged back to the Haast Hut to scout another possible new route in an attempt to take my mind off things. The hut was empty save for a hand crank transceiver for emergencies and weather reports from the Hermitage. It was now too late to tune in for a forecast so, after a simple meal of dried beans and biscuits, I crawled into my sleeping bag, for climbs in the New Zealand Alps start at about 2:00 am.

I have no idea why I got out of my warm cocoon in the wee small hours, for the temperature was below zero, but I felt compelled to switch on the radio. There was a crackle of static and the weak hum of a carrier wave, then a faint voice echoed like a ghost from the small speaker.

'Accident. Empress Hut. Urgent.' Then, silence.

Dumbfounded and now wide awake, I doubted myself and considered that I may, in my sleep-addled state, have imagined those few words and the desperation they imparted. I had to do something, but what? It was the middle of the night; there would probably be no one down at the Hermitage listening in. Nevertheless, I sat astride the hand generator stool, grabbed the two handles and hand-pedalled with all my might, a troublesome affair since it was two-way radio designed for one person to generate power and the other to operate the mic. Despite my efforts, there was no response from the mystery caller or the Hermitage.

At last, I got through to Mick Bowie, the big, quietly spoken chief guide at the Hermitage. With great difficulty, for I was turning the generator with one hand and holding the mic in the other, I breathlessly related the urgent call. Mick suspected it had been made by two Australians—Cooper and Murphy, from the Sydney Bushwalking Club—who had asked him about conditions a few days earlier and had ignored Mick's advice to steer clear of Mount Cook. I, too, had met the Australians just before they left for the Empress the day before, as I retreated to the Unwin hut to wait out the poor weather. Their diary, which Mick's party found later, showed that they had left the hut at 3:00 am on 23 February in overcast weather and reached the main summit of Mount Cook at 7:00 am.

It is about a mile between the high and low peaks, and by the time they had returned to the low peak, the wind had increased. Rain had impaired visibility, while soft snow on hard ice made their descent treacherous. They were negotiating a steep couloir that dropped down to the Hooker Glacier far below when they both slipped and shot down the slope, triggering an avalanche that partially buried them both. Murphy, who had sustained injuries to his head, back and wrist, somehow managed to dig himself out of the avalanche debris but couldn't excavate his friend, and Cooper perished in the snow.

With herculean effort, Murphy managed to climb down a rock rib to reach the hut, where he collapsed on the floor, exhausted. Unable to move, he lay for two days, with the door wide open and snow drifting in. It was during the evening of the third day that I received his message. How he managed to operate the generator, with his broken wrist trying to hold the mic and his other hand turning the strenuous handle, I will never know. I found it almost impossible despite being fit and strong.

Eventually, thanks to Murphy's persistent attempts to summon help and the sheer good fortune of my nocturnal tinkering with the radio, he was rescued by Mick and the other guides and evacuated off the mountain in a distressed state. Sadly, the body of his friend was never found.

During such perambulations on Mount Cook in those years, I had spied a prominent rock ridge, which was yet to be named. I had good knowledge of this steep part of the mountain, and after a solitary recce, during which I encountered a precipitous wall I didn't fancy soloing, I returned the following year with two American pals, Dick Irvin and Peter Robinson (with whom I had climbed the South West Ridge of Nazomi), for an attempt at a first ascent.

We grabbed our chance during a brief weather window, as the sun made an appearance and a wisp of cirrus passed across the mountain's face like a teardrop.

Our plan was to climb the virgin ridge via a series of steep individual buttresses, each about 1,000 ft high, then summit the highest peak of Mount Cook. As we toiled upwards, the Tasman Glacier snaked sinuously down from the snowfield at a leisurely pace. The sun beat down oppressively and we had to negotiate the maw of a yawning crevasse and an evil-looking avalanche chute like a bagatelle's launching bay. Bypassing a crop of gendarmes resembling portly rock policemen with lichen cloaks, we climbed to the crest via a small glacier, with Zurbriggen's route on our left and the Linda Glacier below. Another crevasse then led to a vegetated wall, where I had to garden my way upwards for about 120 ft to reach a belay. The rock was rotten but, now on easier terrain, we untied our bowlines and took the rope off to save time—we had no harnesses in those days.

We ascended into the rarefied air, delighting in the exposure of an airy buttress on better rock with heavenly views all around. This was what it was all about! Reaching what appeared to be the crux crack, I roped up once again and was thankful for the additional—if predominantly psychological—security, for the fissure proved to be as awkward as I had expected it would be when I had recced it the previous year.

There were several more gendarmes to negotiate in this Alpine cornucopia, but for the most part we opted to save time by climbing unroped, surmising that it was the lesser evil. Despite this, by 12:30 pm we were still only at the junction of the Linda Glacier and Zurbriggen Ridge. Although we were now ravenous, there was no time to delve into our goodie bags, for the summit beckoned, and beyond that we had a long way to go. We pressed on, haunted by our old enemy: time—or rather the lack of it. We finally arrived at Middle Peak and had a breather, with the weather still just about holding.

Eventually reaching the top of Mount Cook, we were surprised to meet two guides from the Hermitage who had battled up Earl's Route, one of the classic climbs on the mountain. They forewarned us that we would have to negotiate steep, hard green ice on the descent, and even though we were able to use their steps, it was still perilous. By the time we arrived at the rocks at the bottom, it was almost dark and we still had to tackle a nasty-looking steep gully. In hindsight, we should have roped up, but with time against us we had a homing instinct to get to the Empress Hut below, rather than spend a night out in an uncomfortable bivouac.

Tired and now struggling to find good foot placements, Peter, whose crampons had clogged with snow, lost his footing and he took off down the slope. I watched helplessly as he tried in vain to arrest his fall with his ice axe. Just at the edge of this slope, the face dropped thousands of feet to the Hooker Glacier and I knew others had fallen to their deaths here. Peter finally managed to get purchase with his axe and he came to an abrupt stop 300 ft below, the cliff edge nipping at his heels. It was a close call indeed. Shaken but miraculously uninjured, save from wounded pride, he stumbled upright—a veritable snowman—clutching his ice axe and yelling that he was all right. Dick and I made our way down to him, now much more tentatively, and conceded that we should stay roped up from here on. It was 29 hours since we had left the Haast Hut and we were done in. We must have been a snowball's throw from the tin hut but we couldn't see it even with our headlamps on and we realised with some dismay that we would have to scrape out a bivvy in the dark. Although it was now raining, at least the wind had dropped. Recalling our miserable, sodden bivvy later, Dick Irwin noted:

'Whilst two of us shivered all night, Hamish, used to such inclement weather back home, slept soundly!'

The next day, we trudged downhill amidst soggy, poultice-like clouds. The technical difficulties were over, but we knew we needed to stay alert, for there were enough hazards to ensure that another slip would have serious, if not fatal, consequences.

As we approached the sanctuary of the Hermitage at last, I recognised the formidable figure of Mick Bowie, who glared at us tightlipped, pipe in hand. Grateful for the sight of a familiar face, I waved to him and yelled,

'Hey, Mick! I hope you don't mind, but we just named our new climb 'Bowie Ridge' after you!'

I thought he was going to drop his pipe as he described how he had watched our unroped progress across the ridge through his powerful ex-U-boat binoculars and had prepared a full-volume bollocking for us upon our return.

'But how the hell can I tell you blighters off now when you named a Mount Cook ridge after me?' he cried, exasperated.

There have been many accidents and over 200 fatalities on Mount Cook over the years, with hypothermia, avalanches, lightning, rockfalls, heart attacks and plane crashes all listed as contributing to the tally. Many years after our ascent of Bowie Ridge, I was involved in an epic rescue on Middle Peak, probably one of the most dramatic and protracted rescues in the history of mountaineering.

Phil Doole and Mark Inglis were two fit young climbers from the National Park's Alpine Rescue Team, who, in 1982, had flown by ski-plane to the Plateau Hut on the eastern flanks of the mountain. Travelling light, they were hoping to bag a quick ascent of the classic East Ridge on their days off. The route is a painstakingly long climb over snow and ice to the summit of Middle Peak, and the pair had set off at 5:00 am to do battle with unconsolidated snow and hard ice on the upper sections. The wind was whipping up spindrift as they approached the summit at around 6:00 pm, but they hoped to force their way across and reach the relative safety of the western side via Porter Col. Unbeknownst to the two climbers, the Southern Oscillation Index, a measurement of the relative strengths between the Australian-Indonesian low and the high-pressure system east of Tahiti, had entered into one of its periodic shifts, generating devastating cyclones across the Central Eastern Pacific. The climb along the East Ridge had been relatively sheltered, but by the time they reached the summit of Middle Peak at over 12,000 ft, Doole and Inglis were at the mercy of a violent storm, the wind having accelerated as it squeezed over this gigantic barrier. Frozen and unable to reach Porter Col, they crawled into a small depression—a bergschrund affectionately known as Middle Peak Hotel—to wait out the storm. 'Hotel' implies some sanctuary, but there are no facilities here other than partial shelter the size of a single bed and lots of snow.

Over the next few days, the pair made repeated attempts to reach the col from where they could descend in relative safety, but they were forced to retreat to their tiny crevasse as the storm raged on.

Back at base, concerns were growing for their safety, and a rescue team that had been training in the area was scrambled. Searches at Mount Cook are managed by the Chief Ranger and usually involve helicopter support due to the scale of the mountain. Along with the air force, local civilian pilot Ron Small, who had an Aerospatiale Squirrel, was drafted in to assist, amid intense media coverage.

By day four, all other search and rescue work was suspended while the park team geared up and waited for a break in the storm to try to reach the stricken climbers. This pattern was repeated day after day to the immense frustration of the team.

Meanwhile, Doole and Inglis, frostbitten, had realised that self-rescue was now impossible and were trying to conserve all their energy in order to survive, remaining mostly motionless and eating and drinking minimally.

After the seventh day, a brief lull in the storm and lifting of the clouds enabled Ron Small to make reconnaissance flights up the mountain, although he too had a near miss when his helicopter almost collided with the ridge.

Finally, the weather abated just enough to allow an air force Iroquois helicopter to ferry rescue party members above the Empress Shelf, a snow plateau some 1,500 ft below the point where radio contact had been made with the stranded climbers. But as the pilot prepared for landing, the rotor blades drew up drifts of snow, blinding him and causing him to catch the tail of the machine, which flipped over. In a scene reminiscent of some clichéd disaster movie plot, tailplane and rotor were now suspended over a 1,000 ft precipice to the lower Empress Shelf. Miraculously, all passengers managed to extricate themselves from the teetering Iroquois, but now required to be rescued by an exasperated Ron Small.

With dogged determination, the rescue team battled on and finally, 14 days after their ill-fated attempt of the East Ridge, Doole and Inglis were winched from their tiny refuge as another wall of snow showers rolled in and the clouds began to spill over the mountain tops once more. Alive but severely frostbitten, both climbers had to have their lower legs amputated, but a few months later Inglis was back at work at Mount Cook National Park and Doole embarked on an expedition to the Peruvian Andes.

Entering the Whale on Rakaposhi

11. RETREAT FROM RAKAPOSHI

The reason Rakaposhi hadn't been climbed before Mike Banks and I attempted it in 1956 was that, logistically, it was too hard. Situated in a remote part of the Karakoram mountain range in the Gilgit-Baltistan territory of Pakistan, Rakaposhi rises up from arable fields to 25,551 ft, and its traditional moniker 'Mother of Clouds' reflects the mountain's great scale and exposure to intense weather systems. Mathias Rebitsch, of early Eigerwand fame, had planned an earlier summit attempt and even had porters' medals pressed in anticipation of the final conquest. In the end, though, he decided that the risks were too high.

Our attempt on the mountain had been a serious business from the outset, crammed full of drama amid blizzards, tottery seracs and a network of crevasses, all of which led me to question then, as I often do now, why we climb. Overwhelmed by the sheer number of avalanches, we finally realised that our adventurous two-man assault on Rakaposhi was over when Mike pointed out that we were almost out of food.

Having stashed gear and food at Camp 4 the day before, we had descended back to Camp 3 in a whiteout to wait out the storm before heading back up to prepare for our attempt on the summit. It soon became clear, however, that this was no passing flurry, and we realised that the ferocity of the wind and sheer volume of snow ruled out any prospect of going back up. In the interest of self-preservation and hoping that the bamboo markers were still in situ, we resignedly packed our rucksacks at Camp 3 as the wind screeched like a banshee around us and the snow crept up over the tops of our gaiters. Besides our personal gear—sleeping-bags, air-beds, crampons and the like—we had a tent and two cine-cameras, which brought the weight of each rucksack up to around the 60 lb mark.

Wind drove the falling snow slantwise into the ground, and visibility was down to about 20 yards, with only occasional glimpses beyond.

In this blank white room, we tentatively picked our way down along the line of the ridge, knowing that any deviation, even a few feet to the right, would take us perilously close to overhanging cornices and could see us hurtling down the mountainside to the Biro Glacier far below. To our left, crevasses lay in wait.

We could barely see through our sun goggles, and eventually we had to take them off, risking snow blindness from the ultraviolet light from the sun, which is more potent at altitude. I theorised, without much conviction, that the light would be diffused by reflecting off every particle of falling snow and would therefore be harmless. At any rate, we had to take our goggles off to see where we were going, so the argument was academic.

In good conditions, it takes quarter of an hour to cover the distance from Camp 3 to an island of rock where the ridge dips to its lowest point, but that day it took us over an hour of hard-going slog, even though it was downhill. Forlorn-looking bamboo canes here and there reassured us that we were on the right track, but we were constantly straining our eyes in the featureless white void, trying to make out the dim line of the cornices on our right or the seracs and crevasses on our left. Eventually, we reached the haven of rocks and gratefully sank down to rest.

The snow was highly unstable, and we were disinclined to climb back over the steep ice above a rocky precipice that we had crossed on the way up. An uncontrolled slip here would have only one outcome. We stopped for a while at the island of rocks, spying out a shortcut down to the glacier that might allow us to avoid an exhausting climb over a subsidiary peak. We set off down this route, but had gone only a short way when I broke through a crevasse bridge. Pulling on the rope, I thrust my axe into the snow and somehow extricated myself, but this put paid to our shortcut. Summoning all our energy, we turned around and ploughed our way up the steep slope we had just descended to reach the site of our old camp once again.

In front of us, the ridge rose slightly and then flattened out along the traverse. We arrived at the last protruding patch of rock, and Mike climbed out onto the fluffy snow that blanketed the ice. Calling out that he didn't much like the look of the slope, he entreated me to make sure I was secure and to arrest his fall if he slipped. This was a fairly impossible request, for I had no firm rocks to attach myself to, just ineffectual fragments of scree. Making the best of things, I thrust my axe into the loose powder and took a turn of the rope around the shaft.

The surface on which I was now perched was a mountaineer's nightmare. The steepest section of the route between Camps 2 and 3, it was normally iced up enough to offer sharp picks and crampon points some adhesion, but now it was covered in fresh, fluffy snow to a depth of a foot or so. It was equally impracticable either to sweep away the masses of loose powder and cut steps in the hard ice beneath, or to carve out firm steps by step-kicking. Mike was reasonably safe so long as I kept him on belay, but the traverse went on for several hundred feet and soon we would have to forsake our security, such as it was.

As it happened, Mike had progressed only a few feet out onto the slope when a clean-cut slab of snow broke free from the compact layer underneath and began to slide inexorably downhill. I looked on helplessly as he tried in vain to arrest his fall. Made heavier by his cumbersome 60 lb rucksack, Mike swooshed ever more quickly down the icy face and, realising the shortcomings of my belay, I braced myself for the strain that would eventually come on the rope. When it did, the axe whipped out, and our ensuing descent toward perdition was interrupted only when my pick bit into a pocket of slightly less fluffy snow. We lay there in crumpled heaps for a few moments, afraid to move for fear of setting off another slide that would surely sweep us over a precipice not far below. At last, Mike shuffled tentatively across to the scree, where he found a belay of sorts and brought me over to join him.

Although now on safe enough ground, we were in a serious predicament, with neither food nor fuel. It would have been nigh-on impossible to pitch our tent on so steep a slope, and in any case, the weather was still atrocious and likely to remain so for several days. Faced with the devil or the deep blue sea, I gathered myself, moved back out onto the powdery snow and tried to create passably sound steps, moving as silently and delicately as possible, slowly transferring my weight before gingerly kicking the next step. After an eternity, I reached a small nook where I allowed my heart rate to settle a bit before burrowing into the snow and fashioning a meagre stance from which I could belay Mike across.

It took courage for Mike to quit the security of his rock belay and quest out on to the slope. With a silent glance at one another, we both tacitly understood that we had renounced our last surety and that if one of us fell, the other had a snowball's chance in hell of holding on. What use was the rope, then, other than a morale boost or a suicide pact?

Pitch by pitch, we carried on in the same manner: kicking steps, scraping snow off and cutting icy belay stances. Slowly, oh so slowly, the angle of the ridge relented until we knew we were approaching the broad ice slope leading down to Camp 2, about 1,500 ft below. By now, we were physically and mentally nearing the end of our tether. All this time, it had snowed mercilessly, penetrating our windproof outer garments and our down jackets and wetting us to the skin. Mike must have been wearing warmer clothing than me, for I was shuddering violently. I suggested camping, but there was nowhere to pitch our tent, and we had to force our weary, overladen bodies on.

Without regret, we turned our backs on Rakaposhi for the last time. Groping onwards, crablike, toward the safety of Camp 2, we tried to catch a glimpse of any identifiable feature as stinging icy needles stabbed our eyes.

Out in front, Mike suddenly noticed a crevasse running parallel to our course, but on his left, where there should have been only the unbroken surface of a snowfield.

'Hell's bells, Hamish!' he cried. 'We're standing on a ruddy great cornice!'

At that stage, I was almost too cold and tired even to care, but we scuttled back to safety.

At last, and with undisguised relief, we found the bamboo cane marking the top of the final steep plunge before the easier scree slopes above Camp 2. I led down, kicking steps as best I could in the creaking snow. After that traverse, it seemed like child's play, and I was about to make some lighthearted quip when, without warning, I found myself whizzing down the slope. Still tethered to me, Mike immediately kicked his crampons and rammed his ice axe into the snow as hard as he could, but they met with little resistance in the soft, newly-fallen powder. Bracing himself, he waited for the rope to tighten. In a moment of infinite stillness, the rope stretched to capacity with an almost audible creak. A pause... then Mike was jerked backwards and began somersaulting madly down the slope toward me, his axe dragging uselessly through the snow. I had managed to drive the pick of my axe into an icy patch on the way down, but I observed somewhat dispassionately that Mike was quite out of control, and I had a vivid conviction that we were heading straight for the Biro Glacier as he tumbled past me before, miraculously, gently coming to rest in a heap of avalanche debris. We were now opposite the isolated boulder marking the top of the screes, having fallen about 300 ft. Most of the avalanches that we had seen coming down this slope had charged right down the mountainside past Camp 2 and carried on down the gully toward Camp 1—a considerable distance. Mike remarked that this particular one had been considerate to stop just when it did. Perhaps Rakaposhi had taken pity on us.

Afraid that the least twitch might set the loose mass of snow moving again, we trod delicately, like cats, and a little later we gained the security of that benign hunk of rock where we had rested gratefully so many times before. We lumbered on to Camp 2, darkness chasing after us, and arrived to find the tents drifted over, so I crawled inside and set about preparing a meal while Mike shovelled snow. When he shuffled into the tent later in anticipation of sustenance, I had to confess that I couldn't get the stove to work at more than a flicker. It needed pricking, but for the first time on the expedition, there was no instrument to be found either with the stove or within the recesses of our rucksacks. Sopping wet to the skin, we crept miserably into our sleeping bags and waited for an eternity for the water to warm. Darkness fell and we lit a candle. Mike said it was burning so brightly that it hurt his eyes to look at it.

Some time later, I was awoken by an anguished cry: 'Hamish, I think I'm going snow-blind!'

And so was I. At first, we felt the pain only when looking at the candle, but soon our eye-sockets felt as though they were filled with hot, burning sand, and we began to weep copiously.

We had been so confident of regaining Camp 4 that Mike had left his medical kit there. I suggested the well-known remedy for 'welder's eye'—pressing tea leaves against our eyes—but it was useless, and we lay awake and in agony most of the night, listening to the gale tearing at the canvas and piling ever more snow over the tiny tent.

Neither of us knew how long the blindness would last, but we realised we would need to wait until we were at least partially recovered before negotiating the gully down to Camp 1. The next morning, Mike could only keep his eyes open for a few seconds at a time. I was slightly better, for I had been wearing a cap with a small peak that had shielded my eyes a little. Tearfully, Mike held the Primus while I wrangled with an ice-piton and managed to change the nipple of the stove. We were assured of a hot meal, at least.

The storm continued to rage all day as we lay inert in our sleeping bags, letting the warmth of our bodies dry our clammy clothing. The soundtrack to our suffering came in the form of avalanches hissing down the slope above us and continuing along the gully. We contemplated why our own had stopped halfway and found no answer. Again, we slept.

By the next morning, our eyes were much better, and we were able to keep them open if we kept our goggles on to cut down the light. Forging down the gully through deep new snow, we were wary of every sibilant murmur on the slopes around us. Just as we reached the bottom of the gully, there was a rumble above us, and we raced to one side to let an avalanche pass to our left; a few moments later, another passed to our right. Mike observed wryly that they were Rakaposhi's final parting shots to the impertinent trespassers who had invaded her sanctuary.

After surviving this final punishment, we arrived tattered and bruised at the place where our base camp had once stood, only to find the place deserted. Surely our porters were a little hasty in giving us up for dead so soon! In the debris around the site, I found my old pyjama bottoms.

Later, the porters reappeared: they had been sheltering from the storm down the valley at Darbar, where they could enjoy plentiful food, a fire and a shepherd's roof over their heads. They were carrying eggs, fruit and some joints of mutton, and they prepared an enormous feast for us.

As darkness fell, we hurried through the pines of Darbar to gain a meadow on the far side. Issa, our head porter, whose already prodigious energy was heightened by an end-of-term feeling, pelted ahead and lit a great roaring campfire to welcome us. Beyond the bottom of the valley, the glinting paddy fields contrasted with the unclimbed snowy barrier behind. Rakaposhi would remain unmolested, at least until the following spring.

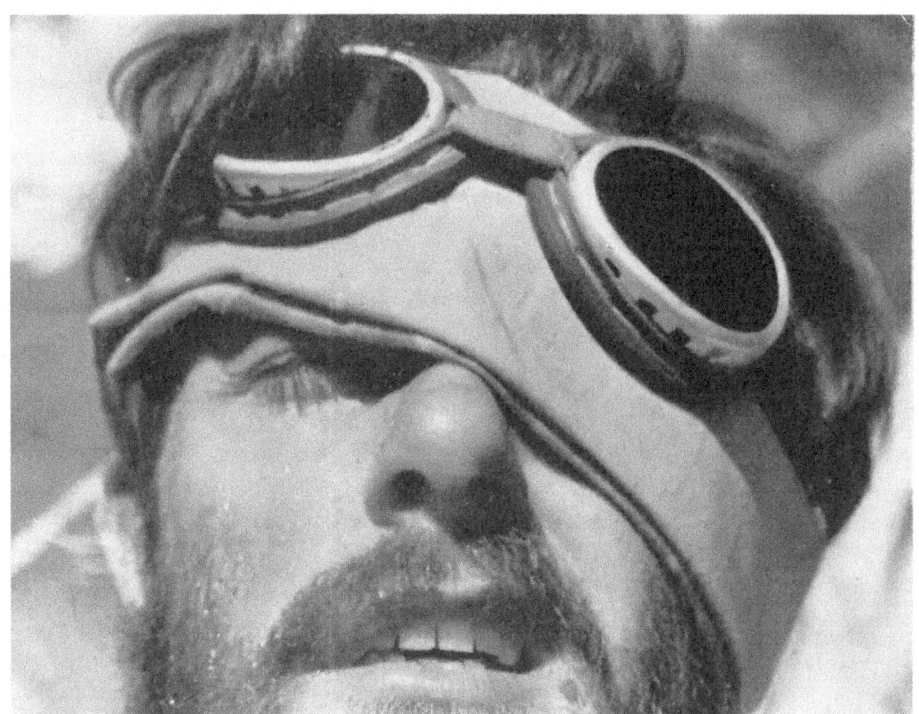
A snow-blind Mike Banks

RECOLLECTIONS FROM RAKAPOSHI

By Mike Banks

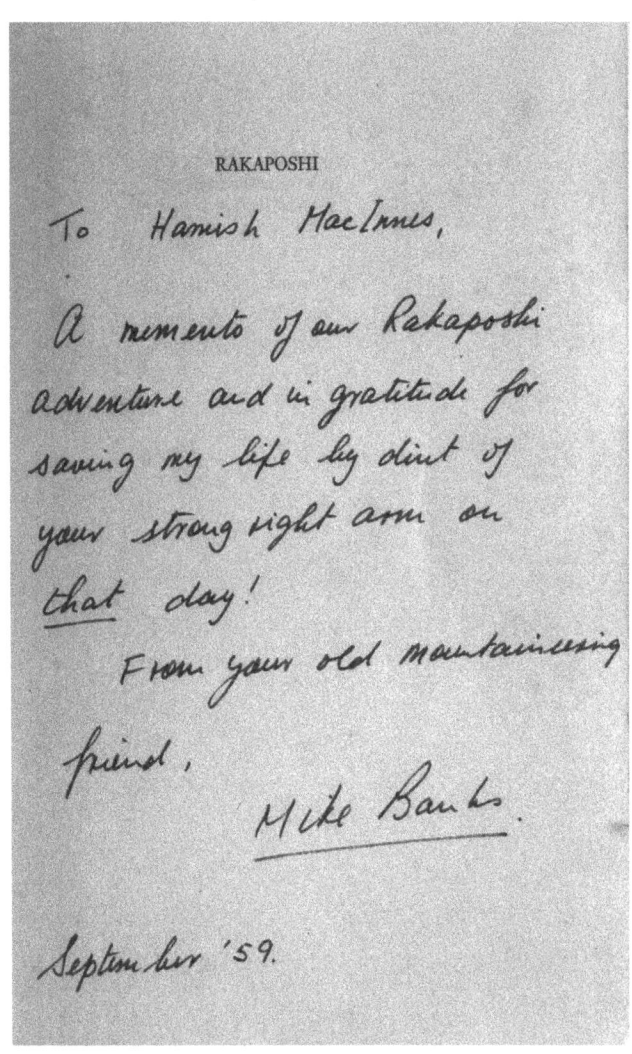

Mike Banks's inscription in the copy of *Rakaposhi* that he gave to Hamish

Despite our retreat, there is no one I would rather have attempted Rakaposhi with than Hamish. We had complete trust in each other's snowcraft and sense of balance. As one climbed, the other was able to relax mentally and think, 'If he can do it, then so can I.' In that sense, we leaned heavily on each other.

He is a truly remarkable man, full of contradictions, yet still the most likeable of persons. He is, for instance, utterly indifferent to personal comfort and health and claims immunity to all diseases and ills, carrying no medical supplies and depending on his robust constitution and hypochondriac friends. Yet he is fastidious about personal cleanliness and tidiness. At the height of a blizzard, his tent would be spotlessly clean and neat, with every particle of snow, stale food, or dirt carefully swept out.

He also has the gift of making his own amusement. During lengthy storms, his mellow baritone would rise above the soughing of the wind, chanting Highland songs, or, incongruously, IRA dirges, the latter to evoke my ire, to the glee of our companions. In the evenings, he would recite his latest poem before a critical audience.

His endurance and energy, too, were remarkable. I have never known anyone to walk uphill so fast and with so little fuss, and he is undoubtedly a master climber. Conventional people have often condemned Hamish and certain of his fellow spirits for being rash and suicidal. This is simply not true, for the very valid reason that if they were, they could not possibly remain alive and unmaimed today. There is much of the canny Scot in Hamish, and before he embarks on any ostensibly madcap scheme, you can be sure he assesses the chances very shrewdly and then takes into full account his formidable personal mountain prowess. This combination of prudence and enterprise makes him the most exhilarating and reliable companion on an expedition. Nor has he wife, job or responsibilities to burden him. Clanking off to the hills, his rucksack full of jingling pitons and poetry books, he is a truly archetypal Scottish adventurer, with that love and affinity for wild lands, that sort of yearning that might be expressed musically in the majestic yet harrowing theme chords of Wagner's *Flying Dutchman*.

Upon our return, we sometimes talked of our shared adventure on Rakaposhi, crystallising our feelings in the aphorism of, 'Well, we had a bloody good try.'

The Mir of Hunza

12. THE KINGDOM OF HUNZA

The Kingdom of Hunza is a charming place, an oasis in a necklace of mountains in the Karakoram range. After Mike Banks's and my unsuccessful attempt on Rakaposhi, I set off toward the settlement on horseback, as the approach to the Hunza River was via a precipitous path hewn out of the rock. I was aboard His Highness, The Mir of Hunza's white stallion and my cap was touching the rock roof. I dismounted, tying my rucksack to the saddle, something which, I learned later, displeased the Mir, who regarded it as demeaning his personal steed.

In modern times, when the Karakoram Highway was being built, an Indian surveyor was working on this gargantuan construction, which excavated the mountains in a series of huge vertical steps to prevent rock falls from demolishing the road. The steps were hundreds of feet high—the exact height of the Chinese rope supplied for the labourers. At any rate, the surveyor fell in love with the daughter of a village elder who lived some distance away from the highway. The elder said he wouldn't give his daughter's hand in marriage unless the road was diverted through his village, which would mean the residents would be eligible for compensation. By altering the drawings, the engineer complied with this, and I suppose they lived happily ever after.

I made my way to the Mir's new palace and was met by the great man himself, who was standing at the ornately carved front door, dressed in an immaculate drill suit. He was too polite to pass comment on my bizarre, filthy attire, which by now included my old pyjama bottoms.

'Welcome from Rakaposhi, Hamish,' the Mir said. 'Come—refreshments.'

'Thank you,' I faltered, overwhelmed by the opulence.

A white-robed bearer offered me a clear liquid from an oriental jug. This was the first—and not the last—encounter with Hunza Pani, the national alcoholic brew. The Mir smiled benevolently and sat down on a divan. I gave him a present of 16mm colour film, surplus from the expedition.

'Sorry, I have nothing more presentable, sir,' I said, somewhat sheepishly.

'I will make good use of it,' he replied magnanimously.

A dignified lady entered, dressed in a stunning embroidered Chinese dress.

'This is my rani. She has some fresh apparel for you up in the guest-house.' The Mir stood up. 'But I didn't realise you were so tall, Hamish. I hope they fit.'

I was shown to a guest house on the grounds and had a much-needed bath. It was good to have clean clothes at last, but my lower legs extended past the cuffs of the trousers, and the shirt sleeves only reached my elbows. Ah, but the thought was there. After a sumptuous meal washed down with Hunza Pani, I retired to bed and watched the amber glow of Rakaposhi, spotlit against the fading azure sky.

Surfacing just after dawn, I was presented with a selection of home-grown cereals and cold ibex steaks, and after breakfast, the Mir suggested that I accompany him in the fields and meet some of his workers. We travelled to the old fort and were greeted by some Hunzacuts, dressed in homespun clothes, who were over 100 years old.

As he turned to admire the view, the Mir said, 'I have been thinking, Hamish, we could have a joint expedition. I would hunt for ibex and supply the food... and the mountains.' He swept his hand round in a wide arc. 'After all, these snowy peaks are mine.'

I was dumbfounded to learn that he had dominion over this entire mountain range.

'I am certainly interested,' I enthused. 'I'll see what I can organise when I go back home.'

I spent several idyllic days in the Kingdom, often in the company of the Mir, other times speaking with some Hunzacuts who had been on Rakaposhi with me. They had a smattering of English, and I, Urdu. There was much laughter.

All too soon, it was time to go, for I had arranged to meet up with Mike in London for a reunion, a reminiscence of our hardships on Rakaposhi. I bade farewell to the Mir and his family. The Mir's rani gave me a pullover, which she had knitted from the inner hair of a herd of ibex. Unfortunately, when I wore the pullover back home, I was surrounded by amorous dogs. In the end, I donated it to the British Museum.

Back in the big smoke, Mike and I had a good party, but eventually, I had to excuse myself, for I had pressing business: I had come back with a hot KTT Velocette racing motorbike, faster than any police car, and I was eager to ride it north on the A1—the closest thing we had to a motorway in those days.

I often regret not accepting His Highness, The Mir of Hunza's offer of a joint expedition. Unfortunately, it clashed with one of my annual Amazonian jaunts.

Alas, the Hunza I knew no longer exists. Gone is the benevolent rule of the Mir; Hunza is now promoted in brochures as a place with good value accommodation, scenic tours and cafés—'All credit cards accepted.' The artery of the Karakoram Highway roars beside the Hunza River, and tour buses shuttle eager armchair pundits around.

Hamish and Chris Bonington's camp at the top of the Montenvers Railway, before they ascended the Bonatti Pillar on the Petit Dru
© Chris Bonington Picture Library

13. IN THE FOOTSTEPS OF THE MASTERS

Few climbs hold such special appeal for mountaineers as the Walker Spur on the North Face of the Grande Jorasses. That great Italian master, Riccardo Cassin, made the first ascent of this formidable pillar back in 1938 with companions Esposito and Ugo Tizzoni, and to this day, it is an Alpinist's dream. Long and extremely demanding, the Walker is still considered a serious undertaking, and it should only be climbed when the mountain is in excellent condition and one is fit and acclimatised.

When Don Whillans joined me in Chamonix in 1959 during a promising season with little snow, we had high hopes of being the first British party to succeed on the route. In anticipation, we established ourselves in a hut which later became known as Chalet Austria. Occupied by a mountain recluse who thought he owned it, it was, in fact, an old goat herder's bothy, close to Montenvers and the Mer de Glace.

Hearing that our Austrian bothy friends Walter Phillip and Richard Blach were setting off that evening for an ascent of the Nant Blanc, Don, who was keen for a training climb, hurriedly packed his rucksack and joined them at the Rognon Bivouac. His recollection of the climb, done in record time—invective excluded—was of strained ankles and aching legs. 'They climbed unroped like robots,' he muttered. I was glad I hadn't gone.

I had been confident that the Walker was in decent condition, but the exhausted Nant Blanc party reported heavy snow on the summit, which somewhat dampened my enthusiasm. We returned to the fleshpots of Chamonix for a couple of days, during which time Don did his best to embroil us in a fracas or two as we awaited the arrival of our friends John Streetly and Les Brown.

As soon as the weather in the mountains settled, our quartet, well-nourished with *vin ordinaire*, set foot on the Mer de Glace. The crepuscular stillness enveloped the valley and long shadows stole out from the boulders strewn over the ice as we headed up to the ruins of the old Leschaux

Hut for our attempt of the Walker. The hut, torn apart by an avalanche some years before, offered only spartan lodging, but gave us a perfect view of the spur's forbidding countenance. It looked like a daunting adversary, and we had to reorientate ourselves to its scale.

Our gear was dated, to say the least, and Les was in a state of destitution, having lost everything on the North Ridge of the Peigne a few days earlier. For once, I was looking unenviously at someone worse off than myself. Although Les was without ice hammer, windproof trousers, crampons and bivvy sack, it didn't dampen his, nor our, enthusiasm. At any rate, paucity of equipment was a matter of course for me after my two-man attempt of Everest in 1953 with John Cunningham, when our total expedition budget had been £40.

Mercifully, a fellow climber and the only other occupant of the ruins, took pity on Les and donated a huge black sombrero, as well as a pair of capacious trousers so vast that they formed a moat when suspended from his sturdy braces. At well over 6ft tall, Les looked like a gargantuan Mexican brigand.

Unlike Les, John Streetly was small of stature. An ex-Cambridge University graduate and domiciled in Trinidad, he had explored the Mato Grosso in Brazil for both oil and Colonel Fawcett's last resting place, and had solo climbed a mesa called Iron Dyke via a tunnel that took him to a summit littered with agates. Not only that, he was the first to attempt the Prow of Roraima in South America, long before Don, Joe Brown, Mo Anthoine and I set foot on it. He was a talented climber and a good man to take along.

As we bided our time in the hut, a full moon rose above the Col des Hirondelles, flooding the surrounding peaks in gold. The fire sparkled, there was no shortage of timber, and as we had a brew, I recalled my last visit to the Leschaux Hut with a young Chris Bonington, when we had aspired to climb our present objective only to be thwarted by heavy snow.

Sleep can be difficult on the eve before a big route, as if giving you time for second thoughts. Then, when you get to grips with the climb, the doubts evaporate, except for worries about the weather and perhaps the yawning bergschrund ahead. Leaving the hut at 2:00 am, we saw early-bird lights on our climb and hoped that they wouldn't knock any rocks down. My pack felt too heavy, and I resolved to lighten it at the first opportunity.

Too late, we realised that we should have recced the approach better, for we were soon in a maze of crevasses and bergschrunds guarding the toe of the spur, and we wasted valuable time reorientating ourselves.

We moved from steep, grotty scree to precipitous, icy rock, which at least offered several possible lines with platforms for belaying. Don, climbing with Les, moved effortlessly up a technical-looking corner, or dièdre, with the ease of someone climbing stairs. This was the famous hundred-foot pitch, one of the main crux sections on the route.

I found this crux pitch unusually difficult as I seconded John on it, for I was feeling weak and uncoordinated, as if suffering the effects of the altitude. This was probably the legacy of a head injury I had sustained on the Bonatti Pillar on the Dru the previous year, since when I had suffered periodic blackouts. On that occasion, a shower of rocks had swept down upon us with an attendant firework display, before a whine with a distinctly fateful tone had presaged an axe-like blow to my head. As I had slipped in and out of consciousness, Chris Bonington had wrapped a bandage over the oozing wound and tied the ends together under my chin so that I had resembled a macabre housewife. With few options for retreat, for we had traversed so much on the ascent, we had continued to the summit, Don hauling me up the steepest sections. After two bitterly cold bivvies, when our sleeping bags had filled with spindrift and a single packet of soup had sustained six of us, we had descended to the Chamonix

Hamish and Paul Ross on the Dru
© Chris Bonington Picture Library

valley with the first British ascent of the Bonatti Pillar in the bag. Ever since then, I have been forever grateful to Chris and Don, without whose help I would no doubt have remained on that lonely ledge on the Bonatti.

A re-enactment of that unfortunate episode now seemed destined to unfold as an orchestra of whines and thuds heralded a bombardment of falling rocks. Some were high-pitched, like petulant children, others strident and aggressive, intent on destruction. Luckily, none of us was directly hit. Both Don and I were wearing workers' bonnets lined with a new type of impact-resistant felt, and we didn't feel a thing, but we later learned that two climbers who had been ahead of us received no fewer than seven head injuries each.

Once the blitzkrieg subsided, John set off again, running out 300ft across steep slabs smeared in icy patches like transfers. Snowed up sections allowed us to gain the crest of the spur before we reached the foot of another long, steep dièdre which was pierced here and there with pitons. Our route followed verglassed slabs, a choked-up chimney and some daunting overhangs, after which an abseil would take us to the Grey Tower but, as we moved upwards on grotty snow, we unwittingly bypassed the true route. This was apparently a common faux pas, and we spent some time relocating before some complicated manoeuvres allowed us to establish ourselves on the route proper, then tension traverse to the fixed abseil. John disappeared into the depths. My admiration for Cassin and his compatriots grew as I imagined attempting such an intricate and demanding climb with no route description and only rudimentary equipment.

Eventually, we reached a bivouac ledge at the top of a particularly arduous pitch, where we could see the summit shrouded in banks of ominous clouds. It seemed an uninvitingly long way off. Out of the corner of my eye, I spied a soggy packet of Smarties, not renowned as a traditional French delicacy. Knowing that Don and Les hadn't taken Smarties with them, I swore violently. 'Robin Smith!' I suspected that my friend and fellow Scot, with his pal Gunn Clark, had been aware of our objective and had got there first, leaving the memento behind to torment us. Feeling somewhat dejected at the thought that we had been pipped at the post, I pulled out of my rucksack a hefty tin of meat that had been sticking into my back all day and gratefully devoured my share of the meagre repast. We made a brew from a tin of Horlicks that we found on the ledge and consoled ourselves with decent grub and an unrivalled view. I mused on the name 'Walker', which was surely a misnomer.

Tenacious fingers of mist now clung to the rock face as the temperature plummeted. We left the ledge for a pegged traverse, which took us back to the edge of the ridge. Now on more vague terrain, some time-consuming meandering forced John to hammer in a peg for security. In fact, we only inserted two pegs on the whole route, although nowadays this great face has suffered the fate of all its compatriots, with pitons and wedges that lead nowhere documenting years of inexpert route-finding.

Darkness enveloped us while we were still on difficult ground, and it became imperative to find a ledge for the night. We reached a patch of scree just as the black curtain came down and the wail of a falling rock close by further chilled our bones. I tried calling out to Don and Les but received only echoes in reply.

With the communal stove sputtering contentedly and a reasonably comfortable ledge anchored from above with slings, we considered ourselves lucky. We relaxed and sipped an insipid brew from the meat tin, and I had the sensation that I was on a ship ploughing through a frothing sea and guided by a solitary star. Later, we learned that our friends hadn't fared so well, and had to spend the night slung in upright positions on a tiny sloping ledge, with no brew, and in Les's case, no sleeping bag or bivvy bag. There is always someone worse off!

Ensconced in my large plastic bag, I spent a fitful and colourful night replete with gompas and astral projection, probably due to oxygen deprivation. Les told me later that he was so exhausted that he had been sick and had spent the hours of darkness fighting off demons. Privately, I thought that any demons would have fled upon seeing such a strange apparition in a sombrero and vast pair of trousers.

By morning, I felt much better. Breakfast was soup and breadcrumbs, and we soon discovered that the ledge above us was the belay stance for the final pitch up the Grey Tower. It was bitterly cold, and we creaked into motion, noting with relief a line of pitons leading upward, which eased our progress to the top of the Tower. A jammed sling looked suspiciously uncontinental, a bitter reminder of the two Scotsmen who had beaten us to the route and who would now be in a café down in Courmayeur, laughing. The grade of the climbing was now about Severe, and the route much more obvious, an airy and exhilarating snaking ridge. I spied Don and Les immersed in a steep chimney above, and we quickly caught up with them for a ritual brew on some unstable snow as rocks fell all around us. Despite the onslaught, deep double bass of thunder and dark clouds monopolising the view, we were nevertheless enjoying ourselves!

After some more technical climbing, we moved upward together like tourists on the summit ridge, eventually breaking through a cornice, beyond which a trail of footsteps led into the white void. Then, the footprints divided, with those to the left stopping at the edge of a yawning crevasse. Were the printmakers entombed? No, the tracks continued off to the right, skirting the edge of another cornice.

As if in anticipation of our arrival at the summit, the wind whipped up in applause and snow swirled like confetti all around us. But there was no celebratory whooping as we reached Pointe Walker, and we immediately turned our thoughts to the descent. The perilous nature of the terrain meant that we had to stay roped up, which slowed our progress, and as the weather worsened, we were soon compelled to bivouac once more.

We were then assailed by the full force of the elements, with thunder like an express train and lightning flashes resembling carriage windows hurtling by. Don, diminutive as he was, had a voluminous bivvy bag, though it was not quite big enough for all of us. Neither was the ledge we were on, and as I had my own plastic bag, the others suggested that I vacate to another spot. Don, with his broad plumber's accent and a hint of gallows humour, drawled, 'You buggers from the Highlands don't feel the bloody cold anyway,' which received a cheer. I fashioned a snow hole on another ledge, which almost resulted in frostbite, but once cocooned in my bag, I relished the chance to escape the fug of cigarette smoke and I was soon fast asleep, confirming Don's observation.

By dawn, we were all soaking wet from the condensation in our plastic bags. Although I had slept fairly well, my companions had had an uncomfortable night. We had to fight our way down through deep powder and I called out to Don, 'Not as bad as descending the Dru last year,' to which, with obligatory fag in his mouth, he replied, 'Thank the wee man for that.'

The descent of the couloir was an obstacle course, as anyone who has experienced it can testify. In lieu of breakfast, our menu comprised seracs, crevasses, snow bridges and bergschrunds, in that order. In pouring rain, we arrived at the rocky outcrop on which the hut was located and were greeted with a spectacular lightning display, which caused my metal-shafted North Wall hammer to hum and emit sparks.

By evening, we were down in the metropolis of Courmayeur, where we met up with the two friendly rivals who had beaten us to the first British ascent of the Walker Spur. Who had left the empty packets of Smarties for us to find? I never did ask Robin.

Hamish (with torn breeks) ascending the Grand Jorasses

The Shkhelda Ridge
in the Caucasus

14. THIRTEEN DAYS ON SHKHELDA RIDGE WITH FOUR DAYS OF FOOD

George Ritchie dropped in at my cottage in Glencoe one day to tell me that, after several years of negotiation, the Scottish Mountaineering Club had received an invitation to send a joint party with the Alpine Club to the Soviet Caucasus. Departure was in three weeks' time. Was I interested? I was not a member of the illustrious club, but George felt sure that he could overcome such a triviality. When I raised concerns about the costs involved, George generously offered to drive us out and said he would meet any expenses beyond my current resources.

At the time, I was making films for Associated Rediffusion (now known as ITV), and when producer John Rhodes agreed to accept a 30-minute documentary on the Caucasus, it was the clincher. George was delighted and promptly began organising the trip in a frenzy. Everything associated with George happened at double speed, and he was invariably involved in several schemes simultaneously.

After the usual trauma of obtaining visas and supplies and finalising logistics, we set off across Europe on a virtually nonstop drive in George's Mini, which he drove like a scaled-down Ferrari.

Going through the Iron Curtain really did feel like rolling into another world where life took on a grey, metallic hue. Even the false teeth were made from raw stainless steel. It was disconcerting to drive along the deserted East German autobahn and find bomb craters in the road like old untreated war wounds.

We entered the USSR at Brest, where a grim-faced soldier guarded the frontier bridge, his scowl suggesting that he'd been deprived of his vodka ration for some weeks. Turned away from an official campsite for not possessing the necessary paperwork, we snatched a few hours' kip by the side of the road.

At last, three days after leaving London, the ornate, majestic buildings of Moscow rose out of the plain like a mirage. It was a moving and unforgettable sight. In our sleep-deprived states, the Russian capital assaulted our senses: there were traffic lights everywhere and within minutes police were yelling at us through loudhailers. If only we could have understood them. Eventually, we were rescued by a friendly British tourist who took us to the Leningradskaya Hotel, where we had been told to report. It quickly became apparent that we couldn't afford a room there, and we made haste to the nearest campsite, which still wasn't cheap. Everything was provided, however; the tents had slatted battens over the groundsheet, and there were camp beds and electricity.

Back home, I had picked up an ancient English/Russian dictionary in a bargain lot of books at an auction. As I thumbed hastily through it to find the necessary word for some transaction, a crowd of onlookers gathered around me, for the dictionary was unique. My mangled pronunciation of some of the arcane suggestions had the Russians howling with laughter. In some ways, Moscow reminded me of Glasgow, which was probably why I felt so at home there. Apart from shared humour and fondness for alcohol, there was the same genuine concern for the visitor. The selflessness of the people was striking: nothing was too much trouble for them, and we had only to ask someone for directions and they would immediately guide us there personally.

A couple of days after our arrival, we sought out the premises of the Mountaineering Federation of the USSR at Skatertnyi Pereulok. A conscientious citizen, not content with taking us three miles to our destination, insisted on accompanying us up the lift and into the reception before he bowed and left us.

It transpired that accommodation arrangements had been made for us, and we were taken to a spacious suite of Edwardian splendour in the Hotel Metropol. With its fountains, chambermaids, oriental carpets and gilt and crimson plush furnishings, it was fresh from the pages of an Agatha Christie novel, and the same price as the campsite. We had business visas, which apparently gave us very special concessions, so we absorbed the luxury of the hotel like two dry sponges before flying the next day to Mineralnye Vody in a TU-104 jet.

Air travel in the Soviet Union was as cheap as rail travel back then, and even peasants from farming districts frequently travelled by plane to sell their products. In a country where—to borrow a phrase—'all pigs are equal', we found ourselves more equal swine than most and were ushered aboard first and given our choice of seats. A small but important deputation of Masters of Sport travelled with us. These highly esteemed Russian mountaineering experts were to join us in the mountains as advisers. Eugene Tur was an engineer from Gorki, and Igor Bandurovski a schoolteacher from Odessa. There was also a special mountaineering reporter who would be with us throughout our stay. We later christened him The Wasp, due to his bright yellow and black football jersey and in recognition of the industrious way in which he buzzed around us.

From Mineralnye Vody we set off on a hundred-mile drive through fields of tobacco, maize and sunflowers, and past cowboys on horseback until progressively dustier and bumpier roads took us into the heart of the Caucasus. The trail stopped at Spartak Camp, and feeling more like rusty jack-knives than climbers, we creaked into motion and stumbled out. Above the trees, the mountains rose like an icy dream. This was what we had come for! The air was keen, replete with the perfume of pines and wildflowers, but the serenity of the scene was abruptly shattered by a Tannoy system calling out an official welcome parade.

We were rudely awoken at 6:00 am the following morning by Big Brother's metallic voice booming from the loudspeakers once again, announcing the hour for physical training and instructing everyone to be joyous. Camp residents were expected to tumble out of bed, full of joie de vivre, and generally disport themselves in an energetic fashion. I stared malevolently from beneath heavy eyelids as a boisterous youth, brimming with vitality and clad only in swimming trunks, charged into our room and urged us to join the youth of the Soviet Union in worshipping the equivalent of Aurora.

'Bugger off, Jimmy,' I said with as much goodwill as I could muster. 'We don't go in for this sort of thing where we come from.'

Sometime after the eager cries had subsided from the playground, we eased out of our pits and staggered somewhat shamefacedly over to the dining hall to see what we could scrounge by way of a late breakfast. A conference was held to decide how we would spend our time there, and I mentioned that, in order to pay for the expense of my trip, I would have to make a short film. The Masters of Sport, no doubt taking pity on me as a victim of capitalism, promised to help.

A discipline has been instilled into Russian mountaineers, which, for the average Westerner used to the freedom of the hills, is hard to understand. For us, part of the charm of the mountains is the complete absence of bureaucracy, the chance to get away from rules and the thrum of society. In Russia back then, you could only undertake climbs in line with your previous experience and skills, and you were issued a control time for each route. When applying for permission to leave the camp, you had to justify your proposals to a Panel of Honoured Masters of Sport, indicating how long you anticipated that particular route would take. These Masters were generally elderly tigers with blunt claws, though still very much with it. They came from all walks of life, but attaining this grade took many years of hard training and a host of serious climbs. If they were satisfied with your plan and the weather report, you received permission and supplies. If you failed to return within the stipulated time, a rescue party was sent out to find you. Progress on a route was also monitored by the use of flares and by walkie-talkie. These measures may seem far fetched and alien to Westerners, but even with such precautions, there were a great number of accidents. When mountains of the altitude and the severity of the Caucasian peaks are popularised, serious incidents will inevitably occur, and even during our short stay at Spartak, several people lost their lives.

After a conference at which our proposals for new routes were firmly if politely rejected, our hosts sent Eugene to suggest that we should do the traverse of Shkhelda, a barrier of precipitous peaks rising to a height of about 14,000 ft, which could take as long as 13 days if the weather proved unfavourable. It was, he said, a very hard tour at the top grade and hadn't yet been climbed by Westerners, but he and Igor would accompany us.

Both George and I had a habit of underestimating potential difficulties, and we brashly stated that we should be able to do the climb in three or four days—particularly since the first traverse of the ridge had only taken five days in 1940. Why, even some of the greatest Alpine routes didn't take that long, we reasoned, unaware at the time that the first ascensionists of Shkhelda had started on Aristov Peak, a point halfway along the ridge.

As we were cheered off by the camp residents, we couldn't help feeling that we were about to engage in mortal combat with a formidable adversary. Shaking their heads at our supplies, which comprised chocolate and some powdered Complan, our hosts insisted that we take two small aluminium containers of Black Sea caviar. We estimated that we had enough food for four days.

Our stroll up through the idyllic forests and abundant flora of the foothills toward the edge of the Shkhelda glacier still lingers in my memory.

Wild bears and wolves roam there, and the forest felt like a bountiful paradise in dramatic contrast to the frigid-looking peaks above.

It was a leisurely day, and we set up camp on the edge of the moraine below the first peak. The Shkhelda glacier flows from the skirt of the magnificent Ushba, one of the finest mountains within the range and indeed anywhere. It then tumbles down in a steep icefall between Pik Schurovsky and the far end of the range at East Shkhelda, brushing the base of Shkhelda for most of its length before veering north toward Spartak. We had two light, waterproof Russian tents, possibly the best items of equipment they possessed, and we pitched these in a hollow by the south side of the glacier. We had carried up some wood for a fire, so before the shadows had marched across the ice from the peaks, a thin column of pine smoke was spiralling upwards as we dined extravagantly on caviar and fried eggs. It was pleasant on the moraine with the flames playing in the boulder hearth. Warm and relaxed with a hearty meal inside us, we savoured our good fortune.

Eugene and Igor told us that the route went directly from our glacier to the summit of West Shkhelda, a journey that, from our current vantage point, looked unfeasibly vast. We had refused to take a bulky walkie-talkie but carried a Very pistol and a supply of flares, which Eugene had arranged to set off at intervals to indicate our progress to the observers at Spartak Camp.

We were surprised when the Russians suggested an 8:00 am start, for we had expected to be away before dawn. Although we had a tendency to laze about at Spartak, it wasn't our usual policy in the mountains. The four of us set off toward the steeper slopes of First West Shkhelda as clouds spilled down the mountains, and soon it was snowing heavily. Lightning began zapping the surrounding peaks, so, soaked to the skin, we manufactured a bivvy ledge from frozen scree. Avalanches thundered by, and I managed to break my all-metal Message ice hammer levering large boulders aside. Camped on a steep, exposed slope after breaking a further two ice axes—a serious loss—George remarked to me, 'This place isn't safe, Hamish. Don't you think that lot might move during the night?' He was right; underneath the snow was unstable scree. It was like being on the flank of a steep coal slag, so we moved higher up and further away from the increasingly laden slopes. It seemed that Shkhelda was making an example of the Scotsmen who had the temerity to underrate her and take only four days' food supply. As it happened, we were gifted with three stormbound days to contemplate this tactical error.

But all bad things come to an end, and at last we awoke to a glorious morning; everything was crystal clear, as if the landscape had just been scrubbed white. Ahead, Ushba reared from its bed of ice like the twin horns of a rhinoceros, and the serrated edge of Shkhelda snaked like a giant cross-cut saw. Behind us, elegantly obese, rose Mount Elbrus (18,510 ft), the highest peak in Europe. We waded our way upwards. There was no going back this time, we resolved.

In the immediate foreground was the Ridge of the Buildings—rickety buildings, we were soon to discover, cemented together largely by the recent snow and resembling a steep cathedral roof incongruously connected to high-rise blocks. The exposure was nauseating; in places, the edge of the ridge could be grasped between forefinger and thumb. We traversed painfully along these sections *à cheval*. Several gendarmes had to be turned directly, and there were various abseils required. We became so absorbed in the technical problems that we failed to notice time slipping by. Although we had finally convinced the Russians that we needed to leave our camp at dawn, it was now late afternoon, and a bulk order of clouds steamed up from the Caspian, heralded by peals of thunder. We picked up the pace and abseiled to a minute snow ledge, which overhung a breathtaking drop of 6,000 ft. Here, we built a platform of stones cemented with ice produced from the only ready supply of warm water we had available and pitched the tents as the first languid snowflakes fell. Lightning soon bounced enthusiastically off the gendarmes like flashes from a sorcerer's wand, and blue sparks fizzed from our pitons and ice axes. Dinner that night was a weak brew of tea, washed down a spoonful of Complan.

The next day, we continued making painfully slow progress along the narrow technical crest. The heavy accumulation of snow required constant vigilance. At one point, a small cornice gave way underneath George's boots, but he managed to stop himself from launching into space just before the rope tightened. The day wore on.

We camped on a steep snow slope in a high-speed blizzard, and two days later, we were still there. Like a chronic invalid, the weather had taken a turn for the worse, and with virtually no food except minute quantities of Black Sea caviar and a trowel's worth of Complan, we were gradually starving to death. I realised I wasn't enjoying myself anymore: we seemed to be concentrating too hard on surviving.

The following morning, I abseiled down a vertical cliff that curved into a wide chimney as rocks whistled past, narrowly missing my head.

Many thousands of feet below lay the wild isolated snows of Svanetia, and ahead of us lay the main difficulties: the two high peaks of Shkhelda, either of which would have posed a formidable climb back home or in the Alps. We considered trying to descend directly down the face to Svanetia, but the avalanche risk was too great. Some passing Red Army climbers who were en route to Central Shkhelda took pity on us and gave us two tins of meat—an absolute godsend. Our gratitude at their immense generosity was tempered by our embarrassment at depriving them of precious supplies: they would be without food for several days before they got off the mountain.

A party from Ukraine joined us at a bivvy spot and built two platforms for their tents. All level space was now occupied, and every movement required the use of safety ropes. The new arrivals were a cheerful bunch, and despite our predicament, there was much merriment. That evening, we had a bizarre tea party. The Ukrainians' tents faced each other on a catwalk ledge, and when I went for a visit in my socks, I slipped on the glassy surface where someone had taken a leak and almost called in at Svanetia sooner than anticipated. Ten of us crammed into the tiny two-man tent, and George and I chuckled as the Ukrainians belted out some of Kipling's imperialist songs. Of course, Rabbie Burns is a passport anywhere in the Soviet Union, and the crags of Shkhelda soon echoed with fine baritone versions of *Auld Lang Syne* and *Scots Wha Hae* in broad Slavic accents. It was just as well there was no vodka that night, or we'd never have made that icy traverse back to our tents safely—it was at least Severe in socks.

In the morning, the weather had deteriorated further, and it was decided that I would continue to lead and fix the rope while the Ukrainians used it to follow as quickly as possible. Our traverse had now become more like a siege, and we all tacitly understood we couldn't survive such atrocious conditions for much longer. I plunged onwards directissima and George—with my 60 lb rucksack—cursed as he followed: a point snapped off each crampon, axe in the wrong hand, rucksack swinging wildly and balaclava slipping down over his eyes.

The next section, the ascent of the Central Tower of Shkhelda, was slathered with ice, and I could barely make contact as I inched my way up the steep gully. It was like Scottish ice-climbing on a grand scale, and the runouts were 150 ft at times. I didn't use any pitons for the simple reason that I couldn't find any placements for them. George followed, but the others made their way to the belay ledges, hand over hand up the fixed rope like a commando assault group. The swirling snow reduced visibility to a few yards and the wind whipped round the ridge from the north. Eventually, I broke out left onto the crest of the ridge and climbed it for a while before returning to the continuation of the couloir. Normally, this section is dangerously loose, but at the time, everything was well bonded with layers of ice. We made our way erratically upwards like a procession of ants on a wedding cake, and when we finally arrived at that hard-gained summit, we were shattered.

Eugene told us that, on long climbs such as this, students from the camps take emergency food up to individual summits. One of the Ukrainians unearthed a great black sausage, and we cut it open gleefully only to find that it was rotten. Even the Alpine choughs which had suddenly appeared wouldn't touch it. But there was also a tin of sprats and some condensed milk, vital sustenance as we pressed onwards in search of another bivvy site. The Ukrainians had decided to cut short their journey and descend into Svanetia via a subsidiary ridge, but George and I were determined to finish the damn thing, if it didn't finish us first. We had been unable to send any flare signals to our faithful watchers at Spartak due to the poor weather, and as it was now approaching our control time of 12 days, we asked the Ukrainians to tell the camp officials that we were all right.

The following morning was lung-bitingly cold with the usual formulae of wind and blinding snow. Now ravenously hungry, I found myself wondering why the hell I was there. The condensed milk had somehow got spilt over the Ukrainians' sewn-in groundsheet, and through the spindrift, I spied one of them licking the foul mess—now reinforced with bits of wool and dubbin—with relish. Its distinctly jaundiced tinge also bore witness to the man's inaccurate aim when using his pee tin.

An abseil brought us down to a col, where two gendarmes between Central and Eastern Shkhelda had to be turned. Ordinarily, this would have been no problem, but in atrocious weather it was bivouac time before we reached the East Peak, the final obstacle on the route. We hacked ledges out of the frozen snow like ice-encrusted old-age pensioners digging our own graves. And to think that less than two weeks previously we had boasted that we'd knock Shkhelda off in four days!

That night was our coldest on the climb. We were frozen to the marrow, and our clothes resembled a collection of oil drums and stove pipes in the morning. Though we kept our boots in our sleeping bags, they too were solid, and we had to strong-arm our feet into them. The tents folded like cardboard and acted like sails on top of our rucksacks. Our gloves looked like small spades, and we couldn't grip our axes properly.

Traversing on tiny holds across an exposed slab, we headed for a patch of sun, which, though off route, was as essential to our well-being as drink is to an alcoholic. On the steep wall high above the Shkhelda glacier, a small ledge glimmered. It looked like paradise, and we shuffled like zombies toward this oasis.

The ledge was the size of a chessboard and sloped slightly downhill to a sheer drop. But we were soon secured and able to take our boots off and massage our feet in the blessed sunshine. Slowly, our clothing changed colour from a matt white to a dirty grey before finally starting to steam. The panorama of the Caucasian range lay magnificently before us and, even in our exhausted and frostbitten state, we felt exhilarated being in that lofty place. Our respite was short-lived, however; time was marching on and we had to get back on the route.

The following pitch seemed as hard as anything I had ever climbed previously: a fragile, ice-filled overhanging crack on shoddy pegs. We then surmounted a series of overhanging chimneys until a 50-degree ribbon of ice ran parallel with a rising rock rib forming a continuous ceiling. I hammered every piton I had into the rock and the rope hung out in space at an alarming angle. After a battle of wills I almost lost, I finally hauled myself over the last bulge of rock and brought up the others, who were so frozen that their coordination resembled that of marionettes. We staggered to the summit of East Shkhelda and were overjoyed when Igor uncovered another buried cache of food—for the last couple of days, a single tin of condensed milk had sustained the four of us.

Shattered and relieved to have completed our mammoth tour, we spent a pleasant night in relative calm bivouacking at the end of the rock ridge, and in the morning, we ran the gauntlet of the Ushba icefall. lthough it had taken us almost two weeks to complete the route, we were buoyed by our success, and in no time at all, we arrived back at Spartak. The entire camp turned out to greet us, showering us with flowers. A local artist had created a superb oil painting especially for our arrival, upon which the words 'Conquering heroes' were emblazoned in Russian. We were in dire need of the feast that had been prepared for us, having each lost about 21 lbs during the climb.

Our protracted expedition had put us behind schedule, and I still had to make a film to pay for my holiday. The Russians hadn't forgotten, however; Abalakov and Rotentaov, two very senior Masters of Sport, quickly organised things for the following day. The whole camp was put at our disposal, and a movie depicting the training and way of life there was made on a nearby glacier and around the camp grounds. It was later screened back in the UK, and I found a Soviet commentator to present it with me—a collaboration that was almost unheard of back then.

After a day of recuperation, we reluctantly said goodbye to our new friends and made our way back to Moscow to retrieve George's Mini. Needless to say, after being abandoned for so long in Revolution Square, the battery was dead, but a posse of genial Muscovite taxi drivers soon gathered round and, in high humour, pushed us across the square as they derisively chanted some revolutionary song.

We pelted our way back along the great straights of the Soviet Union en route to Poland. It was harvest time and the land was golden. The barrier at Brest clanged behind us. Near Warsaw, a drunken cyclist weaving his way along a dirt road veered out in front of us. George had no chance of stopping, and bicycle and cyclist sailed up in the air. Mercifully, the cyclist, perhaps thanks to his drunken state, landed softly enough, and he issued forth an unmistakable stream of obscenities as he gestured wildly at his buckled wheel. A small crowd, including several horses and carts, soon gathered and divided into two camps: those for and those against the foreigners. One chap pulled up in a car and said helpfully to George, in broken English, 'You pay him £30 and forget about it!'

'Not on your life,' George retorted. He had actually read the small print of the State Insurance, which we had taken out at the frontier. So he called the police, a move that received enthusiastic applause from the pro-Scots faction. Half an hour later, a police car drew up and out tumbled an insurance assessor, a judge, an interpreter and a policeman. Court was held on the public highway.

'How much damage to the car?' asked the insurance assessor.

'About £3.50,' George replied, surveying the damage with a critical eye.

The damage to the bike was some 70p, apparently. George magnanimously declared that, as the cyclist was evidently a poor man, he would pay for the wheel. Upon hearing this proposal translated, the drunkard leapt up and grabbed George by the shoulders, planting wet kisses on both cheeks.

It was settled. We all shook hands, and George and I folded ourselves back into the Mini to a chorus of farewells.

I was sorry to drive back across the Iron Curtain, for we had made a lot of friends in the Caucasus, and renewing my climbing partnership with George had brought back fond memories of our time together as less experienced mountaineers. Our adventure on the Shkhelda Ridge cemented a great friendship that lasted a lifetime. At an age when many men would have been contemplating retirement, George had made a most congenial, steadfast companion, enduring protracted hardship without complaint while I felt like eating my boots and threatened to give up climbing altogether. Several years later, I visited George at his Edinburgh home and I was surprised to see a familiar sight amid the shrubbery—the infamous Mini. It was now a rusty playpen for his children.

Fifty years later, I received a visit from my nephew, Douglas, now himself in his 60s. He confided to me that, as a small boy, he loved sneaking up to the third floor and slipping into 'Uncle Hamish's Stores'—a spare room in my sister's house, full of tents, ropes and ice axes, and smelling of boiled wool, boot polish and paraffin. Douglas admitted that one of his great joys—which only a small boy would find appealing—was prying open my tins of Complan and sticking his tongue in to coat it in the powder. He recalled that it tasted thoroughly disgusting, but he found it thrilling all the same, imagining that this was what real explorers lived on as they roamed the wilds of the world in search of the Abominable Snowman.

A SHEPHERD'S TALE

By Walter Elliot

Walter and Moss in Glen Etive

I vividly remember it was the height of the Suez Canal Crisis. 1956. We (The Elliot Family) got word there'd been a bad accident on Buachaille Etive Mòr in The Chasm—a nasty place round the back of the mountain, down Glen Etive. That's a long way from where we live at Achnambeithach in Glen Coe.

Petrol was still under ration at the time, but because we lived the 'farming life' we had access to fuel, so we took our Austin 12 and drove round to Glen Etive.

The victim lay just below the Devil's Cauldron. He'd fallen a long way and he had an open leg fracture above the ankle, but he was conscious and he'd be ok.

Not long after we arrived, we saw two folk above us—this would be Hamish and John Cunningham. They'd been climbing on Bidean nam Bian nearby and had also heard about the accident, so they'd run across the mountain range to see if they could help. We were all in our mid-twenties and this would be the first time I met John or Hamish. They were keen to help, but Hamish being Hamish wanted to know if we could give them a lift back round to Glen Coe afterwards. This we did, for the Austin had plenty of room for all of us, including the casualty. So began my life-long friendship with Hamish.

Up until this point, the local Glen Coe shepherds and their families handled most of the rescues and searches, for there were few folks on the hills, and if it was a technical rescue, the climbing clubs from Glasgow would be called in to help. But things began to change, with more and more folk breaking out of the cities on weekends and heading to the mountains. With them came more searches, more accidents, more rescues.

A group of us got together—Hamish, myself and Donald Duff—and decided it was time to establish a 'proper' local mountain rescue team. And so, the Glencoe Mountain Rescue Team was born.

Catherine MacInnes training rescue dogs © John Cleare

Local crofter and shepherd Huan Findlay and the Glencoe Mountain Rescue Team © John Cleare

Buachaille Etive Mòr

15. THE GREAT HERDSMAN OF ETIVE

I have found that every mountain tends to have its own personality. For all its grandeur, Ben Nevis seems to withdraw reclusively into itself, and for most of the year it's in purdah, shrouded in a wet veil of mist. The diminutive Cobbler in the Arrochar Alps, on the other hand, reminds me of a troupe of dancing dwarfs, mica schist like wrinkled skin, while Cìr Mhòr on Arran resembles a young bride, its pale, elegant granite train enticing walkers and climbers alike.

Buachaille Etive Mòr, Gaelic for Great Herdsman of Etive, has the presence of a dignitary. It glows with the healthy complexion of rhyolite, and when approaching from the flatlands of Rannoch Moor, it stands like a prize exhibit for all that is great in Scottish mountaineering: impeccable rock, deeply etched gullies and stately majesty—much like a monarch presiding over her dominion—that gives one an exalted feeling when scaling one of the mountain's lofty routes. 'The Buachaille' has provided pleasure for generations of hillwalkers, rock gymnasts and ice technicians. I think of it as a great curved bookshelf, where every ledge holds a story of high adventure, where adrenaline has flowed like the draught ale at the nearby Kingshouse Hotel, and where the dull clink of hobnailed boots has given way to the rasp and spark of Tricounis and, later, the scrape of crampons or the purposeful quietude of sticky rubber.

Bill Murray's historic account of his first winter ascent of Shelf Route in 1937 was a classic Buachaille adventure. He and the redoubtable Bill MacKenzie pioneered this radical winter route, which slices the side of Crowberry Ridge like a celestial axe wound. There were no dropped picks or 12-point crampons in those days. Not that one can condemn those trusty Tricounis: in some situations, they were superior to crampons, but the challenges of climbing with this ancient gear are hard to overstate. Worst of all was the rope, usually Italian hemp or manila, which would freeze solid and feel akin to wrestling with a steel hawser when tying on or belaying.

Looking over the expanse of Rannoch Moor, it's easy to imagine it covered in a great sheet of ice several kilometres thick, with glaciers spilling down through what is now Glen Coe and Glen Etive. After the ice retreated, the vast Caledonian forest stretched far beyond the distant peak of Schiehallion. Aeons later, drovers with black cattle, riding over the hill above Allt Chailleach, would have seen The Buachaille rearing up out of the moor as they made their way down to the Kingshouse.

Before mountaineers treadmilled The Buachaille, only the occasional hunter ventured on its lower slopes, the poet Duncan Ban MacIntyre amongst them. VIPs such as Queen Victoria and Charles Dickens may have gazed up and passed judgement, but I doubt they gave a passing thought to the possibility of scaling the red ramparts of Stob Dearg, the mountain's summit top.

It wasn't until 1895 that the great North Buttress was climbed, quickly followed by Curved Ridge, with Original Route and Crowberry Gully falling three years later. The slow race was on, and climbing history was being made each year as new climbs were pioneered in both winter and summer, even during both world wars.

Jock Nimlin and company made one of the most notable pre-Second World War ascents when they climbed Raven's Gully in the summer of 1937. At that time, mountaineering was mainly the preserve of the professional classes, but Jock hailed from the working classes of Glasgow. A crane operator by profession, but a climber and lover of nature by inclination, he was lured by the distant call of Ben Lomond and the hills near Arrochar, whose panorama represented freedom and adventure. On weekends, Jock would sling his Bergen rucksack over his shoulder and head for the caves above Arrochar, sometimes walking from Glasgow. There, he and his mates would sing songs about the Spanish Civil War as they sat round a campfire. The Cobbler, a working man's mountain, was his and the Creagh Dhu Club's favourite stomping ground.

It was, therefore, with some deliberation that Jock stole a march on the establishment that was the Scottish Mountaineering Club and bagged Raven's Gully, which was one of the most formidable climbs of the day. Despite repeated attempts over the next two years, it repulsed all comers vying to make the second ascent. Even confident rock technicians from south of the border failed, usually peeling off the notorious fourth pitch. Many years later, in 1953, a youthful Chris Bonington and I took advantage of excellent conditions to bag the first winter ascent of the route. Although we managed to tick off the technically harder Crowberry Ridge Direct a day later, this was before front-pointing and Raven's Gully was probably more demanding, with a reputation of being the most difficult winter route in Scotland at the time.

There have been many tragedies on the flanks of The Buachaille and some remarkable escapes. I can recall at least two falls of over 1,000 ft in winter where the victims somehow survived after dodging jagged rocks en route down gullies resembling steeply tilted Cresta Runs. One man slipped a snowball's throw from the summit and free-fell over Central Buttress, eventually coming to a stop where the heather pushed up through the snow on The Buachaille's aprons. Remarkably, he lived to climb again, albeit some time later.

With each generation, the standard steadily rises, and today there are many new and serious routes on the mountain. In winter mountaineering, there was a quantum leap with the advent of the dropped pick and a profusion of cams and other protection that enabled the climber to progress relatively safely. On the whole, this advance in standards has run parallel with improvements in safety, but those who follow 'The Grand Old Masters' have the benefit of a springboard from which to leap.

The inimitable Tom Patey perfectly sums up the myriad adventures on The Buachaille and its compatriot hills in *The Ballad of Bill Murray*:

> *In the gullies of Glen Coe, they trod the virgin snow*
> *With Mackenzie to lead in the van*
> *With hawk nose distended and blue eyes flashing fire*
> *He was more like a God than a man.*
> *They plied the ashen shaft, applied their native craft*
> *Standing square, hitting home, hard and true*
> *And they climbed their hardest routes in Tricouni-studded boots*
> *There was nothing that those heroes wouldn't do.*

The Aonach Eagach, with Ben Nevis beyond © Hamish Frost

16. THE GLENCOE SCHOOL OF WINTER CLIMBING

The word 'avalanche' encompasses everything from rock falls to soggy masses of slithering mud and earth. Avalanches can take the form of ice, powder snow, wet snow and windslab, or indeed combinations of all these. Just one of many dangers sprung on the unwary mountaineer, they can descend with devastating force, but they are not always in a hurry. A small, wet avalanche can tumble down a slope as if it had all the time in the world, but its flightier brother, the airborne powder avalanche, can reach speeds of over 200 mph, ripping up everything in its path, including reinforced concrete, and reducing villages to their foundations. Until the early 1960s, even though climbers were injured and killed by avalanches in Scotland, they were by and large considered to be an act of God and given very little attention. This changed when the ice climbing revolution got underway in the mid-60s, however, as the number of mountaineers on the hills in winter rose dramatically.

When I began to take an academic interest in snow science in the early half of that decade, I had already fallen foul of three avalanches, so I had more than a passing interest in them. Better late than never, I read all I could on the subject. Some might wryly point out that since I've subsequently been engulfed by three further avalanches, my studies haven't done me much good, but these encounters were either in the Himalayas in bad weather or during rescues on terrain I wouldn't normally have ventured into.

I resolved to do something constructive about avalanche awareness and rescue in Scotland after searching for a buried climber, one Professor Lata, who had been swept down the Aonach Eagach Ridge in Glen Coe. It had been an apology for an avalanche, really—a narrow ribbon of snow that had slid down like a stair runner for 1,000ft. But it was wet snow with virtually no air content. Burial in such liquid porridge, when there is little or no trapped air, is usually fatal. I had my dog with me when we started searching for the buried climber, but in those days we had no specially trained dogs, and when Tiki started to dig enthusiastically at the edge of the debris, I thought it was an unlikely location and called her away. To my dismay, the next day we found the Professor's body where Tiki had been digging. After this, the Scottish branch of the British Red Cross sponsored my visit to a centre in Switzerland that specialised in running courses on avalanche rescue using dogs, and when I returned home, I established the Search and Rescue Dog Association (SARDA). We held the first training course in Glen Coe that winter, incorporating both summer and winter search techniques. We had made a start.

I wasn't the only person with an interest in snow science at this time. Eric Langmuir, then the Principal of Glenmore Lodge, an outdoor training centre in the Cairngorms, was fascinated by snow in all its forms, and he later became a leading authority on avalanches in Britain. Through his keen interest in the structure and behaviour of snow, Eric became acquainted with Miloš Vrba, an avalanche expert with the Czech Government and a member of Horská služba České, the country's national mountain rescue service. Miloš was invited to Scotland to lecture on the subject and deliver

A rescue on the Aonach Eagach

practical demonstrations in the mountains around Glen Coe. After he had taken a snow profile, he surprised us by saying that he considered the snow unstable and dangerous that day. The slope avalanched overnight.

Miloš and I became good friends after that, and Eric and I visited him in Czechoslovakia. Our whistle-stop tour with the Horská služba team included a short stay in the Low Tatra, terrain not unlike the Cairngorms, with rolling, spacious hills. In winter, they are pleasingly snow-clad, and in the forests on the lower slopes, the silence is broken only by the soughing of the pines. It's the sort of place where one might imagine Good King Wenceslas with a foot-weary page hirpling through oxter-deep powder.

My concern for the number of accidents occurring in Scotland as a result of avalanches was also a big part of my decision to establish the Glencoe School of Winter Climbing in the early 1960s. Aspirant winter climbers from all over the UK had been decrying the lack of facilities for instruction in the basics of mountain safety, and many people were being killed simply because of a lack of knowledge. The school was the first in Scotland to provide instruction in step-cutting and what is now known as ice axe arrest, as well as tuition on snow structure and avalanche awareness. The Scottish Youth Hostel Association was eager to assist and kindly offered accommodation at Glencoe for pupils and instructors.

I established a nucleus of top winter climbers at the school over the 20-odd years of its existence. Safety was paramount, and despite running many hundreds of courses over the years, we never had an accident. Allan Fyffe, Paul Nunn, John Grieve and even Tom Patey were just a few of the well-kent faces there, and most of the climbers in the Glencoe Mountain Rescue Team, including Graeme Hunter, Rob Taylor and Ian Clough, also instructed.

I met Ian when I was the instructor employed by the Mountaineering Association to run a winter climbing course back in the 1950s. He was quiet and unassuming, with a natural affinity for moving on steep snow and ice. I knew immediately that he was taking this winter business seriously and would make his mark on many a mountain, for he already had a modern short ice axe and crampons, which, remarkably, were frowned upon by some at the time.

Later, Ian joined forces with me running the Glencoe School of Winter Climbing during the week, and we climbed together on weekends. He was a model instructor on our courses, but he had a mischievous streak and would often seek amusement at his pupils' expense. One such pupil was Raymond Japhet (AKA Scoop), a sub-editor of a well-known Sunday tabloid. Scoop plagued mountaineers from the Cuillins of Skye to the dank heights of Snowdonia as he charged around seeking a story, grasping his notebook as if it were an Olympic torch. His clarion cry for 'copy' was to the detriment of all those seeking tranquillity, but he meant well and probably loved the mountains as much as we did. Although not a climber, Scoop had aspirations to write a book, and he enrolled on one of our winter survival courses for research purposes. When the students were snowbound in the Charles Inglis Clark (CIC) hut on Ben Nevis one day, Ian sought to give the others some peace and quiet by convincing Scoop that, in order to pass the survival course, he needed to construct a snowhole and tunnel his way out. Dressed only in his underpants, with a notepad tucked into this waistband, Scoop set about his task with customary zeal and claimed the first successful ascent of the icy corrugated roof of the CIC hut in crampons.

My time with Ian at the Glencoe School of Winter Climbing is now a distant memory, a blur of sunsets, bivouacs, cold dawns, rescues and avalanches. It was a pleasure and a privilege to have known him—a modest man now with so many others in the Hall of Fame. Sadly, Ian was killed by a falling serac on the very last day of Chris Bonington's British expedition to the South Face of Annapurna in 1970.

Ian Clough, 1967

THE MACINNES STRETCHER

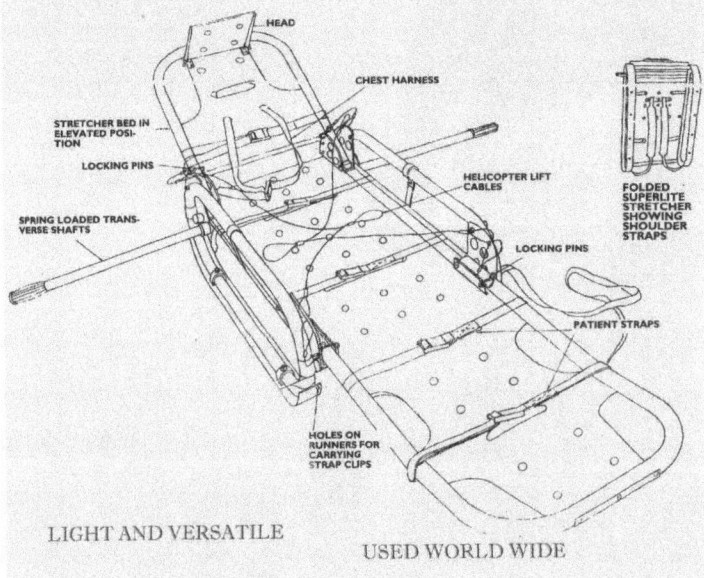

MacInnes Superlite Stretcher

This lightweight stretcher has been developed due to the extensive use of helicopters in Mountain Rescue work throughout the world. It can be carried speedily to the scene of an accident by one person and is ready for use in seconds. There are no projecting parts to foul when being winched by helicopter and lift wires are standard.
Even though it is one of the lightest MR stretchers ever developed, it can still be used for the rough and tough carry-out situation should helicopter assistance fail to materialise. It is equally suited to cableway and cliff use. The alloy patient bed gives maximum protection together with excellent rigidity for spinal/neck injuries. A fold-flat head protector is standard. Patient contact surface is coated in closed-cell foam.

THE SUPERLITE STRETCHER HAS ADJUSTABLE BACK AND OPTIONAL SPRING LOADED TRANSVERSE SHAFTS. THE TRANSPORT WHEEL CLIPS ONTO THE RUNNERS WITH HOOK BOLTS. STAINLESS STEEL DROP PINS ARE USED FOR LOCKING THE STRETCHER IN POSITION.

LIGHT AND VERSATILE   USED WORLD WIDE

In the early 1960s, evacuating injured walkers and climbers from troublesome mountain locations was a major headache for rescue teams. Helicopters often couldn't access these places, and the rescues themselves were usually strenuous, requiring careful negotiation over precipitous and unstable terrain. Traditional single-unit stretchers were bulky and heavy, and carrying them uphill required two rescue team members.

I pondered this problem and tasked myself with designing something more efficient that would make life easier for rescuers and improve the prospects of our unfortunate clients. This led to the genesis of the first folding stretcher, made from aluminium alloy to minimise weight. The two-piece Mk6, as it was known, had special frames that doubled as harnesses for transporting casualties. Jumbo-sized wheels allowed it to move over rough ground effectively and shock cord acted as dampers. Later modifications included quick-release buckles, a detachable head guard and a helicopter winch harness cable, which clipped onto stainless steel anchor pins. This stretcher was used on five expeditions to Everest, and thousands of injured climbers around the world have been evacuated using variations of the original Mk6 over the last 50 years or so.

But even the weight of half a stretcher, with all the associated equipment, is near the limit of what one person can carry and move quickly with, and the original design has undergone many iterations over the years. In 2002, I was fortunate to meet Richard Glanville, an Inverness-based sailor and professional architect who had built the first all-carbon fibre reinforced sailing yacht. We soon developed a friendship and mutual respect for each other's abilities, and our collaboration led to the creation of a new compact, lighter version of the Mk6, which we imaginatively called the Mk7. Constructed from high-strength abrasion- and impact-resistant material that could withstand very low temperatures, the Mk7 was ideal for military operations and disaster work when helicopter transportation is often required, and over the years it has been successfully deployed on many international rescues. Richard and I were pleased and surprised that we were able to whittle the Mk7's weight down to a mere 11 kg. This was mainly due to the development of the stretcher's composite tub shell, which Richard's father, in his late 80s, helped us refine during the production process.

Hamish with his SARDA
dogs © John Cleare

17. A MINI, A TRAIN AND A CORPSE

When I got a call from Donnie Smith of the Northern Constabulary, I knew it was going to be a long day. A climber had been reported missing in Inchnadamph, an area of Scotland famous for its intricate coastline and array of spectacular sandstone mountains.

Dedicated mountain rescuers, my then wife Catherine and I set off in my Mini with our pre-packed rucksacks and our hounds Rangi and Tiki, agog with excitement in the hold and seemingly cognisant of their impending adventure. At that time, SARDA was itself a puppy. My dogs had accompanied me on several rescue call-outs over the years and had proved their worth on more than one occasion, so I had recently paid a visit to an avalanche dog training course in Switzerland, where I immediately recognised the possibilities for developing a similar specialised branch of mountain rescue in Scotland. A dog's sense of smell is thought to be a thousand times more sensitive than a human's, and, as is commonly known today, they can be trained to use this to detect human scent in the air, even in the case of deceased victims. They are also fairly impervious to bad weather and can work in all conditions, day or night, quickly covering huge areas. Together, a dog and its handler make an extremely efficient team.

After several hours travelling at breakneck speed in my little tin box, we arrived at the Old School House at Elphin, which was lit up as if for a Christmas rehearsal, with trucks and cars everywhere. Looking altogether too cheerful in their bright yellow anoraks, Donnie was framed in the doorway alongside Chief Inspector Charlie Rhoden.

'Good morning!' Charlie boomed. 'It's gae snell, how about a stroupach [cup of tea]? I've just had a call from HQ to say that there's been an incident in Torridon; disnae sound good—screams! Can you head over there with your dogs instead?' He didn't stop to hear our reply. 'Marvellous! I'll have bacon and eggs on standby.'

'A couple of hillwalkers thought they heard cries for help high on up on Liathach,' Donnie advised us as we devoured two vast all-day breakfasts. 'For some reason, they didn't report it. It was the driver of the wee bus that goes to Diabaig who raised the alarm when he heard the lads chatting about the cries.'

'Anything else?' I mumbled through a mouthful of scrambled egg.

'Aye. Splitpin, the bobby from Kinlochewe—you know, skinny bloke with the big heid? Well, he drove doon Glen Torridon and found a Ford van parked at the bottom of Liathach.'

'Hmm, it doesn't sound good,' I admitted, thinking of those great sandstone terraces, most of them overhanging. 'We'll head off immediately. He may still be alive.'

Catherine and I made fast time to Garve, which comprised a junction, a hotel, a railway station and damn all else. From here, a road snakes west into the wild and beautiful country of Achnashellach and Torridon, a paradise of lochs, peaks and ancient forest.

As I accelerated uphill flat out, we reached a wide glen and came parallel with a freight train, belting along and belching smoke. The driver blasted his whistle and gave a cheerful wave. I responded with an embarrassing squeak of the Mini's horn.

I don't think that either the train driver or I intended to race, but it soon became clear that's what we were doing. Although my Mini had a boy-racer instinct, I was hard-pressed to keep up with the train. *God help us if we meet someone coming the other way*, I thought, as I put my foot to the floor. One minute the train was ahead, then I would overtake, horn squealing like a piglet in distress. For a while, we were neck and neck, blasting and squealing in unison. This went on for miles with, thankfully, no audience other than some bemused-looking red deer.

We finally reached Achnasheen, my Mini the runner-up, beaten by half a train length. The winner doffed his dirty cap and gave a final blast as a cheerio.

Descending into Glen Torridon, we resumed a more sombre attitude as the mighty Liathach hove into view, rearing up in great steps to its jagged summit. We released the dogs and surveyed the formidable massif. Resembling a high-angled paddy field, the ancient sandstone ridge of Liathach is grand in scale and fiendishly complex, especially in suboptimal conditions. It is not a place for the inexperienced or fainthearted.

On some flat moorland nearby, crofters were cutting peat, unaware of any drama above them. A whisky bottle glinted in the morning sunlight: lubrication for the day ahead, no doubt.

Within 40 minutes we had reached a point close to the summit ridge and the dogs were ranging around on precipitous rock, intent on demonstrating their superior tracking skills. There was no sign of anyone, so we stopped for a breather, and I said to Catherine I would take a look over some steeper terrain we had avoided on the way up.

As I clambered down a weakness in the face, Rangi stopped on a small ledge and sniffed the air, every sinew trembling with the intensity of the task at hand. On the ledge was the imprint of a cleated rubber sole. Suddenly, Catherine shouted from above, 'Tiki's found him, Hamish! He's up here.'

Joining Catherine at the top of a steep scree slope leading to a precipitous gully, I saw the crumpled heap of humanity, limbs at an unlikely angle. Sadly, he appeared to have perished only recently. With his greenish-brown clothing, the victim was almost invisible, even from a few feet away. His watch had stopped at 12:55pm, the time that the two young lads had heard the calls for help.

I sent up a flare, which arced above us and exploded in a mass of red smoke, and we sat in the sunshine waiting for the reinforcements to arrive. Far below, we could see the RAF Kinloss Mountain Rescue Team led by John Hinde, and a cluster of rubber-necking tourists. With what I fancied to be totemic significance, a golden eagle drifted by silently.

Soaked in sweat, John and his team finally arrived with the rescue equipment. Although the corpse was only a short distance away from where they had gathered, none of them could see the well-camouflaged victim, and we had to point to where he lay.

The stretcher lower down those great steps of Liathach was gruelling and dangerous even for seasoned rescuers. Terraced ledges soon gave way to full-blown cliffs and we had to send one of the crew out in front as a scout, to see if it was possible to set up the complex lowering systems that were required to prevent both pallbearers and stretcher shooting off down the mountain toward the enthralled onlookers below. Tiki and Rangi, ever faithful, were eager to contribute and would dart off in one direction before returning with canine news of an impasse or avoidable hazard. Eventually, our sombre cortege reached the road, shattered after such a physically and manually demanding evacuation, which was all the more traumatic for the victim's untimely demise. We ignored the avid spectators and slid the corpse into the waiting ambulance.

Rangi and Tiki were the first two Search and Rescue dogs in Great Britain. Some time after our unfortunate call-out on Liathach, Catherine and I were called upon to search for an overdue climber in the Mamores mountain range in the West Highlands. We had heard reports of a massive avalanche in Steall Gully in Glen Nevis, and I suspected the two events might be connected, so I left Catherine to sweep the lower slopes with Tiki and set off with Rangi to explore the upper section of the gully. As it reared at a near-vertical angle above me, I could see it was swept clean right down to bedrock with not a patch of snow left in it. There was little further threat of avalanche here, and next to no chance of finding a victim. With Rangi at my side, I was about to descend when I heard a tremendous crack from above, as a subsidiary gully, only a metre or so wide, suddenly shed its load. I managed to scramble up some nearby rocks but Rangi was swept away with the full force of the avalanche and instantly buried. Catherine hurried across to the debris site and Tiki quickly found Rangi, alive but paralysed with a broken spine. I picked up the dog and carried him in my arms down to the base of the gully. There was nothing to be done for him but to put him out of his misery. Rangi was a wonderful dog and, in so many ways, proved to be the inspiration for SARDA.

Catherine and the dogs on a training exercise in Glen Coe
© John Cleare

OBSERVATIONS ON A RESCUE
By John Cleare

The very first lift of a MacInnes Stretcher in the 1960s

Returning south one winter from a *Highlands Magazine* assignment, I'd lodged overnight with my friend Ian Clough in Glencoe village. Around 3:00 am, there was a rescue call-out. 'The team will need you, John,' insisted Ian. It was official.

It seemed that a climber was missing on Buachaille Etive Mòr. This was long before mobile phones, and the climber's companion had descended the mountain in the dark to raise the alarm.

The system was well-oiled. We picked up team members as we drove through the village and up the glen, pausing only to collect Hamish at Allt na Reigh. It was sleeting as we pulled off the road at Jacksonville. Everyone knew their task and what to carry, and we set off by torchlight, splashing through the burn and on up the mountain.

Hamish was well prepared and had already debriefed the missing climber's companion. Late completing their climb, the pair had lost contact with each other as they tried to descend unroped over easy but icy, exposed ground in poor visibility. Knowing the terrain as well as he did, Hamish had a fair idea where the accident had occurred and could guess the outcome. Nevertheless, we moved as fast as we could onto more difficult rocky ground, Hamish pressing on ahead to recce as dawn bleached the sky.

It was as he thought, and there was now no hurry. The missing man was lying below a steep pitch near the foot of one of the great gullies that slashes The Buachaille's north face. He must have tumbled almost 1,000ft. In the half-light, we scrambled across to the gully and abseiled into the cauldron below the pitch. There was blood in the snow as Hamish pulled a tarp over the body. Coffee thermoses were passed round.

I'd encountered death on the mountain before, but the experience left me squeamish. For the team, though, it was merely another sad job, not a hoped-for life-saver. I noted how respectfully the body was handled, and as an unusual favour, Hamish agreed that I could take pictures on the proviso that I embargoed any that depicted the casualty for at least 20 years.

The task now was to wrap and evacuate the body. Hamish gave his instructions and the team sprang into action, everyone aware of what to do. The loaded stretcher with a 'barrow boy' guiding it was carefully lowered down the gully walls onto steep, snowy scree. Then the ropes were coiled, the gear packed, and the site cleared of any sign of the fatal incident. We set off down the hill toward the road, frequently changing bearers, and I noted that a dead body seems somehow heavier than a live one.

Unlike other rather haphazard rescues I'd observed elsewhere, this had been an impressive operation. With clinical efficiency, Hamish, like a surgeon in an operating theatre, commanded a team of dedicated friends who trusted him completely as they relied on each other to carry out their duty to help others.

Avalanche probe line on Ben Nevis

Lowering a casualty on a technical rescue on Bidean nam Bian

Tending to a casualty in Glen Coe

Observations on a Rescue

Tom Patey on the first winter traverse of the Cuillin Ridge

18. THE CUILLIN RIDGE IN WINTER

Originally written by Dr Tom Patey for the Scottish Mountaineering Club Journal *in 1965, with commentary from Brian Robertson and Hamish MacInnes added in 2017. This newly revised version is available thanks to the kindness of the Patey family.*

It was a frosty moonlit night in February, and snow blanketed the hills around the head of Loch Broom. I had just finished my evening's work when the phone rang. Anticipating a late-night visit, I lifted the receiver with weary resignation.

'Hello there! Is that you, Tom?' said a familiar voice. 'I was thinking of pushing over to Skye tonight for a look at the Cuillin Ridge. Naturally, I thought you might like to come along.'

The enthusiasm crackling along the line left no doubt as to the owner of the voice. Who else but Hamish MacInnes would phone at this hour with such a preposterous suggestion?

'It's great to hear from you again, Hamish,' I replied cautiously. 'Could I perhaps phone you back in an hour? I would need to make a few trifling arrangements, you know.'

'Of course, of course,' he conceded magnanimously. 'Perhaps an hour would be sufficient, and if I haven't heard from you by then, I'll just set off.'

Sixty-five minutes later, I rang him up. 'Hello again, Tom, I thought it might be you,' he bellowed cheerfully. 'You're just in time. We're about to leave.'

'We? Who is "we"?' I asked suspiciously.

'Davie Crabbe and myself, who else? Didn't I tell you? Oh, of course, you wouldn't know. Well, when you didn't phone back I asked him to come instead. It's unfortunate that you've got everything fixed up.' His voice took on a sententious tone. 'Three is a bad number for the ridge—far too slow and they eat too much. Why don't you find a fourth? Anyway, I can't stop to talk now. See you tonight at Sligachan? The last ferry from Kyle leaves in three hours, so you might just make it if you hurry.'

I swore violently as the line went dead. My mind went back to the occasion several years ago when I had received a postcard that briefly announced, 'Meet me at Molde on 25 June at 3:00 pm.' Molde is a tiny place somewhere up a Norwegian fjord. I already knew of Hamish's capricious fits of enthusiasm, so I had thought of phoning him at his home in Glencoe on the appointed day and announcing my arrival in Molde. I had abandoned the idea. He would have commiserated briefly and then asked about the snow conditions. (N.B. from Hamish MacInnes: I was indeed in Molde on the afternoon of 25 June—Tom was nowhere to be seen.)

I remembered, too, the scraps of information scattered haphazardly through Hamish's letters, which had a simplicity often shattering in its impact—viz: 'If you receive no reply to your next letter, you will know that I have gone up the Amazon in search of a new species of long-tailed monkey. It promises to be a really interesting project.' To be fair, I found out later that the tale of the long-tailed monkey was true.

It had been eight years since our last climb together. That was a red-letter day in February 1957, when, with Graeme Nicol of Aberdeen, we made the first winter ascent of Zero Gully on Ben Nevis, at that time the most difficult winter route on the mountain. Curiously, we had never joined forces again.

My annoyance at MacInnes's premature departure for Skye was eased the next day by the news that he had got stuck in a snowdrift near Cluanie and had retreated to Glencoe to carry out essential repairs on his car.

That same evening, a small, wiry individual wearing a climber's safety helmet arrived at our door looking for a 'doss'. It was none other than Brian Robertson. He had hitch-hiked from Fort William in a fish lorry and wore the keenly expectant look of a man who has wandered many days in the desert and suddenly stumbled upon an oasis. His arrival could scarcely have been better timed.

The following evening found us at Sligachan. We had chosen to attempt a traverse of the ridge from the north as this would enable us to abseil several sections where the reverse direction would involve very severe ice climbing.

We phoned MacInnes in Glencoe and told him snow conditions appeared excellent and we would be starting at dawn. If he hurried, he could just catch the late-night ferry. It says a lot for his superb sangfroid that he was able to accept this information with no outward show of emotion and to inform us in a detached tone that he would be unable to leave for several days due to previous commitments.

The 'Winter Traverse' had become something of an out-of-season attraction as so many rival groups of climbers vied for the honour of being the first claimant. I had already made an attempt, and I knew of at least a dozen others, including six made by Hamish himself with different companions. The essential ingredients for success appeared to be a heavy snowfall without an accompanying wind, followed successively by a thaw and an equally rapid freeze. The weather would also need to remain favourable for at least two days, and all these conditions rarely concur because of the maritime climate.

It is hardly surprising, then, that I had had to wait so long after my first attempt before returning to the fray, when, as events were soon to prove, the only thing out of condition was the climbing party. In direct contrast to my previous visit, there was no snow at all below the 2,000-foot contour, but above this level, the fantastic jagged skyline of the main ridge was crusted as white as a Christmas cake. The conditions were perfect—iron-hard névé, ideally suited to front-point cramponing—but an unduly late start and a comedy of errors and misadventures quickly put paid to our Cuillin adventure. I might not have been so despondent had I known that we would be returning to Sligachan before the week was out. I phoned MacInnes, as I had promised, with the news of our defeat.

'So you didn't get up,' he remarked before I had even spoken.

'How on earth did you know that?'

'Well I heard that conditions were almost spring-like, so I knew you wouldn't bother pushing on with it. Quite right, it would have been daylight robbery to claim a first winter ascent.'

'What do you know about it?' I replied huffily, 'You weren't even there.'

'Ah, you forget that a friend of mine, Peter Thomas, lives at Glen Brittle,' said Hamish in his 'matter-of-fact' voice.

I returned the gauntlet. 'If that's what you think, go over and see yourself.'

'All right,' he said thoughtfully. 'I think I will. I'll find Davie Crabbe and we'll be on the road in an hour. See you at Sligachan...'

Wee Brian was persuaded to attempt a rematch, so we set off once more for Sligachan. From the road outside the hotel, MacInnes was prepared to admit he was wrong about the conditions, but that was about all he would concede. 'Tom, I hear you're thinking of getting Peter Thomas to carry the bivvy gear up to Sgùrr na Banachdich, which is all very well, but Davie and I have been thinking and we reckon it's cheating. You know, of course, what everyone will say?' he said darkly.

'You think it's cheating? Well, look at it this way—I've already carried a heavy rucksack as far as Bidein Druim nan Ramh and that's almost as far as Banachdich. I'm damned if I'm going to do it twice in a week merely to keep the records straight. I want to enjoy the climb, and so does Brian. If we happen to find a couple of rucksacks on top of Sgùrr na Banachdich just before dusk, we shall accept their existence as an Act of God and put them to good use. Peter Thomas is agreeable?'

'Oh yes, he is quite willing to help out but wonders if you are happy about the ethics of the thing.'

'Overjoyed,' I said, 'and so will you be when we take your packs off you after you've collapsed with exhaustion.'

Once more, we stood at the top of the abseil from the Bhàsteir Tooth. The weather was perfect, the snow beyond reproach. Only the time of day differed from the last visit—it was 11:00 am. Our rapid progress was due to two factors. First, we had our own recently-made tracks to guide us. More importantly, there was also a hint of rivalry between the two pairs of climbers—the merest suggestion, but sufficient to cause a gradual and insidious acceleration in the combined speed of the party. All the way from Sligachan, we had been forced to put up with MacInnes's lifemanship gambits. He appears to be entirely unaware of his talents in this particular field, so his comments are usually unanswerable.

'That was a tricky bit, eh, Davie? The boys made it look quite easy! It only shows how carrying a pack can upset your equilibrium. Makes an easy pitch Very Severe.'

Or:

'Please don't let us hold you up, lads! It's going to be a terribly cold night for you if you don't reach Banachdich tonight. I know quite well you're both keen to get ahead.' He was hammering along like a steam engine at the time, and we had considerable difficulty keeping up, but we had a measure of excuse for our poor showing. MacInnes and Crabbe had gone religiously to bed at 9:00 pm the previous evening, while Robertson and I had stayed up until 2:00 am at a ceilidh, exchanging stories with my host, John MacLellan, a former Scottish Heavy Events champion. Several other convivial Sgiathanachs had joined the group around the fire. An accordion, a mouth organ, a tape recorder and a bottle of whisky were ideal ingredients for an impromptu ceilidh. The whisky circulated briskly. Robertson had been unable to resist the fiery creutair and the temptation of getting something for nothing. We had been roused by an alarm clock at 5:00 am, but we could have slept till midday, and it was a long time before I could convince myself that we had slept at all. On the way up the mountain, Robertson had stopped every half mile to be sick, and I imagined he might give Sgùrr nan Gillean a miss since he had climbed it only a few days before.

I soloed up the gully leading to the final col on the Pinnacle Ridge and then made my way with some difficulty up the most direct route to the top, being forced to cut steps for the last 400 ft. Despite this, I arrived a little in front of MacInnes and Crabbe, who had climbed the West Ridge, finding the gendarme tricky.

The four of us were climbing unroped and Robertson and I were ahead of the others by about ten minutes when we reached a crucial abseil. I was halfway down the aerial section when a freak knot appeared on the rope below me. The next minute it had jammed squarely against the karabiner at my waist and I was left spinning round on the rope like a frustrated marionette. Desperate situations call for desperate measures, and I eventually solved the problem by hammering the knot through the karabiner.

It was only when we were about to retrieve the abseil rope that I realised that the knot was on the 'wrong' half of the doubled rope. Sure enough, it jammed again in the eye of the abseil piton. There was no easy solution this time. We would just have to wait for MacInnes and Crabbe to free it.

Then I noticed they were preparing to abseil down an altogether different part of the wall somewhere in the neighbourhood of Naismith's Route.

'Climb down a bit this way. That's the wrong route,' I called up persuasively.

'It looks okay to us,' said Hamish, 'and will save minutes in any case.'

'You realise that if the rope's only 150 ft long, it won't reach the bottom?'

'Of course it will. I happened to measure this pitch last summer. It is exactly 135 ft from top to bottom.'

MacInnes has such an impressive array of facts and figures at his fingertips that one occasionally doubts their authenticity. However, his voice carries such conviction that it is difficult to argue with him.

'Actually, it would help us if you could come down the same way; our rope is jammed, and you could chuck it down to us.' I felt like the small boy who asks for his ball back from the garden next door.

The practised lifeman never exploits such an obvious confession of failure. Instead, he pretends to ignore it altogether, although his face shows that he has had to make a conscious effort to do so.

'Pity about that,' remarked Hamish, in an abstract way as he handed us a neatly coiled rope. 'We must have lost at least ten minutes on that little mishap. Can't be helped, of course. These things happen.'

We mumbled our apologies and offered to take our turn of carrying the packs.

'I'm feeling fine,' said MacInnes, who indeed looked it. 'How about you, Davie?'

'Never felt better,' replied that stalwart with his usual loyalty.

'Thanks all the same, Tom,' the gallant hero continued, 'but you have to get to Banachdich for four o'clock and we'll manage to struggle along.'

I was beginning to question which pair of us was labouring under the bigger handicap. Without rucksacks, we should have been half as fast again as they were, but with Hamish in his usual superb physical condition, this was an impossibility.

I must admit, too, that we were dismayed to discover how effortlessly Davie Crabbe was keeping pace with MacInnes. For a man who had only recently entered the limelight, he was making light of snow and ice problems that would have caused most veteran Alpinists to demand the protection of a rope. I had always understood that although reigning tigers might surpass their elders on short routes of extreme technical severity, they lacked experience of moving quickly and competently over averagely difficult terrain. I was now finding out, like many others, that this is another myth as ridiculous as the tale that the modern climber only betters the achievements of his forebears by excessive use of pitons and slings. In climbing, as in any other competitive sport, a person's ability and achievements must be measured against the yardstick of his contemporaries.

At the top of the snow gully between the central and west peaks of Bidein, we grappled with our first pitch of actual rock climbing. Even so, the vital holds were hidden under blue ice and had to be bared with axes. Although merely a 'muscle-loosener' in summer, this was now a pitch of

Severe standard. Having duly appropriated the central peak, we abseiled back to the col, passing the other pair on the way up.

From here to Sgùrr a' Mhadaidh was no more than a walk. That is to say, you could have fallen and escaped with your life. This could not be said of any other part of the Cuillin Ridge in the conditions we found it. There was a sufficient depth of iron-hard névé on most of the ledges to incorporate them into the uniformly steep slopes which fell away from the snowy knife-edge. We could never hope to find more perfect climbing conditions.

Two successive abseils from the twin towers of Sgùrr a' Mhadaidh launched us upon the long middle section of the traverse, which leads successively over the summits of Sgùrr a' Ghreadaidh and Sgùrr na Banachdich. While there are no outstanding rock problems, a steady succession of minor difficulties would greatly reduce the pace of a roped party in winter. Fast progress on this part of the ridge is essential if one is to complete the route in two days. Indeed, if a climber has not the confidence and experience to cope with this section unroped, he would be ill-advised to attempt the full traverse.

Some climbers advocate moving together and carrying coils on this kind of terrain. My own view is that in these circumstances the rope is rather a hindrance and a hazard rather than a means of protection: if no belays are taken, then any protection is largely illusory. Quite apart from this, very few climbers move with the same margin of safety if they are clutching a coil of rope in one hand. Wee Brian Robertson remembers things differently, however: 'As an inexperienced 20-year-old, I was aghast when I saw Tom's rapid movement over this ground as I realised a mistake would mean curtains.'

Although now enveloped in mist, our party continued to advance in loose order. Robertson was still vomiting periodically, about 20 minutes behind me. At least half an hour behind him were MacInnes and Crabbe. Why they were no longer challenging us was not obvious. Later, it transpired that a disastrous thing had happened: Davie Crabbe had broken a crampon. For a time, MacInnes even considered abandoning the attempt. In effect, Crabbe was climbing with one foot and a heel, the toe of his unprotected vibram-soled boot stubbing uselessly against the glassy surface. He roped up behind MacInnes.

I knew nothing of this, and by the time I reached Sgùrr na Banachdich, sounds of pursuit had long since faded. Visibility was down to ten yards and I was aware of a gnawing doubt whether we would ever be reunited with that all-important rucksack containing the bivouac gear and food rations for the next 24 hours. Supposing Peter Thomas had left it at the wrong place? We had only an hour of daylight to seek our salvation.

Suddenly and quite unexpectedly, I came upon some dog footprints followed, a few yards further, by a trail of clearly defined human footprints leading toward the summit of Banachdich. I heaved a profound sigh of relief. The supply party—consisting of Hamish's wife, Catherine, Peter Thomas, and Hamish's two Alsatian dogs—had passed this way an hour earlier. A few more steps and I came upon the rucksacks, neatly stacked against the summit cairn. It was a poignant moment.

As I had not seen anyone for several hours, I was quite relieved when Robertson appeared about 20 minutes later. By this time, I had discovered a well-protected ledge for a bivouac, and when the other pair dropped in half an hour later we had already excavated a level platform capable of holding four in some discomfort.

'It looks a bit cramped,' MacInnes remarked critically. 'I rather fancy digging a snow hole. How about you, Davie? It would be good practice if nothing else.'

I waited with interest to see if Hamish intended to carry out such a prodigious threat. In the end, he settled for another smaller ledge a few feet to the side.

A vague element of contest still coloured the remarks that wafted across the icy no-man's-land between the rival bivouacs:

'This is excellent soup, Davie. What's it called?'

'What's after the baked beans, Brian?'

'I don't know whether I could eat any more if I tried!'

'This is a palace!'

'I could live here quite happily for a week!'

'I reckon the packs were worth the effort. Makes you feel that you've earned it all.'

'That was a great idea getting the packs sent up. Organisation! A pity we had to stop; I could have gone on for hours!'

And so on.

In fact, the organisation was far from perfect. We had assembled the contents of Peter Thomas's rucksack in a hurry on our return from the ceilidh. Our choice showed little discrimination and a lack of consideration for our porter's feelings. Catherine MacInnes told us later that he had eventually opened the rucksack out of curiosity and asked with disgust, 'Is this a bivouac

Hamish in relative luxury at the bivouac, by Tom Patey

or a birthday party?' There was some truth in his complaint. The contents included three packets of margarine, a large tin of salt, and a half-gallon can of water.

We had selected a fine vantage point for our bivouac. Anchored by ropes and pitons, and secure in the warmth of duvets and sleeping bags, we could pass away the evening by identifying the numerous lighthouses off the west coast of Skye. Nearer at hand, the lights of Glen Brittle offered a friendly beacon. How easy and pleasant it would be to glissade down the long slopes of Banachdich! In an hour, we could be sitting by a warm fire. In the morning, if we rose early, we could be back on the top by dawn and nobody would know we had deserted our posts…

At some unearthly hour, I was awakened by a light snowfall and the dawn ushered in a cheerless morning. Grey tentacles of mist clung to every cranny on the ridge and fresh hoar frost covered the rocks. It had been one of the coldest nights of the winter. Although I had fallen asleep in comparative luxury, I awoke in misery. Condensation inside the polythene bivvy bag had soaked inexorably through my sleeping bag, duvet and trousers. As soon as I got up, my clothes became as stiff as cardboard. Then the primus refused to work in the cold and we had to borrow Hamish's butane stove. It was almost 9:00 am before we finally got under way, climbing with the agility of four knights in full armour.

Fortunately, it was an easy start to the day. At the col between Banachdich and Sgùrr Dearg, we jettisoned all the spare rations and bivouac gear. MacInnes, ever cautious, placed his rucksack under a prominent boulder; I slung my own with utter contempt in the direction of Glen Brittle and watched with gay abandon as it finally disappeared from view, 1,500 ft below, in one final gigantic arc. Robertson followed suit, although with mixed emotions. It was the first time he had willfully abandoned his precious ironmongery, and there was a nostalgic look in his eyes. (Happily, both rucksacks were recovered intact the following morning, less than an hour's walk away from Glen Brittle.)

We now had to keep our first appointment of the day. The Inaccessible Pinnacle of Sgùrr Dearg was an unpleasant customer to meet so early in the morning. Easily the most impressive summit pinnacle in Britain, it is considerably more intimidating in midwinter. We began by examining the north end of the Pinnacle, the so-called 'Short Side'. It was plated from top to bottom with black ice. The ascent can be quite awkward on a wet day in summer, yet

Hamish was confident that he could force a way up even in these conditions.

It promised to be a struggle, and I do not enjoy watching life-and-death drama for the same reason that I would not pay to watch circus acrobats: I become too personally involved. Consequently, I left the other two spectating and walked round toward the other end of the Pinnacle. Suddenly, I had an impulse to investigate the 'Long Side'. Although reputedly a much easier climb than its counterpart, it is at least twice the length and might now present similar technical difficulties, for the angles of both routes are roughly comparable. After 50 ft of climbing, undertaken purely for reconnaissance, I became unpleasantly aware that I was now committed to the climb. After 100 ft, I would have given a great deal for rope protection and a belay. There was little time to cut extra holds. The very edge of the arête had been denuded of snow by the sun, but even so, there was less than half the summer quota of holds. When I came to the short vertical step where one usually pauses before stepping up on to a rather thin bracket, I decided that it was time to enlist Robertson's assistance. Unfortunately, he was out of sight and apparently beyond recall because nobody appeared to investigate my shouts. There was no sense in hanging on indefinitely for a last-minute reprieve, so I chose to continue while I still had some strength. As so often, no sooner had I made this resolution, when everything suddenly clicked. Crampon points bit tenaciously into thin wafers of water ice, woollen gloves clamped down firmly on rounded verglassed holds, and before I even had time to consider the penalties of failure, I was already over the difficulty and scrambling up the last few feet to the top. Total time for the ascent: ten minutes. Standard: a good Severe. I had to suppress an urge to dramatise my sudden appearance on the top of the Pinnacle. It was gratifyingly effective nevertheless, as MacInnes was at grips with the 'bad step' and in a position to appreciate a top-rope, although, knowing Hamish, he would have fought his way up in time. I pulled up an extra length of rope from the base of the Pinnacle and belayed MacInnes from one rope, leaving the second for use as a handrail.

'This fixed rope isn't much good, Tom. It will swing clean off the rock. Can't you flick it across to your left?'

'All right, I'll do that,' I said, 'but I'll have to let go of your rope. Okay?'

'No! Not on your life! I'm relying on this rope for support.' Most odd, I thought. I am obviously belaying him with the wrong rope. By ordinary standards, Hamish ought to be in mid-air.

After jugglery, we had a second rope secured top and bottom, and the rest of the party made free use of it to clamber up and down the Pinnacle.

The first of the two redoubtable strong points of the Cuillin Ridge had been outmanoeuvred and overcome. The early morning mists were dispersing rapidly, the sun shone on a dazzling landscape, and for the first time, we dared to contemplate success. If the weather was not going to stop us, nothing else would.

We glissaded down the long snow chutes of An Stac and climbed the twisting aerial stairway to Sgùrr Mhic Chòinnich. From the summit eyrie, one after another we spun down the 150-foot abseil, which hung clear of the cliff like a spider's thread. Soon to Sgùrr Thearlaich by a left-flanking traverse on 300 ft of creaking snow that threatened to avalanche but held firm. At the top of the Great Stone Chute, we turned aside to pay homage to Sgùrr Alasdair and a magnificent viewpoint.

We were all impatient to come to grips with the last difficulty on the ridge: the Thearlaich-Dubh Gap. It needed only a few seconds' inspection to confirm that its ascent under present conditions would be exceptionally 'thin'—corresponding to a summer grading of Very Severe and rating high in that category. An evil veneer of ice obscured every wrinkle on the wall. Without crampons, any ascent would have been out of the question, but where were there big enough incuts to support the front points of a crampon? I did not fancy peeling off backwards, as someone had some years ago and paid for it with his life. A glance at the jagged boulders that lined the floor of the gap recalled this incident.

We were, however, most reluctant to make this diversion, and Robertson prepared to hurl himself at the last hurdle in a fervour of martyrdom.

At that moment, MacInnes, who had yet to descend into the Thearlaich-Dubh Gap, made a novel suggestion. 'If you just hold it a minute, lads,' he shouted, 'I might manage to get a rope over to the other side.'

Surely, I thought, someone would have discovered this solution long ago, if it existed? However, few can rival Hamish's flair for improvisation.

'The fact is, I've been here investigating in the summer,' he confessed, 'and there's a pointed rock on the other side that will take a direct pull from below, supposing I get the rope to lie behind it.'

With the very first cast, his rope wrapped itself neatly round a projection at the top of the wall. Most men would have sweated blood and tears to achieve this. Only one thing troubled me. It was obviously not the same projection that Hamish had aimed at.

'How do you know this rope is safe, Hamish?'

'I don't,' he replied in his abstract way.

'Well, how are we to find out whether it's safe if you can't tell us from up there?'

MacInnes was the model of patience. 'Try climbing up the rope,' he remarked encouragingly. 'I'll be most surprised if it comes away.'

You won't be the only one, I thought.

Now came the moment of truth, beloved of mountaineering chroniclers—the throw of the dice that was the difference between success and utter disaster. Even if the whole of my past life did not flash across my subconscious mind as is supposed to happen on these occasions, I still remember the enormous relief when I pulled myself over the top to find the rope securely jammed. We had broken the last barrier. Success was assured.

One abseil remained. Then we coiled up the rope for the last time and each of us wandered silently and independently along the final mile of scree-speckled ridge to Gars-bheinn, the final outpost. Beyond lay the blue Atlantic, warm and inviting in the afternoon sun. Down by the shore, a different world awaited us, full of colour and contrast. In one whooping 2,000-foot glissade, we returned to it gratefully. Our two-day journey across the Cuillin Ridge and the 12-hour 'tarantella on ice', where crampon tips and ice axe spikes had been our only contact with tangible reality, now seemed a strange and wonderful fantasy.

A little older in wisdom, a little younger in spirit, we marched back over the moors to Glen Brittle. Down in Cuillin Cottage, Mrs Campbell would be waiting for us with supper. It was a long-standing invitation that we fully intended to keep.

There are many ultimates in mountaineering, and every generation finds its own Last Problem. The others who shared the first Winter Traverse of the Cuillin Ridge probably feel the same way as I do. There are many harder and more exacting routes, and many more still to be explored, yet I feel confident that this achievement will retain its place as the greatest single adventure in British mountaineering.

It would be presumptuous to be conceited about the success of our own exploit. We can only be grateful that we were lucky to find this superb climb in perfect winter conditions. If any individual honours are awarded, then they should go to Davie Crabbe and Brian Robertson, who completed the ridge on half a crampon and half a stomach, respectively, thereby revealing—in Hamish's phraseology—'determination that is truly Scottish'.

Let us end with a few well-chosen words by Wee Brian:

> *With individuals from Edinburgh, Glasgow, Glencoe, and of course Aberdeen, this was one of the few occasions where all the strands of Scottish climbing cooperated in harmony... despite Hamish's West Coast humour. There was fierce competition for the first ascent, with so many climbers vying for the prize. I was merely along for the ride—and what a ride!*

The team after the climb, by Mrs Campbell

Tyrolean traverse across to
the Great Stack of Handa
© Graeme Hunter Collection

19. STACKS OF FUN

For those of you who have never been to the Island of Handa in North West Scotland, pencil in a visit. It is a desolate, abandoned piece of the western seaboard jigsaw for most of the year, but awash with sunshine and wildflowers come spring. Over 150 ago, there were seven crofting families on the island, and it was famous for its potatoes until the potato famine of 1845 forced the residents reluctantly to emigrate to America; thereafter, the island became the exclusive domain of birds and twitchers.

Not only does spring offer a weather window, but the birds arrive for their holidays—all 90,000 of them! Most reside on or around the Great Stack, a 350-foot-high overhanging monolith of stratified sandstone perched on five stubby legs, under which the eastern Atlantic ebbs and flows. Scotland has a profusion of such sea stacks: ocean-swept fangs dotted around the most hostile parts of our coastline. All were at one time part of our island landmass but have been eroded by centuries of relentless pounding of the waves to form elegant spires.

The Great Stack is separated from the main island by a narrow channel, the width of a rowing boat in places. A seabird La Scala, there is always a full house of immaculate patrons in evening dress with clown-like puffins thrown in for light relief. The place has a Wagnerian feel, especially if there's a swell, for the tide charges through the channel at full bore. Circumnavigation is a seat-wetting experience best postponed for a calm day. Valkyries should have season tickets for lower ledges.

The first ascent of the Stack is an interesting milestone in Scottish climbing history. Climbers in those days (circa 1876) were no fools. They chose the easiest way up, or in this case, the easiest way across, and there was always either grub or cash incentives.

It all started with a colony of great black-backed gulls that used the Great Stack as an operational base for island pillaging, i.e., killing the law-abiding bird population, which was an important source of food for the natives. A contract was sent to some birdmen of Lewis, experienced in both birds and cliffs, to come across the Minch and liquidate the gulls. One Donald Macdonald, the boldest and most agile of the men, took a 500-foot rope round the bay so that it lay over the top of the Great Stack, then he tensioned it and swung hand over hand on the rope for 150 ft to reach the top. His teammates threw a line across, enabling Donald to haul over a hammer and stakes, which he drove into the grassy summit to act as belays. Then, with block and tackle, a breeches buoy was rigged, allowing the rest of the men to come over. Exit gulls and eggs: contract completed. This was a remarkable feat involving technical rope work now known as a Tyrolean traverse, which would not become part of the mountaineering repertoire for a further 100 years.

A fisherman by the name of Alasdair Munro took Graeme Hunter, Douglas Lang and me to the Great Stack in August 1969, when we made the first technical ascent. Alasdair was the official guardian of the area and a local expert who had circumnavigated the avian citadel many times. When we all met up on the strand opposite the mainland, he sized us up and realised that despite two of us being unable to swim, we were not jessies.

As we set off in his boat, Alasdair, a master boatman, leaned on his oars and observed the pulsing swell of the ocean, noting the point where the waves were at their lowest. Suddenly the boat shot forward on a trough and we were in a narrow gap at the base of the five-legged leviathan. The gap was tight, but it soon became much narrower, the width of the boat. We were propelled at speed on the crest of a bore, like surfers, and spat out the other side, where we rowed past two prodigious legs and experienced the strange sensation that restless monsters of the deep were stirring. Alasdair seemed unperturbed and took us round the Rubicon, which separated over 60 fathoms of treacherous ocean from over 300 ft of vertical rock.

The attempt on the climb was about to start! We three were no slouches, and we had our gear in our rucksacks and were roped up, ready to go. We had decided by majority vote that Graeme, the only swimmer, would have the honour of leading the first pitch, which was overhanging, slimy and soaking. He also had extra ballast in the form of karabiners, pitons and a hammer. Weighed down by the ironmongery of modern climbing, he risked being drowned or at least saturated. I had a vision of my good friend John Cunningham, one of Scotland's finest climbers, who sadly met his demise

The final challenge—an abseil back into the boat © Graeme Hunter Collection

on a sea cliff. He too had a full complement of ironmongery with him when he landed in the water. John couldn't swim.

It was high tide with only a gentle three-foot swell as Alasdair manoeuvred the stern of the boat next to the wall. As we bobbed up and down, Graeme worked out the sequence of holds to break loose from the security of the boat. When it reached the high point of the swell, he jumped onto the Stack and climbed up to drier rock, where he quickly placed a piton for reassurance.

Reaching a belay stance on a shoulder about 40 ft above, Graeme brought Doug and me up, where we assembled before tackling the overhanging crux of the climb. Graeme took the lead and climbed up to the overhangs, traversing left past a confused-looking fulmar, which apparently felt sorry for him, for it didn't regurgitate its oily lunch. (Fulmar chicks have the unique ability to project, with great accuracy, their regurgitated fish suppers onto you, so that you usually have to incinerate your clothes and avoid personal human contact until the pong wears off.)

The situation was now exposed and challenging, with little prospect of effective protection in the compact sandstone. By this time, a small flotilla of boats had gathered to watch this spectacular event or just to relish the drama of our predicament. Graeme hauled himself up and left, then thrutched his way over another overhang to reach a small protruding ledge, an exhilaratingly exposed diving board jutting out 150 ft above the waves. After a final short, easier pitch, we all stood on the island side of the summit to the amazement and consternation of some tourists on the main island who had been admiring the spectacular view.

We couldn't stand around entertaining the crowds all day, though, and after briefly savouring our success, we planned our exit strategy. Faced with loose, unstable rock, we realised it would be imprudent to abseil back down to the ledge where we had left our rucksacks and gear, and we returned to the diving board and the prospect of a spectacular free abseil directly into the boat. By this time, the tide had gone out and the swell had dropped, so I shouted down to Alasdair, asking if he could manoeuvre his boat to catch us on the descent.

Graeme had an off-cut piece of my mountain rescue stretcher, which he had fashioned into a large nut. He jammed this into a wide crack and prepared the abseil rope, and I then gingerly lowered myself into thin air, coming to land some time later on a wet, barnacle-encrusted ledge just above the high water. The next trick required swinging out and quickly descending the rope when the boat was in a trough, letting go of the rope at the top of the swell and landing safely in the craft. This worked fine for me and Doug, but Graeme didn't quite get the timing right and had to be winched in with a boat hook, more than a little damp and minus some skin on his hands.

All three of us now safely aboard, Alasdair, who was fond of a wee tipple, produced a bottle of whisky and announced, 'That was grand, lads, a fine thing on my birthday.' So we drank to Alasdair, to the Stack, and a wonderful day. We decided to call the route after him, as he was such a vital member of the team.

Toasting success
© Graeme Hunter Collection

Hamish prospects new ground on
The Buachaille © John Cleare

20. THE EVOLUTION OF THE TERRORDACTYL

In 1950, it was very difficult to buy an ice axe. This was the post-war era when we wore clinker nailed boots and used climbing ropes made from hemp. Early Alpinists had little more than long poles with metal tips for grip.

Out of necessity, I designed my all-metal North Wall hammer. It had a pressed tubular Reynolds steel shaft, which was originally used for making frames for racing bicycles and was very light and strong. This was probably the first all-metal ice axe ever produced, and the robust implement was christened the 'Message' by my friends in the Creagh Dhu Mountaineering Club as it battered our soft steel pitons so much that in Glasgow parlance they 'got the message'. A fine welder in the club, appropriately called The Mank, coated the hammer face with a very hard metal called Stellite, while Tommy Paul, another club member, replaced the pick end with a tool steel insert. With these modifications, my Message served me well for the next decade on many routes all over the world. It didn't have a dropped pick, but its super-strong shaft was a step in the right direction.

In the winter of 1959, I was climbing on the North Face of Ben Nevis with my good friend Ian Clough. We were camping below the face when word came that three climbers were overdue from an attempt on the then unclimbed Zero Gully. Although it was dark and a blizzard was brewing, we set off and eventually found the climbers, who had fallen over 1,000 ft still roped together. All three were dead; two of the men had broken ice axes.

In the morning, we hiked up into Zero Gully, now an avalanche chute, and discovered the third ice axe. It had clearly been used as a belay and, being made of wood, had snapped off at snow level. I was angry with myself because I had been climbing with my Message for nearly ten years and subconsciously knew its potential to help avoid just this sort of tragedy. Within a few weeks, I had traced John Byam-Grounds, a member of the Alpine Club who was the Managing Director of B&S Massey of Openshaw near Manchester, drop

Tom Patey testing the strength
of a Terrodactyl © John Cleare

forgers and manufacturers of massive high-rise presses and hammers. He believed he could drop forge the heads of my Message prototype, meaning the hot steel would be stamped in a die by an enormous press. With sudden enhanced production and my old Glencoe shed for an assembly line, a wide market was soon established, and in 1962, I took out patents for the tools. The pick declined to 78 degrees, which gave it much better holding power, but as is often the case with new ideas, there were objections from some who felt that the angle was too steep. The Message soon proved its worth, however, when Bugs McKeith and Kenny Spence used it on their ascent of the Eiger's North Pillar.

Back then, we mountaineers faced the enduring problem of trying to maintain contact with overhanging ice. The technique at the time was to hang on to ice pitons which were driven in above the leader's head, but this was both dangerous and insecure. Although the all-metal ice axes and ice hammers had straight, slightly declined picks, these weren't sufficiently dropped for direct aid on vertical ice. But ice climbing was about to experience a revolution that is still in progress today. Among the various ideas floating around at the time, one of the most bizarre was from my late friend Dr Tom Patey, one of Scotland's most prolific climbers. He too had been mulling over the problem of ascending vertical and overhanging ice, and one night he telephoned me at about 3:00 am (this was not unusual) and said ominously, 'I've got a great idea.'

'Hmm,' I replied warily, for I was familiar with Tom's outlandish schemes.

'I bought a pair of hand cultivators today. You know, the tools that elderly gardeners use for breaking up the soil between flower beds. All I want you to do is attach straps onto them so that I can fix them to my wrists.'

The rest is history; the cultivators were relegated to Tom's garden shed and dropped picked tools were invented. The angle of the pick was based on the way a kedge anchor bites into the sea floor and I called my new design the Terrordactyl. Ian soon nicknamed it the 'Terror', and Paul Nunn quipped that the profile of my head and nose were identical to its angle. Not only did this short, all-metal ice tool have the strength of an aluminium alloy shaft and a high-quality pressed steel head, it also had both an adze and steeply inclined serrated pick.

I am often amazed at the way similar ideas develop independently in different countries around the same time. In the 1960s, direct aid ice tools were at an embryo stage in Glencoe and America, but in the Great Pacific Ironworks in Ventura, California, the legendary climber Yvon Chouinard had invented a model called the 'Climax', which was based on the radius of the cutting arc, with a curved, serrated pick and a wooden shaft.

The two protagonists, the Climax and the Terror, met in the Clachaig Bar in Glencoe one evening, and Yvon and I planned some sorties that would test our respective wares. The next day, Yvon and his friend Doug Tompkins put the Climax to the test on the first ascent of the highly technical Raven's Gully Direct on Buachaille Etive Mòr, and the Terrors swiftly followed suit on a nearby line.

Dropped picks retained their popularity thanks to their efficiency. Ian Nicholson of the Creagh Dhu Club used Terrordactyls to make successive solo ascents of Point Five and Zero Gully on Ben Nevis and was back down at the pub in time for lunch. The Terrors also accompanied Dougal Haston and Doug Scott on their first British ascent of Mount Everest. Eventually, the accepted norm for modern ice tools evolved as a combination of a steeply dropped Terror-like pick with an upward curving tip like a reversed Climax, otherwise known as a 'banana' pick. For the next two decades, this simple modification would prove to be the secret weapon on thousands of increasingly difficult ice and mixed routes.

Bent shaft tools, however, arrived much later, although my good friend Rob Taylor recalls how Don Whillans was probably responsible for its prototype about a dozen years before it formally appeared on the scene. Don arrived at my house in Glencoe on a small motorbike having just returned from one of his protracted journeys across Asia, clad in a leather safety helmet, leather jacket and billowy baby-blue pyjama bottoms, which were stained and filthy.

Rob was toiling outside in the raspberry patch and recalls that when Don dismounted, he was smaller standing than when he was perched on the bike. With his diminutive stance and red hair and beard, he resembled Tolkien's dwarf, Gimli. Don, in his usual dry caustic manner, drawled, 'What a pleasant change—good to see the locals doing some constructive work rather than their usual thieving.' Perhaps on purpose, Don ran over Rob's rucksack as he departed two hours later. Lashed onto the rucksack were two Terrors, one of which wedged beneath the frame of the bike and bent. Rob helped lift the bike and Don was on his way... but not for long. On the A82, near Tyndrum, he pulled over—the Terror had gotten its revenge and punctured his rear tyre.

Master engineer at work
© John Cleare

Chris Woodall beneath
the North Face of Pik
Shchurovsky

21. A FIRST ASCENT IN THE FROSTY CAUCASUS

Over one billion people saw the North Face of Shchurovsky on the opening television screen shot of the Sochi Winter Olympics in 2014, yet, to this day, the mountain remains an enigma. In another place and time, it would be revered for the epic climb it was, much like the first ascents of Everest or the Eiger. A consistently overhanging mixed face dripping with icicles, it was considered 'impossible' before our early free ascent, even by the Soviets.

I first became involved with the British Soviet Caucasus Expedition to Pik Shchurovsky by default. Dennis Gray, a well-known English climber, had originally agreed to lead the trip but, due to other commitments and the sheer risks associated with the undertaking, he pulled out. Trying to obtain permission to climb in the Caucasus was like attempting to win the National Lottery. Paul Nunn and Tut Braithwaite, old climbing colleagues, asked if I would accept the mantle. They hoped that I could exert my influence, such as it was, with the Russian authorities, for I had enjoyed good relations with them since my previous visit to the region with George Ritchie in 1961. Reluctantly, I agreed.

There were six of us. Paul Nunn, the genial, unflappable Friar Tuck of the climbing world, who could float gracefully up the most delicate route. A mine of not-always-useful information, Paul could opine at length on a wide range of crucial topics, such as the distribution of wheat in Georgia in the 16th century. Richard McHardy was a talented solo climber with an exuberant sense of humour and the appetite of a dinosaur. Tut Braithwaite, a superman disguised as a long-term hunger-striker, had the energy of a nuclear reactor. A decorator by trade and an entertainer by nature, Tut was at the forefront of a generation of Alpine hard men. Chris Woodall, by far the quietest member of the team, was an unassuming physical training instructor, strong and reliable, with the earnest face of a teacher and the temperament of a philosopher. Finally, Peter Seeds, our assiduous Scoop, was a small, gregarious man with a zeal for news and life in general. A features writer on the *Sunday Mirror* and an old acquaintance of Paul's, he managed to persuade his paper to subsidise our trip. Every expedition should have a Seeds; he was a born storyteller who sowed a little of the freedom of Fleet Street throughout the breadth of communist Russia.

For some reason, we decided to make the ludicrously long journey by car, and our motley crew met in London to load up two vehicles which Fiat of Turin had naively loaned us for the trip.

The Fiat 125S—incongruously, the 'S' stood for 'Samantha'—was produced by the revered design firm, Vignale. She was a rally car of considerable pep, but with her compression suitably lowered for low-octane Russian petrol. The other vehicle was a Campagnola, the Italian equivalent of the Land Rover: a sturdy workhorse. Both motors were stuffed to the gunnels with the contents of Paul's garage, which had been dubbed Smaug's Cave for its accumulation of supermarket goodies ranging from beer to skittles.

Lifting the canvas cover on the Campagnola, I saw that a substantial amount of space had been given to cans of Newcastle Brown Ale. I don't drink beer, so I pointed out that this was an unnecessary luxury and proposed an on-the-spot party to dispose of enough cans to at least make room for my rucksack. Several empties later, we duly settled down for our marathon drive.

Our plan was to journey to the Caucasus via East Germany and Poland. Within the Iron Curtain, I saw many improvements since my last visit in 1969, when I had been a guest of Horská služba České, the Czech Rescue Service.

Poland is a country that immediately draws you into a giant bear-hug. When we arrived at a small border village late one evening, we were besieged by welcoming locals inviting us to their homes and pressing us with drinks. With regret, we resisted their hospitality and slept by the wayside beneath the fruit trees and poplars bordering either side of the high cambered road. Nearer Warsaw, it was too built up for this nomadic approach, and Richard asked a passing priest where we could find a suitable campsite.

'Follow me,' replied the priest in good English. We fell in behind the holy man like a funeral procession, and he took us to a seminary where we were welcomed like repentant sinners. We were provided with beds with clean sheets, a simple meal and use of the homemade swimming pool, which, after the dust of the Polish roads, was a welcome luxury.

We were short of Polish currency and always seemed to arrive at banks when they were closed. In the shadow of the lofty Palace of Culture in Warsaw, we resorted to exchanging currency with a shady-looking local who left us looking furtively in different directions in the middle of a thoroughfare while he set off in search of someone ominously known as 'Mr Big'.

The drive itself was like a cabaret act. Paul's great bellowing laugh would rise above the din of the Campagnola as Tut, with the aspirations of a budding Grand Prix driver, steered a collision course with all oncoming traffic, chuckling as he granted his passengers a last-second reprieve. Our progress toward Russia was more of a touristy amble, and we frequently lost our way. Clouds of dust would engulf us as we leapt from one pothole to the next, and the road eventually dwindled to a track and then open ground. Low hills rose ahead, with no sign of a highway.

'Hey, look up there.' Peter pointed to a pillbox on stilts in the distance. We were right on the Russian border.

'Hmm,' I said nervously, 'I'm sure the Russians don't usually welcome tourists arriving cross-country in a military-type vehicle.'

We caught up with the others at Shaginia, the official frontier post which is now part of the Republic of Belarus, and Tut shouted across from the other car: 'The trouble with you, Hamish, is that you can't read the signposts. They're in very clear Polish.'

The next morning, we took to the long, straight Russian roads. There was no better way to appreciate the scale of the Soviet Union than to drive across it. The horizon seemed limitless, merging in a haze with the skyline. Roadside camping was discouraged, so we stayed at the clean, official campsites where Paul, who was a lecturer in economics and an armchair expert in political theory, would engage in heated discussions with Russian students preaching Leninism. This was the centenary year of Lenin's birth, and there were huge posters of the great man everywhere.

With Kiev, Kharkov and Rostov behind us, we sped along the sun-drenched Georgian highway, a ribbon of melted tarmac lined with poplars. The foothills of the Caucasus rose in front of us in the shimmering, oppressive heat; even the metal of the vehicles was too hot to touch. Thankfully, the heat seemed to deter the 'snots', as we called the traffic police. There had been one at every road junction all the way from Poland, and at Baksan a posse of them adamantly informed us that we could go no further. Four hours later, we finally persuaded them to let us pass.

The road up the Baksan River snakes through deep gorges and pleasant woodlands; the country is suddenly Alpine, the air pure. This region was a popular vacation area in the Soviet Union, frequented by two classes: the dedicated climber and the tourist. Many of the latter were German holidaymakers, and they arrived from Moscow with the attitude of people determined to enjoy themselves. Climbers, by dint of circumstance, are spartan, and as we drove up the road approaching Mount Elbrus, we were somewhat daunted by a huge hotel that sparkled into view, ultramodern even by Western standards. This was the Itkol, the new tourist hotel that was to be our home for the next few weeks.

Six filthy climbers, sprouting anaemic beards and caked in the dust of the plains, creaked from the two vehicles and were ushered into this sybaritic glass palace. We would have been happier in a frugal mountain hut. The ancient, traditionally dressed Cossack porter jerked upright and gave us a grandiose salute. Later, this man became partial to the Newcastle Brown Ale I had failed to offload in London and received the moniker Ivan Beershiftsky. He was armed to the teeth with antique weaponry and told us candidly that he was a dishonest man and we would have to hide all our equipment, for he couldn't hold himself responsible if it went missing. With the expertise of slum dwellers, we succeeded in lowering the tone of our three luxury rooms in a matter of hours.

It took us a couple of days to unwind after the long drive, but accommodation at the Hotel Itkol was conducive to easy living and the place grew on us. We had breakfast in the goldfish bowl dining room and cooked the other meals in our suites or on the verandah. I met Rotentaov, the senior Master of Sport I had befriended during my last visit to the Caucasus and good-humouredly nicknamed Rotten Tie-off, a reference to a short section of nylon tape that is used to tie round the neck of a piton that can't be fully driven into a crack. Rotentaov was now acting as an adviser to climbing guests at the hotel, and I hoped he might help us overcome some obstacles that confronted interloping climbers in the Soviet Union.

It had been my ambition for some time to visit the valley of Svanetia, that turbulent region I had contemplated when attempting a direct descent from the Shkhelda Ridge a few years previously. At one time, Svanetia had been an anarchic stronghold where each house had its own protective tower. Without too much hope, I requested permission for a visit. Rotentaov refused but suggested instead that we plan an ascent of the North Face of Nakra Tau, a 4,000-foot wall first pioneered by that great Russian climber Abalakov after he had lost most of his toes and fingers to frostbite. Neither my remark that it would make a good acclimatisation route nor the boys' irreverent reference to it as 'Knackery Tau' were well received by Rotentaov, but we got our gear together and waited for the weather gods to authorise our plan.

Richard, always on the lookout for difficult rock to climb, remembered a fearsome cliff he had spied on the way up from the plains near Tiernauz, and after obtaining permission from Rotentaov, he set off to climb this with Peter. On the crux of the route, as Peter grappled with an intimidating, overhanging crack, a bionic voice boomed across the valley via a powerful Tannoy system. It was some snots shouting in Russian, demanding to know what the hell they were doing.

Despite his enthusiasm, Peter didn't have the experience for a technical north face, however, and as the rest of us prepared for Nakra Tau, he went exploring.

On a clear, bright day with barely a wisp of cloud in the sky, we scampered across the glacier toward the mountain, which had a rugged demeanour and a face as furrowed as a shepherd's.

'Hell's bells. Look at that serac overhanging the lower part of the wall. It's got our names all over it!' Tut was eyeing the route through his binoculars.

The others seemed as apprehensive of this great tottering block of ice as I was, but we said no more about it as we traversed the glacier moraine in search of a bivouac. We found a crashed helicopter (thankfully without any bodies) where we spent a surreal night sleeping in a deep freeze with a spectacular view. The next morning, after a breakfast of dehydrated food that looked and tasted like toenail clippings, we shouldered our packs, switched on our headlamps, and set off as the morning light caught the wires of a *téléphérique* on the lower slopes of Mount Elbrus, illuminating them like fine strands of gossamer.

A short time before the trip, I had designed my Terrordactyl: a new lightweight ice climbing tool with an aggressive dropped pick that gave it superlative cutting and holding power. This was the first time that my 'Terrors' had been used at altitude on such an extreme climb and we were itching to see how they performed on steep ice.

First light saw us soloing up a ramp of steep snow. Richard, who had suffered from headaches since a fall while solo climbing, announced he was heading back. We sympathised, but there was little we could do to help. There were few technical difficulties on the descent, especially for someone of Richard's ability, so no one offered to accompany him.

I looked up apprehensively as we approached the icy wall leading toward the serac we had been so concerned about the previous day. Suddenly, there was a crunch like two ships colliding, followed by the roar of falling debris above us. Had we been roped up we would have been obliterated by this bombardment. Even though the slope was tilted at an angle of about 50 degrees, we stampeded, dignity gone to the wind, in an attempt to gain the top of the snow ramp we had recently abandoned. The serac was probably no bigger than a church steeple, but it brought down a ton of snow and ice and set off a substantial airborne avalanche. A blast of cold air was followed by a lingering cloud of fine snow particles.

It was only once we were safely across that an awful thought occurred to us: Richard! The avalanche had fallen to the snow ramp below and swept the slope that he had just descended.

Meanwhile, Richard, who had reached the base of the ramp and was safely on the snowfield below, had witnessed the whole thing as if it were a horror movie scene in slow motion and he hadn't seen us scuttling like scalded cats to the side. Never mind cats, we returned to the Itkol like dogs with our tails between our legs, deeply relieved to discover we were all still intact.

Rotentaov was not amused by our escapades as we celebrated our survival with an ample supply of vodka that Peter had brought back from his tourist jaunt. Then Rudy, the leader of a group of East German climbers, arrived with some of his friends and drank a toast to Lenin. After a first-class evening, Tut volunteered to drive them back to their camp in the small hours, but the snots on duty outside the hotel were firm: there was to be no driving that night. Rudy and his pals had to walk. Of course, the police were quite right, for we had all had too much to drink, but the only pedestrians about at that time of night on those lonely roads would have been Caucasian bears.

At that time, with the popularity of James Bond sweeping the West, we imagined that every room from the bogs to the dining hall was bugged, although what the Russians would have found interesting about our drivel is hard to imagine. Nevertheless, it provided us with humorous diversions.

'Haf you heeden infrared film, Paul?' I would ask when we were tucked away in bed.

'Yes, ees in sealed coffee tin.'

'Very good, but vee must get seegnal out.'

On it went, in deplorable Slavic accents. Perhaps it was our imaginations at work, but Peter did seem to have some trouble sending copy out to his editor.

We were all raring to go, but the weather gods were forever conspiring against us. Down in the lush valley of Baksan, however, it was tropical, and while we were hanging about, I was stricken with sunstroke, something I had fallen foul of at various times in seemingly impossible conditions, including the Himalayas in winter.

Eventually, we obtained permission to attempt a new route on Ushba, and we made several sorties to the German bivouac—the first base for this climb and others in the area—but we were turned back by storms. Time was running out, and we marched back and forth to the bivouac like the Grand Old Duke of York's henchmen. When all hopes of doing a route on Ushba were abandoned, I beat a trail to Rotentaov's door with another request: permission to attempt the 14,000-foot Pik Shchurovsky, whose North West Face looked compelling. It was the hardest looking wall we had seen in the whole area, and as Tut observed, 'So bloody steep there's nowhere for snow to land.'

Meanwhile, Tut and Richard had asked if they could attempt the direct route up the West Face of Shkhelda from the Shkhelda glacier, just across from the German bivouac. This 6,000-foot wall would afford them plenty of verticality and sport.

With only a few days left of our planned holiday, we were champing at the bit and eager to salvage some success from the sponsored Caucasus trip. Weather be damned, Chris, Paul and I set off on a fair morning for the German bivouac in the fervent hope that the weather would hold. The bivvy site was busy; it was a weekend and there were several Masters of Sport, both men and women, having a busman's holiday in the mountains. The sun came out and chased the snow into the furthest crannies, and we passed a sociable evening, swapping gear and ideas. The Russians made some very good titanium equipment at that time, for many of their climbers were also engineers.

Our proposed route up Pik Shchurovsky was parallel to one put up by Abalakov some years previously. Any climb up the wall would be difficult, and the more time I spent in the Caucasus, the more I respected the ability of Soviet mountaineers. I didn't object to their restrictions toward mountaineering, and I couldn't help feeling that something similar might be welcome in the Alps, where a dozen parties make a beeline for a route as soon as the weather clears, and unless your party is in front, you suffer the inevitable penalty of either being held up or bombarded by rocks. Shchurovsky was obviously not on most Russians' tick list, and the local climbers at the German bivouac doubted the feasibility of the climb. They wished us luck, however, and in the morning, with a frost lifting our hopes, we made the short distance across the ice to come to long-overdue grips with a Russian mountain.

As usual, we didn't rope up until we were on a steeply angled slope and it was almost too difficult to do so. Until now, we had been weaving our way through a labyrinth of shallow gullies and steep tongues of snow but, suddenly, we broke out of these and found ourselves at the base of an overhanging section.

'How about heading up through those icicles, Hamish, then breaking right?' suggested Chris optimistically. I soon gathered that this was because he was expecting me to lead.

'Yes, it's just like a Scottish gully,' Paul added quickly, backing up Chris's opening gambit. 'It'll be a good test for the Terrors!'

'Well,' I said with resignation, 'I thought when I was asked to come on this trip I was a figurehead. Now I see I am the dunderhead.'

Upon closer inspection, I realised that forging a route straight up the overhanging wall would take hours—time we did not have. Discounting the bulging wall above, I sped off rightwards on an icy horizontal traverse, my Lawrence of Arabia neckshield flapping in the breeze. Where it led, I could only guess, for its far edge lay out of sight around a corner. It was incredibly airy—reminiscent of the Traverse of the Gods on the Eiger North Wall, but on perfect ice. Occasionally, I would snake the rope behind a rock flake or a spike cemented into ice, protection that was largely illusory, but the climbing was straightforward enough. My hunch had paid off.

Paul Nunn immediately christened the pitch 'Traverse of the Yobs' as he and Chris followed. It was a rather devious route involving no small amount of jiggery pokery, including standing in slings to gain a steep snow gully above that led to the central ice field.

It was barely noon and we were nearly halfway up the face. Confidently, I led off up the short but precipitous central ice field, hacking away enthusiastically with my Terrors. The sun had passed behind the mountain and the ice was firm. I cut a few steps beneath the only weakness—a small dimple in the overhanging icicle-festooned Great Barrier that loomed overhead.

Like assiduous generals planning the siege of a fortress, we had studied the face on many occasions through binoculars and had anticipated that this pitch would be the crux. From our current vantage point, however, it looked far worse than we expected—any exposed rock was an overhang with a fringe of icicles and everything else was plum vertical and sheathed in verglas.

The morning's punishing output, dehydration and the constant gripping of axes had left me with terrible cramp in my hands. I remembered the tablespoon of salt I had liberated from an ancient ration box in the German bivouac, and Paul and Chris looked on in disgust as I pulled out this crumpled bit of paper and unwrapped it. I flicked off mouse droppings, devoured the salt, and set off again, ready for the battle above. For many hours, I forged my way upwards; it was without question the most difficult and desperate climbing of my life.

Paul and Chris shivered in the cold, deep shadow on the belay ledge as I fought for every inch of headway. I wove an intricate line, hooking and chipping over icy overhangs and along hanging gangways and grooves with scant protection. Eventually, I reached an inverted hanging V-gully, which I conquered by bridging my feet and hooking my Terrors into the thin vertical ice. I marvelled at the technical capability of my new-fangled tools and concluded that it would have been impossible to negotiate that terrain without them.

It took me about three hours of hard climbing on insecure ice and loose rock to reach the top of the Great Barrier. The climbing was typical of the hardest British winter routes, and on a north face in the Caucasus it felt profoundly serious. By late afternoon, after following a small ledge system, I broke through to easier ground. Now it was Paul and Chris's turn to follow, but as I prepared the belay, the bandolier holding almost all of our protection suddenly snapped, showering my companions with our precious ironmongery, which then tinkled off into the gloom. Suddenly, the whole tone of the climb changed. Any possibility of retreat was now out of the question. Vitaly Abalakov, in the valley below, would not invent his ingenious V-thread for some years yet, and we were totally committed to reaching the summit. Paul and Chris, clinging on desperately as they followed on a top rope, agreed that the climbing was harder than anything they had done in winter previously. In a moment of clarity, I understood the impact the Terrordactyl would have on modern climbing henceforth. Thanks to its unique dimensions and steeply inclined serrated pick, the most impossible-looking line was now feasible—even if it was still desperate.

Finally, we were huddled together on a small ledge above the Great Barrier, standing on each other's boots. I use the term 'ledge' generously here, for any self-respecting eagle would have turned its beak up at such a landing site.

'It must be late,' I said. 'It's time we got some shelter.' It was snowing like Christmas.

'Well, this place won't get three stars for comfort,' Paul commented. I was leaning heavily against him, and we were all secured to a single peg at knee level.

'How about moving up a short way to see if there's any better lodging, Hamish,' said Chris. 'I like you better at a distance.'

I moved diagonally upwards to a further icy step that would have to suffice as a ledge, and on this frugal perch we settled ourselves for the night. We had two options: we could either let our legs overhang the drop, for the ledge, once cleared of ice, was the width of a mantelpiece, or we could tuck our knees up to our chins and clasp our arms around our shins. With these two positions offering alternating discomfort, we spent the night like a row of miserable garden gnomes.

For the ever-stoical Chris, the discomfort of spending a night on a narrow ledge with his feet swinging in space was eclipsed by the misery of severe dehydration. The matches had gotten damp, and with no way to light the stove, there was no possibility of a hot drink or any food. The Caucasus is indeed a frosty place to bivouac, and the next day we had mild frostbite, but we got going and soon found ourselves on enjoyably steep mixed ground. Although heavy snow had fallen overnight, it hadn't adhered to the steep face of Shchurovsky.

By early afternoon, pale clouds steamed in from the Bezinghi region and lay like a blanket on the glaciers below us. More clouds slipped furtively over the peak, and after a while it began to snow steadily once again.

Chris took the lead, for I had tired myself out the previous day, both mentally and physically. Our progress slowed as new snow accumulated on top of the old stuff and clung on insecurely, ready to slough off with the least provocation. As I climbed up to Paul's stance, I shovelled hail like loose change from the holds.

We speculated that we had perhaps only 700 vertical feet remaining before the summit. Chris's strength and ability now came to the fore, and he pressed on in the sub-zero inferno, ploughing upwards as avalanches of powder drowned his yellow cagoule and periodically obliterated him from view. Only occasional tugs of the rope communicated to Paul and me that it was our turn to follow—Chris was totally lost in the maelstrom, swimming up a trough of bottomless, insecure snow.

The final pitch was a deadly-looking avalanche slope, and Chris was forced rightwards toward a ridge line. From our tiny stance, Paul and I watched as, hanging from ice screw to ice screw, Chris bulled his way across the top of a vertical couloir, fighting against the heaving snow as it tried to cast him off into the abyss. Midway along this, a blast of airborne powder wrenched the ice axe out of hand, and we watched in dismay as it cartwheeled into the void.

As you might imagine, Chris was distraught at the imminent danger he now faced without his precious tool. But his anguish was deeper than that. The ice axe had belonged to my close friend Ian Clough, who had died barely a month earlier on the last day of a successful Annapurna South West Face expedition, and I had lent it to Chris for the duration of this trip. Chris didn't know that, by nature, I have little time for sentimentality and none whatsoever for objects—the axe was merely a tool; it was people, not things, that I cherished. I passed no comment on the loss of the axe, and with encouragement from Paul and me, Chris regained his composure and reached the safety of the ridge line. We christened this penultimate pitch 'Traverse of the Screws', and swarmed up the easier rocks and snow of the North East Ridge.

Suddenly, there was no more mountain above us. We could just make out the edge of a cornice snaking away as we stood on the knife-edge summit like three disillusioned snowmen hoping for an early thaw, relieved by the fact that we were up but now concerned about the prospect of getting down.

'What will we do?' Paul yelled. 'Bivvy?'

'It's a bit early,' I shouted back. 'It would be more like a siesta. How about going on a compass bearing along the ridge?' The uninviting alternatives were a vast cornice on one side and an avalanche-prone slope on the other. I took up my compass and racked my glazed brain for an approximate bearing to the plateau of Ushba, the great snowfield at the base of the mountain. We leaned against the wind and prayed we were going in the right direction.

Sure enough, the ridge started to decline, and in a short time, we could see slopes leading toward the plateau below us. Crevasses appeared, grinning like old friends, and we zigzagged our way through them until the sky turned to ink and it was time to bivvy once again. This time, instead of the steep wall of Shchurovsky, there was only a wide, open snowfield. We were on the Ushba plateau, but where, we didn't know. Thankfully, the clouds lowered again, giving us the comforting sensation of wearing blinkers, and we experienced that sense of detachment that people often describe before they succumb to exposure.

We soon discovered that Paul, who was already suffering from the altitude, was also severely hypothermic. There was nothing to be done but bed down—and quickly—for he was in a bad way: pale, blue-lipped and disorientated. It had happened suddenly, as if someone had pulled a switch, so right there and then we dug pits in the snow. I had never been fond of snow-holes, believing them to be time-wasting contrivances for character-building schools. That night substantiated my doubts. Although we were inside our bivvy bags, the spindrift, blown by a strong wind, built up around us with relentless determination. It would have been suicidal for us all to have gone to sleep, even if we could have, for we would have suffocated. But the trouble with oxygen deprivation is that it affects alertness, and it is easy to drop into a somnolent state. From time to time, one of us would call out to see if the rest were still awake before removing the accumulation of snow that engulfed us.

We shivered and awaited the dawn. At first light, we set off down the glacier toward the German bivouac like homing pigeons, reaching the crevassed maze of the icefall. We found the food we had cached for our abortive Ushba climb, but we were too shattered to eat. Although the conditions had hardly been conducive to convalescence, Paul had nevertheless improved somewhat overnight and I admired his resilience and powers of recovery.

The Ushba icefall required focus, with crumbly snow bridges and giant seracs suspended above us like baited traps. At one point, we had to assemble a 50 ft free abseil from the top of a tottery serac before running like hell toward the German bivouac. We arrived late that afternoon and were met by an anxious Richard.

'One of Rudy's mates has fallen into a crevasse down on the Shkhelda glacier.' He pointed. 'I've come up to collect blankets from the bivvy, but it doesn't look good.'

The crevasse was on our regular trail up the ice. It was only about 18 inches wide but around 70 ft deep, and the unfortunate climber was apparently up to his waist in water and stuck as if in a vice. Tut, Rudy and some Russians had tried unsuccessfully to bail him out, and any hope that he was still alive was fading fast.

We hotfooted it down the glacier and joined the sombre party that had gathered round the insignificant-looking slot. By now, they had managed to drag the man out of the slot, but he had the waxy, translucent pallor of a corpse. I felt for a pulse as Paul wrapped blankets around him, but there was bugger all there. I was quite sure he would not recover in the normal course of events, for it would be at least six hours before a rescue party reached him and a helicopter wouldn't attempt to fly in such poor visibility. I decided then and there to risk administering a cortisone injection, something I had done with severely exposed climbers back in Scotland, often successfully. I gave the shot, and we sat in silence for several minutes until, with a delighted yelp, I noticed a slight rise and fall of the man's chest. Within 15 minutes, I felt a weak, fluttering pulse, and with little more to do, we left him wrapped up in blankets with his friends and took to the glacier once more, now wary of every fissure in the ice. The next morning, the sky cleared, and a helicopter managed to reach the glacier where, miraculously, our friend climbed aboard unaided. I breathed a sigh of relief, for I didn't relish the prospect of answering awkward questions in a Russian court of inquiry.

Russians are lavish with their hospitality, and our safe return was celebrated with a banquet at Itkol. The ban on alcohol was lifted for the evening, and we indulged in numerous lengthy toasts, standing up and sitting down like Jack-in-the-boxes as the tributes became ever more impassioned. Paul, who had to go and collect some gear from Rudy, vividly described this 'Last Supper' in terms that would have shamed Bacchus.

By then, we had had enough adventures in the Caucasus, but we still had to make the return journey... with Tut at the wheel of the Fiat. Tut was endearingly polite, and even if the person with whom he was conversing was in the back seat of his car, he would turn to address them as he drove. I heard he had demolished and rebuilt more than one wall for irate farmers back home. We were only a few miles within the Czech frontier and Tut was driving at about 70 mph in the Fiat at dusk, with his usual scattered attention to the road. I saw the dim outline of a cart and had just enough time to clear my throat and berate the carelessness of peasants who took unlit horses and carts onto public highways before my sentence was cut short and we ran slap-bang into the rear of the rustic contraption. All hell broke loose, water and antifreeze gushed from the radiator, and fragments of hay floated down through the air like confetti. Miraculously, we were uninjured, but the peasants were scattered on the ground, projected by Tut's arse-end assault. Their invective, which rose like an approaching storm, was no less equivocal for its foreignness. The two horses, which had been harnessed on either side of the single draw shaft, were thankfully unhurt. In fact, the Fiat had come off worse. The front was staved in and the radiator and bodywork were mangled.

By the time the police arrived to take statements, a large crowd had assembled, for it was Friday night and the locals were eager for some light entertainment. After all, it wasn't often that a peasant cart collided with a car, especially one that had large capitalist posters all over it advertising the *Sunday Mirror* Caucasus Expedition.

Suddenly, I had an idea. 'The chewing gum, Chris! Where's that case that was left over from the trip?'

'In the back of the Campagnola,' he replied warily.

'Let's have it,' I said with enthusiasm.

'Oh, not another bloody idea,' Tut groaned.

I opened the case of Wrigley's gum and began handing it out to the bemused onlookers. I tried to convey by miming that they should all chew like mad and hand the gum back when the sweetness had gone. Thirty chewing Czechs! The babbling mass of a few minutes earlier was now a silent choir with jaws going like fiddlers' elbows. Soon enough, we had a gigantic wad of sticky, saliva-covered gum. Handing half of the gloop to Chris, I instructed him to give me a hand sealing the car's radiator. Half an hour later, we had done a good plastering job, but we soon discovered that there was also a crack in the water pump flange.

'Well, it was a good try,' I said petulantly, as Tut shook his head.

'Not only are we without a bloody car now,' said Chris in despair, 'we are also out of chewing gum.'

Meanwhile, Paul, ever congenial, had struck up a conversation with a pretty local girl who spoke excellent English. She was getting married in two days and would Paul like to be her best man? My mind boggled as to what might have been proposed had their acquaintance extended to half an hour! Calculating that there might be an advantage to our current situation, Paul said that he would need time to consider the offer and was there somewhere he and his friends could stay the night whilst he made up his mind? She and her husband-to-be immediately welcomed us into their home and we abandoned the dejected-looking car beside the road. We'd decide what to do with it later.

We had a raucous night. I'm not sure when we finally went to bed, but we didn't wake refreshed, which is always a good barometer of enjoyment.

We realised that there was no hope of having the Fiat repaired in this part of Czechoslovakia, so we resigned ourselves to a long tow to Austria. Thankfully, the Campagnola was more than capable of this, so we 'roped up' and continued on our long return journey west.

Unsurprisingly, our reception at the Fiat office in Turin lacked enthusiasm, but they generously substituted a pristine model for our crumpled one, and we were treated with greater courtesy than we deserved. We were very grateful to Fiat, for they had done us proud, and we were grateful, too, to the Russians who had been so patient with a bunch of scruffy, unruly Westerners. I suppose I can't really call a journey like that an 'expedition' when we'd had so much fun.

On 6 August 1995, Paul Nunn was overwhelmed by a massive serac collapse while returning from the summit of Haramosh II (21,870 ft), in the Karakoram range. He was mere minutes from the safety of high camp.

Paul Nunn

*Whenever I take the longest drive north
and west at Whitsun I think of Nunn other
then the name that echoes through the guidebook
like his laugh, the indoor bagpipes
of the climbing village, slightly embarrassing,
needing all the space of the Peakland moors,
Sutherland, the Karakoram: 'as the mountain valleys
open up one feels that one is coming home.'*

*Outlandish, like those obscure scraps
of facts he'd pin you down with while
he built a theory between one pint and the next
he'd always offer anyone at hand. Such hands
you'd think grasped summits annually, yet
how often he would return empty-handed home
from home. 'We had no commitments, except
to ourselves, and they were satisfied.'*

*He'd lost friends to a single falling stone,
the sudden moment of the snow slide, sérac crack
we must struggle to accept. 'Someday soon
some must fall. It was a case of grinning
and ignoring them.' Out here, with sea
and mountains meet, where the sky's bighearted,
something is missing and present between sun
and showers in his 'far far away land.'*

The Single Falling Stone
In Memory of Paul Nunn, by Terry Gifford

Roriama seen from a
camp on the approach

22. THE LOST WORLD

I was planning a trip to the Russian Caucasus when I received a letter from my old friend John Streetly, with whom I'd climbed the North Face of the Grand Jorasses. He'd just come back from Guyana in South America and he told me about some spectacular mountains that overhung on all sides for over 1,500 ft. He said there were still unclimbed peaks in the area and the Guyanese government was keen to arrange a trip to Mount Roraima the following spring. Did I fancy it? I told him I'd rather take my chances with the frozen wastelands of the Caucasus than the bug-infested jungle.

Mo Anthoine then got in touch and tried to persuade me otherwise. He was part of a plan to forge a route up the Great Prow of Roraima, whose summit marked the border between Venezuela and Brazil. My old friends Don Whillans and Joe Brown would also be in attendance. It would be a strong team, but my disinclination persisted.

Don made his annual pilgrimage up to visit me in Glencoe the following May in his ramshackle old caravan. He proceeded to boast about the forthcoming trip and how much support they had from the Guyanese government. I recalled John telling me about a peak out there that was strewn with semi-precious stones, so I asked Don if he thought there might be any diamonds.

'Tons of them! It's the second-biggest diamond area in the world.'

Suddenly, my interest was piqued, for I still had the prospecting bug from my time in New Zealand many years previously. My imagination took over as Don droned on about it for a while, lamenting the lack of cash they had to fund the trip. Foolishly, I heard myself saying that I was sure I could swing something with the BBC if we agreed to film the venture.

Roraima had been the inspiration for Arthur Conan Doyle's 1912 novel *The Lost World*, but it had first captured the public's imagination when the illustrious explorer Robert Schomburgk reached the base of the mountain in

1834 after a trek lasting several months. Locals revered the place, calling it the Mother of Waters, as it is one of the wettest places on Earth and usually shrouded in cloud.

Schomburgk had been commissioned by the British government at the time to survey the area and establish the border between British Guiana, as Guyana was then known, and Venezuela. There had been much wrangling over the territory and, unsurprisingly, Schomburgk resolved the matter in favour of the British, thereby deeply offending the Venezuelans and sustaining the dispute. Eventually, the business was settled by arbitration, with Venezuela gaining full control of the mouth of the Orinoco River, which was essential for trade and travel. The summit of Roraima, meanwhile, would demarcate the east boundary between Venezuela, Brazil and Guyana. However, it couldn't be reached from Guyana itself, and the Guyanese government hoped that our expedition would succeed in establishing a pathway through the inhospitable rainforests of the north and gain access for the first time.

The expedition team dynamics were interesting. Mo was cautious by nature and always put safety and friendship ahead of his climbing ambitions. Joe was easygoing, keen to laugh or participate in a practical joke. Highly competitive, he never accepted anything at face value and was capable of rapid and astute mental calculations. Don was blunt, shrewd and introspective, at his best in a desperate mountain situation or holding forth in a pub, where his monotone Mancunian drawl was oddly mesmerising. He usually remained in the background until the odds were against him, when he would deploy almost superhuman reserves of willpower and endurance. Don never beat around the bush, no matter who he was talking to. He had a bad reputation, but in my experience, it was ill-founded. I could not conceive of anyone I'd rather have in my camp in a crisis.

I presented our case to the BBC, and they agreed to fund some of the trip and send out a director and two-man film crew. I would get the footage on the summit. We also managed to secure a helicopter to take all our filming and climbing equipment to base camp, and the Guyanese government had thrown in free interior flights and water travel by canoe.

Not long before we left, a letter arrived for me from a Dr McInnes Fletcher, who took great pains to reel off a litany of jungle hazards we needed to be aware of. The bushmaster pit viper was about 10 ft-long with fangs that could pierce a leather shoe and poison that was deadly in under five minutes.

It was also aggressive, and we would encounter them regularly. Meanwhile, the water camoudi—a boa constrictor—could crush you to death. The only way to survive once it had begun to entwine itself around you was to hack it to pieces. Then there was the kaboura fly—smaller than a Highland midge, but even more voracious, with bites that took weeks to subside. Last but by no means least was the vampire bat, which could transmit paralytic rabies.

Hearing this, I telephoned my local doctor and asked where I could obtain a vaccine.

'For what?!' he said, accustomed to my outlandish requests. 'I must say, Hamish, you have some strange holiday destinations.'

I managed to hotfoot it to Glasgow the following day to get the jab, but it was only after I had received it that the doctor informed me that it wouldn't take effect for six weeks.

As the plans took shape, our expedition team was scattered over the planet on various vacations, so the organisation was haphazard, to say the least. The departure date approached via a series of mini-crises as tickets were forgotten and food and equipment got lost in transit. *God help us*, I thought, as Don appointed himself expedition medic and sent me anti-malaria tablets, which I promptly forgot to take. Joe had raided his garage for ropes, bolts and some hand drills, and I managed to get a hold of some Hilti guns, which would drive bolts home without killing anyone in the vicinity.

Two weeks later, we emerged from an air-conditioned aeroplane into the moist, sticky air of Guyana in the small hours and were met by a tall, distinguished-looking man called Adrian Thompson. Adrian, an official in the Guyana Government Service, had cleared our passage through customs and arranged a meeting with Guyanese ministers who were eager to ensure that our film would portray their country in the best light. Our forthcoming adventure had attracted much attention, and people would stop us in the street to ask about it. Even the local bookies were taking bets on our success.

At our luxurious hotel, I watched Don unpack a spectacular array of colourful apparel. One shirt had multicoloured stripes in the shape of a bullseye. I dissolved into fits of laughter, and Don retorted huffily, 'The problem with you teuchters is that you're so used to rain, bog and mist that you go mad at the first hint of colour. I suppose you'll be wearing your kilt?'

After several days of bureaucratic hold-ups, meetings and expedition planning, we set off on the first flight to the interior. Our pilot was an engaging local man who seemed entirely unperturbable. 'You guys want to see Roraima?' he said, as we rose swiftly above the forest and the mighty Essequibo River. The great expanse of slow-moving water was like a huge camoudi. Occasionally, we spied a lonely shack thrown up in a small clearing on the riverbank or a local paddling a dugout canoe. Although rivers were the motorways of the American rainforest, no navigable rivers passed close to Roraima, so access was only possible by canoe or on foot. Aside from the river, all we could see was rainforest canopy like a green sea, undulating with almost hypnotic monotony. The pilot told us cheerfully that if our plane had to land or if it crashed in the forest, it would be almost impossible to spot from the air. We were soon in the cloud, but we could just pick out Roraima ahead. Great towers rose in the swirling mist toward an immense tabletop summit and waterfalls of great beauty cascaded down from deep ravines.

The geological history of Guyana is fascinating. The basement rocks are comprised of gneiss and schists, which were intruded by granite over 2,000 million years ago. Then the rocks were eroded down to a flat plain before rivers from the east brought in vast quantities of sediments. The vista dominates the skyline between Columbia through Venezuela and Brazil as far as Suriname, grey and pink quartzitic sandstones and conglomerates forming high ramparts that culminate in the broad plateau of Mount Roraima itself. The sandstones surrounding the escarpment have been slowly eroded by rivers over the last few million years, and the surrounding plains probably formed shallow coastal seas, pierced by islands until further tectonic movement raised the whole land surface by some 400 ft.

'Some nice wee slimy overhangs for you doon there, Jock,' said Don. The huge rock faces jutted outwards for most of the way up. At least we'd stay dry on the climb.

We landed in a place called Kamarang, where our equipment had been stashed in the army compound. The place had a Robinson Crusoe atmosphere. A butterfly resembling a flying telephone directory pounded by, and tame parrots flitted through liana vines that hung from mora trees. From here, we set off in canoes on the first part of the journey, casting off from the large fallen palm tree that served as a jetty. Our canoe made a steady nine knots as the skipper navigated submerged logs and rapids. Soon, it began to rain—not just a drizzle but a torrent that hit the water sideways like welding rods. In an instant, we were soaked through and frantically bailing out the canoe with an old tin can. Don managed somehow to continue smoking his obligatory roll-up. 'For somewhere so close to the equator, it feels bloody cold,' grumbled Joe. 'This rain is worse than in Glen Coe.'

The Mazaruni River stole sulkily past like heavy brown ale and dusk fell with a suddenness that startled us. We seemed to be in a trance as the rain beat down and the fireflies flickered around. Arriving at the village of Maiurapai, we skidded around on the steep river bank as we decanted our kit and carted it by torchlight to our huts, which comprised a few hand-sawn boards on stilts with corrugated iron roofs. I glanced nervously at a bat as it flitted past, thoughts returning to paralytic rabies and the knowledge that my vaccine wouldn't have kicked in yet, but I was too weary to bother with precautionary measures.

I awoke, ravenous, to rain crashing down on the corrugated roof. Breakfast was some Dairy Milk chocolate. We left the village and the bulk of our equipment, which a helicopter was to transport to a camp spot known as El Dorado, the furthest place any previous expeditions had made it to. Looking at all the supplies, I felt a gnawing sense of unease at the dearth of food.

Our journey continued for several days, a mixture of canoeing and trudging through swamps. Eventually, we arrived at our third camp. We were now a cast of 5,000, comprising climbers, film crew, porters, guides and scientists. Joe distributed a pack of Havana cigars as we snacked on some gritty homemade bread, and I hoped that we'd find better nourishment at the following camps.

The trails from here were desperate, with tree roots abound and bogs requiring waist-deep wading. Occasional bamboo saplings and broken twigs marking the way were nigh-on impossible to spot amid all the undergrowth. I managed to stumble on a slippery tree root and the long, hooked spikes of a prickly palm pierced my hand as I fell. To add to the growing list of maladies, Mo had developed a nasty-looking blister from some tree sap and Don had a foot injury from stepping on a broken twig. The journey was beginning to feel like running the gauntlet.

Don was keen to move ahead of the main group, as he liked to travel with a minimum of fuss, but we had to be mindful of the tensions within the ever-expanding team. The film crew were struggling to get footage, and the different paces of everyone meant we were becoming increasingly spread out. We also had virtually nothing left to eat, and we needed to stay close to the porters.

Our next camp was a nasty, boggy clearing, and humidity was at saturation point. The trees, having lost the support of their kin, listed dangerously, and moss hung like dirty washing from branches, giving the place the appearance of a bomb-shelled territory. Snake-rooted corkwoods and prickly palms were in abundance and the cages of the stilt-rooted Clusia trees looked sinister. *Probably the home of lethal insects*, I thought morbidly as I swung my snake-deterrent—an old Terrordactyl with a stretcher shaft attached—from side to side. I visualised myself imprisoned in one of these cages, being eaten alive by soldier ants.

Breakfast the next morning was thick, lumpy porridge, much to Don's disgust. Don laboured under the impression that I lived on a diet of porridge and turnips, and I was finding it increasingly difficult to defend our national dish. I worked out that we had enough left for seven more days, and we had just finished all the tea and sugar.

Another crisis ensued. The local porters were quitting, partly because they weren't getting paid enough to put up with all this drama and partly because they were Seventh-day Adventists and had been asked to work on a Saturday. They could easily earn as much staying in the local villages. 'The sooner we get away from this chaotic circus, the better,' said Don. 'We don't want this whole ruddy menagerie. We came here to climb!' He waved his Swiss Army Knife in the direction of the mountain and stormed off.

From here, the trail rose steeply and the undergrowth grew denser. The Great Prow of Roraima hove into view, allowing us to temporarily forget our woes. 'Blimey, it looks fantastic,' said Joe softy. Lianas festooned the upper branches of the trees, forming a gently waving curtain, and hummingbirds hovered ecstatically, their wings whirring like tiny electric fan blades in a blur of light.

That evening, raindrops the size of peanuts bounced several inches off the mud. There was an almighty clatter, as one of the main supports for our hammock system gave way and sent 12 of us crashing onto the sodden earth. A shower of minimally-clad filthy bodies slid around in the mud, swearing profusely. Mosquitoes began their evening rounds, and several bats darted about, but I no longer cared. Eventually, I drifted off, hunger gnawing at my stomach.

The days passed in a reliably monotonous fashion, enlivened only by minor catastrophes. One morning, we heard that there was trouble with the helicopter that was supposed to be bringing in our food supplies. It had broken down, and no one knew when spare parts would be available. Suddenly, we realised the seriousness of our situation. The rain, endless mud and general depression that had been building seemed to be epitomised in that scrap of a message. Our plans were sinking fast.

Later, as we stood in line for our daily ration of rice like prisoners, Adrian called me over. There was only one thing for it, he said. He would return to Maiurapai to collect the supplies and return within the week. This was no small undertaking, and it was not clear he would be able to find enough porters to assist him on the return journey, but there seemed to be no alternative.

We bade Adrian good luck as we set off the next day. As the trails grew narrower, long saplings placed horizontally across rocky precipices made excellent narrow catwalks and strategically placed vines functioned as handrails. We christened the place 'snot forest', for slime coated everything like axle grease and thick mist enveloped us in a clammy embrace. Every spark of life jostled for space on the steep hillside. There were huge bromeliads that would only flower once in their lives and trees with leaves like football bladders. We could now see more clearly above the rainforest canopy. 'Hey, Joe, this is fabulous,' I said, recovering some of my optimism as I swung on a short, slimy vine.

At 6,700 ft, there was a notch on the ridge with a steep cliff above it. Mo slung a rope ladder and we slithered up to a dense thicket before emerging onto white, sticky sand peppered with small stagnant pools. Moss hung like fright-night wigs from the trees, and we had to use great matted pitcher plants as stepping stones. This was the El Dorado swamp.

That night, we turned in as the rain beat down with such ferocity we thought it might sever the flysheet. Our hammocks were a haven in that sea of mud; once inside, we were chrysalises.

We awoke to a dawn of startling clarity. The great tabletop of rock looked as if it had been wire-brushed and the waterfalls tumbled like fresh cream for 1,500 ft. The day before, Mo had gone ahead to assess the cliff and scope out a bivvy spot for us near the base of the Great Prow. We wouldn't even need tents, he said, as it was a sort of natural cave with a rocky roof. We set off with all our climbing gear up the ridge above El Dorado to reach the final step below the main wall, a crest with a drop of around 2,000 ft. Here, we would fix ropes on the steepest sections before retreating back to camp. At last, this was what it was all about!

There are some places I have visited in my life that linger in my mind like half-forgotten snatches of a tune: the Cuillin Ridge on Skye on a crisp February day; a lonely valley in the Himalayas with only a couple of bears for company; and that idyllic path skirting under the 1,500-foot-high sandstone cliffs of Roraima. It was like a lost paradise, albeit a slightly hostile one.

Thrashing our way back through the undergrowth after fixing the ropes in place, we came upon an avalanche of bromeliads several feet deep that had fallen off the main wall, and as we squelched over them, strange noises emanated from them as if they were alive and in pain. It was a reminder of the precarious nature of the untravelled rock we were about to navigate our way up. We bashed our way back to camp and sucked on an opal mint apiece. A few meagre supplies of food arrived later that evening, so we sat and sorted out our gear and tried to clear some of the mud that had caked everything.

Now enthused about the prospect of leaving the jungle behind and ascending some proper rock, we set off with packs laden with the extra gear, including pitons, bolts and drills. The serious climbing was about to start.

The first pitch reared up like the bows of a huge ocean liner, and we jumared up this, hammering in pitons and using natural holds where we could. Clearing the holds required care, for scorpions and other beasties lurked in the shadows, and we used more pegs than we would otherwise have. The slime was so pervasive it clogged up the teeth of our jumars, and the rock was so hard that the self-drilling bolts kept blunting. Above us was the great corner we had called Big Dièdre. The vast amount of energy that Joe spent fixing equipment in place that day gained us only seven vertical feet, but these were crucial, for they had got us to the bottom of the dièdre, and Joe felt it would now 'go' without too much trouble. We arrived back at camp, happier than we had been in days, to hear that Adrian had arrived in Maiurapai in under two days and would be back soon with more supplies, which did much to lift everyone's spirits.

By now, however, the daily privations and constant threats to physical safety were taking their toll, and Joe had developed a hacking cough. Mo was under the weather, too, with a fever and diarrhoea. I woke to retching noises drifting across from Mo's tent, so Don and I sorted out the climbing gear we'd need for the face as we waited for them to recover. Ironically, the designer of the Whillans harness didn't fit into any of the four that Joe had brought along from his shop in Llanberis.

A couple of days later, Joe and Mo were still poorly, so Don and I shouldered our packs, bade our farewells and set off to fix a bivvy spot below the main face. It took us hours to clear the ledge and fix the tarp to the lip of an overhang. I removed some dead bees from a bag of sugar and made a brew. Squinting up at my handiwork on the overhang, I regretted the space I had left between the sheet and the rock. The rain was driving through the gap and running onto my hammock, but the repair job would have to wait until the following day, when we were also going to fix a rope ladder on the chossy pitch at the base of the route.

Just then, Joe and the others arrived. 'I've come to fix your house,' said Joe, the master plumber and builder. Mo, on a dose of antibiotics, was still white-lipped and exhausted.

Don and I set off on the first pitch the following morning. I felt elated to finally be on steep rock and I chanted the *Mingulay Boat Song* as I ascended. Joe mimicked bagpipes droning. As I approached the top of the fixed rope, I noted that it had already begun to fray against the rough rock and was relieved

The mighty Roraima

that we had agreed to put a second rope in place. I moved steadily upwards on my two jumars, knowing that if the fixed rope snapped, the second jumar, connected via a short sling to my harness, would only allow me to fall only a couple of feet. Still, it was airy. Above our heads, the Great Prow rose out at a ridiculous angle, and vast quantities of water sprayed across the face for 100m or so from the waterfall, drenching us.

We pinned our hopes on a terrace far above to the right, which would be about the length of the rope we had available. I was now high above Don on a ledge the size of a biscuit tin lid, and between my straddled legs, I could see the porters and film crew moving around like soldier ants at the camp far below us. My boots were as flexible as sandshoes and my feet were killing me in the nylon loops I'd attached to my jumar. Fixing a few more pitons in place, we descended once again to camp. Dusk was settling in as we eased ourselves into our hammocks. It was bitterly cold and we no longer needed the mosquito nets.

Don's piercing whistle heralded the bright morning as he set off to fix more equipment in place on the route. My now regular early morning sniffles had begun to feel like something more sinister and sweat was pouring off me. Some of the others were also looking gaunt and weak after so long with little food and various maladies. There were now minor skirmishes whenever someone wasted or mis-cooked food, as everyone's nerves were stretched to breaking point. I was used to this from previous trips to Everest, where some members of the party had become somewhat unhinged due to the rigours of expedition life.

The arrival of Adrian and more porters later that morning was a godsend. They had stacks of food with them, as well as the rest of our kit, and we fell upon them as if we were junkies with the imminent prospect of a fix. Joe carefully unwrapped a box of cigars as reverently as if they were family heirlooms.

My swamp flu was stubborn, and as I dogged Joe's footsteps up the trail toward the cave Mo had selected as a bivvy spot, I dwelt upon the folly of the life I'd chosen for myself. My memories of the drudgery and monotony of expedition life had been blunted in retrospect, such are the quirks of the mind. Joe remarked how he had resolved to give up expeditions some time ago as they were so unpleasant, and this trip had merely substantiated his position. The low-hanging cloud gave the place an aura of Rannoch Moor in November and reflected our collective mood. We had been privileged to visit this hidden corner of the world, but it was a frightening paradise. I felt vulnerable and insignificant, and my nerves were jangled from the continual threat of illness and hostile creatures.

As we arrived at the cave early that evening, Don abseiled in like a well-fed spider returning to its lair and spun above us, as if assessing which of us would make the tastiest meal. He and Mo had had unusually kind weather that day and they had been making good progress until a huge tarantula appeared out of a crack and reared up on its hind legs, six inches in front of Mo's face. He had managed to pull his hammer out of its holder and had splatted it, but then spent the rest of the day nervously peering in every crevice lest other arachnids sought to avenge their mate. The rock quality had deteriorated and it had shattered in shards as Mo tried to hammer in more pegs, so he ended up having to grab hold of bromeliads and clamber up them. Don then spied a scorpion sauntering down the rope toward his face and had to swipe it off. A hoped-for ascent of a chimney turned out to be a no-go as it was a watercourse. The only solution appeared to be a smooth sweep of rusty, blank rock leading to huge roofs above, all of which would need to be bolted before it could be ascended.

A porter came hurrying up to the cave the following morning, bearing an ominous-looking scrap of paper. One of the team at the camp below had trodden on a spike of wood and punctured his foot. As he lay in his hammock, the scent of his blood had attracted an army of soldier ants, which had first bitten the camp residents and then proceeded to munch their way through an entire kit bag of food containing at least 30 packets of essential noodles. With one disaster following another, we were reaching the end of our tether. Weakly, I eased myself out of my hammock and struggled upright to send the haul bag up to Don on the face.

I had a good meal going for Don when he dropped in later that day, golden shafts of light picking him out against the vast expanse of forest below. I thought how nice it would be to roam through these lands without stumbling over tree roots, clutching a cutlass or snake stick. Don and I shared a pleasant evening together in the cave, marred only slightly by the invasion of a scorpion, which I casually crushed under my boot. Later, I awoke panic-stricken, thinking there was a snake in my sleeping bag, but it was only Don's foot twitching next to me. In the small hours, Don gave a yell as a spiny rat slunk around his sleeping bag. We let the rat live, for we'd come to regard it as a pet in our new home.

Joe in a hammock on
Tarantula Terrace

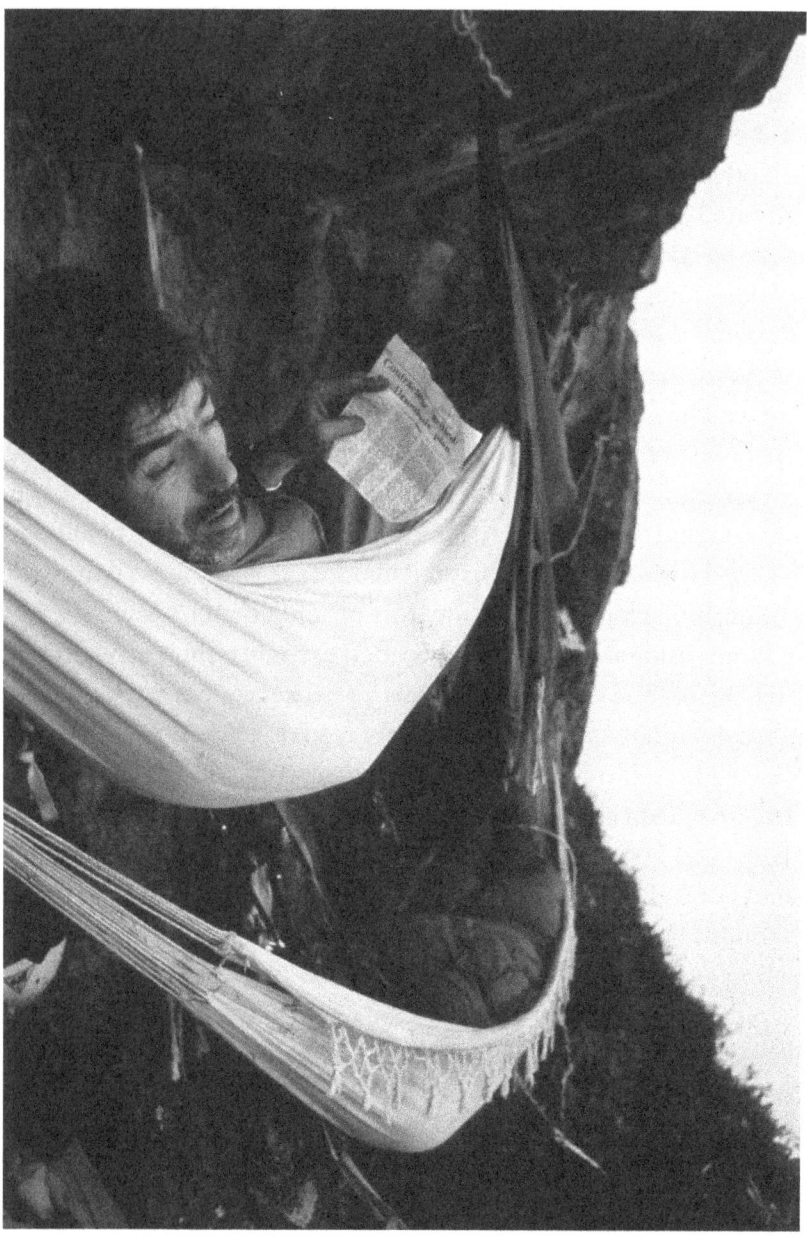

As yet, we had absolutely no footage of the climb and we were already a third of the way up. The following day, I put the cine-camera in a kit bag and tied it to my harness, determined to get some coverage now that I was feeling a bit more human. Surprisingly, I made good progress that morning and headed up to join Mo and Joe on a ledge they'd nicknamed Tarantula Terrace, where they'd slept after a day of bolting. They were still in their hammocks, lazily swaying to and fro. After a brew, Mo started up the fixed rope toward a long flake system. As he balanced horizontally at full stretch, trying to place a peg in the wafer-thin flake, I noted how sensational our situation was. With the luxury of time, good weather and some space around us, I pulled out the cine-camera from my bag and finally got some footage. Mo then yelled down that he was getting terrible rope drag, and he was going to have to untie and climb up on just the sack-haul rope. He made a few moves without clipping into anything, and just as he was about to move up on a peg, it slipped out and he dropped, only just managing to catch hold of the edge of the rock. It was thrilling footage, at least.

We returned to the cave to find we had received new supplies of food, and after a heartier meal than we had had in some time, we felt we should make a push for the next bivvy ledge above a chimney we nicknamed the Green Tower. Mo and Joe, exhausted after their recent efforts, which had included a series of traverses and a spectacular and terrifying abseil over a huge roof, needed a day off. Joe had chafing, and he wanted to spend a day smoking cigars.

Don and I started at first light, hauling up food, water and ropes. Don jumared up the alarming roof, his orange jacket billowing out so that he resembled a psychedelic bat. We got the bags up to the terrace that day, but it was clear we weren't going to make it any further and we retreated once more. Discussing tactics over our evening meal, we resolved to make an all-out assault on the Green Tower the next day. Mo and Joe would lead off in front as they knew the route better. As we eased ourselves into our hammocks that night, I pulled the flysheet of the spare tent around me to form a protective wall against the mist and I hunkered down.

When I awoke in the morning, the mist was clearing and a fresh wind was blowing over from Venezuela. We had been well sheltered under our rocky canopy and had slept soundly. We packed our bags for what we hoped would be our final day on the great wall.

Jumaring upwards behind Don, I was alarmed to find the innards of the sheathed rope were exposed like entrails and the casing was completely cut through from contact with the rough sandstone. I tried to quell my rising panic as the sheath slipped down like skin off a snake. Most of the core seemed intact, but it measured only a quarter of an inch in diameter.

'Don, the bloody rope's nearly cut through!'

'What's that, Jock?' Don's head appeared, blue cap pulled down over his eyes like a guardsman. There was more than the usual amount of interest in his voice. 'You'd better hurry up then, before it parts.'

I gasped as another strand pinged. I had shifted the upper jumar to the bare cord of the rope, and the sheath was bunched up in the grip of the lower one. Don was only about 10ft above me, poised like Santa Claus on a tiny ledge with the haul bags.

'The other rope's a bit tatty as well,' he warned in a low voice.

Finally, I managed to remove the lower jumar and clip it onto the other rope. Alternating between the two ropes, I shifted the upper jumar onto a sound section of rope and let my heart rate settle. 'You know, Don. I've concluded that this climb is a bit dangerous,' I said weakly, as I clung to a microscopic ledge and watched bromeliads hurtle by. The rock was running with water and a freezing wind plucked at us savagely. Distant yells drifted down from above us. The other two were clearly having a desperate time on an especially chossy pitch, but we had no way of helping them. I wondered what the hell I was doing in such a godforsaken place.

Meanwhile, Mo and Joe were deeply involved in a chimney full of prickly vegetation and blind, shallow cracks. It had taken Mo nearly four hours to lead a single section onto a tiny stance and all the peg placements were marginal. By now they were tired and wet, and Joe had started to shiver violently, doubtful of the integrity of any belay Mo would have been able to find.

The weather had been deteriorating all day, and we were now in a full-scale storm. Horizontal droplets of icy rain gleamed in the light like tracer bullets. The heavy rope tugged at me violently, and we were numbly aware that a tiny mistake could end in disaster. Don and I were already mentally prepared for retreat when Mo yelled down that they too were bailing out.

The next few hours were a series of alarming abseils and sack hauls, with any attempt at communication greedily snatched by the wind. Don and I were relatively sheltered lower down the face, but we knew that Mo and Joe were in dire straits, tangled up in ropes that were nigh-on impossible to sort out in the storm. Joe ended up climbing down the rope bundle so he could work out which ones were fixed. As he abseiled over a sharp edge, frayed rope slid through his descender. In the darkness, he had attached himself to the rope I had so nearly come a cropper on earlier, and he only just managed to grab hold of the rock as another strand gave way.

Don and I tried to lower the haul bags but, in the confusion, we couldn't tell which rope to use. Don, who was usually sanguine in a crisis, was more gripped than I had ever seen him. We were soaked, mentally beaten and utterly exhausted.

Somewhat miraculously, we all made it back to the terrace in one piece and admitted defeat. Mo's and Joe's hands were torn to shreds, and their nails, eyelashes and hair were coated in mud. Joe was pallid and drawn. They looked as if they'd come back from a week's potholing. We shivered around a Gaz stove and prepared some soup. It was all we could be bothered to eat.

As is so often the case after such a violent storm, the next day was fine and clear. We didn't speak much over breakfast, still numb from the previous days' exertions. Sipping our tea in silence, we began to sort out the gear for the descent. Joe was eager to get going, and he set off first as I laboured with the cine-camera at the back. The trail down was terrible, but after the previous day's events, it seemed like paradise. To move unencumbered by jumars and descenders was bliss.

Although we had all agreed to go down, each of us wondered who would moot the idea of a rematch once we had recuperated a little. At camp the next day, Mo sat on a twisted branch outside my tent. We discussed our predicament at length and agreed that after all the effort that had been invested so far, we should give it one more go. Mo and Joe needed to recover some strength, but I would go back up with Don to try to breach the great wall.

A hummingbird hovered outside my hammock early the following morning, as if chiding me to get up, and a squadron of parakeets cheered us on as we left the camp. En route back up to the overhangs, the ropes were even more frayed than before, but we were now mentally and physically prepared for them, with haul bags for rope protection. Don quested up the vegetated chimney, cursing and swearing at the tangle of ropes that had been left in place after our ignominious retreat. It was slimy and horrid, and the ledge at the top of the fixed rope was the size of a paperback novel. I looked sceptically at the shallow pegs that Joe had placed at his high point.

Most of the ropes had languished in Joe's garage for several years before being resurrected for the Great Prow, and while they were fine as fixed lines, it was doubtful any of them would withstand dynamic loading. Reluctantly, I concluded that the only suitable rope to lead on was the one above me, which Joe had descended in the storm and which was now jammed, though how securely it was impossible to know. Then I had a brainwave. If I clamped my jumar upside down onto this rope, then climbed up, bypassing the peg runners Joe had clipped into, I could remain attached if the rope happened to pull free, as the teeth of the jumar would bite into the rope if it was loaded. I knew, though, that the breaking strain of these devices was a mere 1,600 lbs and that even a short fall could generate that force. I shouted down to Don what I was planning to do and asked him to tie off the end of Joe's rope, then I began moving up the dripping rock using the pegs as handholds and clipping a foot stirrup into them every time I moved the jumars between the runners. Water poured in via my anorak hood and out my waterproof trousers into my boots. I reached the narrow section where Joe had inserted a peg, most of which was sticking out of the crack. Suddenly, the elusive loose end of the rope dangled tantalisingly in front of my eyes. I snatched it, tied on and yelled to Don to belay me on this rope. Now reasonably safe, I felt drained from the surge of adrenalin. This was not the best place to be experimenting with new ideas.

 The chimney formed a corner, around which I discovered a groove we'd previously contemplated. I belayed Don up as if he were a baited fish being reeled in. I led off again, bashing in a few more pegs and flinging off some spiders along the way. With water running into my eyes, I tried to move left to get out of the worst of the watercourse, and to my undiluted joy found a superb-looking horizontal crack leading to a vertical pillar. This section looked like it would go, and more than that, it might actually be quite enjoyable!

 We abseiled back down as it got dark, leaving the rope in place for the next day. I forgot to tell Don that I'd attached a kit bag to the rock to prevent the rope chafing, and that one of the abseil ropes ran over this while the other lay under it. As a result, when Don tried to abseil past it, he got stuck and had to spend ages untangling it. In the end, he whipped out his Swiss Army Knife in disgust and severed the offending kit bag from its anchorage with decisive slashes, all the while directing a continual stream of invective at me. I watched the kit bag float across the forest like an exotic bird.

 After our productive day, we persuaded Joe and Mo to join us for another attempt on the Prow. Joe had recovered some of his lost spirits and was boosted by my assurances of good rock above the chimney.

We endured another couple of long days digging and grovelling our way up rock of varying degrees of integrity, hammering in pegs where we could and hurling bromeliads down the face as the water continually ran up our sleeves. At last, at the top of an overhanging chimney, Joe spied a light—a through route, by the looks of it. The top lay tantalisingly close but, once again, we were out of daylight and energy, so we reluctantly retreated to our bivvy.

By now, everything was ingrained with mud. Don slept with his head exposed at the far end of the ledge as the flysheet didn't extend far enough, while I had to lay my head down in a hole. I filled this with boots, pitons and harnesses and set a Gaz stove on top of this as a pillow. Here I reposed for the remainder of that miserable night, three wire prongs supporting my head. A full moon picked out the neighbouring peaks in stark relief. We fervently hoped tomorrow would be our last ascent.

We were up before dawn, donning wet, filthy clothes. I set off first, glad to be moving again after such an uncomfortable night. Soon, though, my circulation began to function, and I moved smoothly up the now-familiar terrain toward the skylight Mo and Joe had seen the day before. I climbed up through a hole like the eye of a needle, dragging my thread of rope with me. The summit was just above, but an overhang would need to be breached first, and my heart sank a little. If we didn't get up the climb today, I doubted we ever would. All our ropes were showing the strain, and I knew that if we kept yo-yoing up and down this bloody face, one of them would snap. Mo was down to his last drill. If it broke, it would be the end of the whole endeavour.

'What's the crack,' demanded Don, seeing my crestfallen face.

'I've got an idea,' I said, after surveying the situation for a few minutes. 'Pass me the end of the climbing rope. See that big loose rock at the top of the crack?'

'Aye.'

'I'm going to try to throw this behind it and jumar up the rope when it jams.' I had used this technique once before to good effect on the first winter traverse of the Cuillin Ridge.

'Right,' replied Don doubtfully.

Tarzan-like, I hurled the rope up with enough slack in my hand so that it would continue its trajectory freely. It arced through the air and fell neatly behind the block, first time. I reckoned there was just enough weight in that block to support me on my jumars.

Mo and Joe arrived at the stance as I gathered up the remaining pegs and krabs.

'Right, I'll get on with it, then,' I said. I tugged at the rope to set it in place, attached my jumars and gingerly applied my weight. It held. I started up, digging my fingers into the dense vegetation and kicking steps as if on a winter route. The next belay ledge was a celebration of flowers, and stalactites of snot trembled from the overhangs. It was straight out of Conan Doyle's science fiction novel.

'I'll lead on if you like,' I offered, 'but I thought you might want this last pitch, Mo. You've led most of the damn thing anyway.'

A few metres up the next section, Mo complained of 'some loose stuff' just before a great mass of vegetation tumbled down, knocking me flat on my back. There was silence for a moment as everyone waited to see how badly injured I was. The difficulties of getting me off the face ran like quicksilver through everyone's minds. I lay there badly winded and in some pain for a while until I was sure nothing was broken, then I urged Mo to keep going. There was no way we were giving up now.

As Mo struggled up the last few feet of the overhang, legs dangling in space, the sun came out and bathed him in exalted light. My final moves up to the summit were slow and painful, but suddenly I was on the great plateau as if I had awoken from a long nightmare and arrived in heaven. When Joe's head popped up, he looked like he was emerging from Hades. From here, the Great Prow looked like the giant bow of a ship jutting out over a verdant sea. We stood on the brink and I set off a parachute rocket up into the air to signal our success to our fellow expedition members 1,000 ft below on El Dorado.

We roamed around in a daze in that strange landscape, our clothes steaming in the sun. There were no roots, no slime, no killer beasties. Just a magnificent panorama of mesas. We looked along the edge of those immense cliffs to the waterfalls tumbling straight down to the Paikwa watershed. White pebbles sat like dinosaur eggs on the washed and windblown sandstone. We gazed into shallow pools; dark mirrors reflecting human faces for the first time. Deep crevices had been gouged out by the elements to form chambers delicately carved into arches and scrolls. It took me back to the Khumbu Icefall on Everest, where I had tried to find a route through a dangerous labyrinth of tottering seracs.

Summits are often unremarkable, even on a first ascent. They are just isolated points on Earth where someone else may or may not have been before.

Roraima was different. We were in alien country, with many plants and animals that were hitherto unknown to science. The climbing was as hard as anything we had experienced before, the conditions comparable to the misery of high altitude. To arrive at that fairyland summit after such a gruelling passage made us feel light-headed.

After a while, it began to rain again, and soon we were exposed to the full fury of the wind and rain like welding rods. In seconds, the decks were awash and new streams began to foam and leap toward the edge of the plateau. We no longer had a forest canopy or cave to protect us. We had made it out of a treacherous slimy sea to the security of a huge ship, but now it was time to go home.

Clint Eastwood in
The Eiger Sanction

23. HOBBLING AROUND ON THE EIGER

One weekend, while scoping out the sea cliffs south east of Edinburgh for possible new adventures, I scraped my leg against a sharp rock, incurring a trivial impact injury below my left knee. For such a minuscule bruise, it was inordinately painful, and reluctantly, I hobbled along to the local infirmary. I had enough time in the waiting room for my conscience to get the better of me, however, and with a gait befitting Long John Silver, I snuck away sheepishly. I was getting as soft as some of those I'd rescued over the years, I told myself: hillwalkers and climbers who, as a fellow rescue team member wryly observed, complained of 'twisted eyebrows'.

By Monday morning, the pain was so intense that I was compelled to return to the hospital, where a friendly doctor examined my benign-looking injury. A quick X-ray confirmed her suspicions: I had gas gangrene. It seemed that the offending rock had been contaminated with seabird guano and a microscopic tear in my knee bursa had allowed the bacteria in.

Within minutes, I had a circle of doctors round my trolley. Donald MacLeod, a senior surgeon whom I later got to know well, told me in no-nonsense terms that he would have to operate immediately. As a throwaway line to cheer me up, he added that, of the three cases of gangrene he had encountered, one had lost a leg and one had died.

I had been exposed to life and death situations on many occasions, but these had usually been in the heat of the moment, or carefully calculated when I had considered the odds, not when lying helpless on a trolley like a side of beef. 'Well,' I said with resignation, 'if you can't save my leg, leave it where it is; I might as well go to the pit with it.'

Donald, skilled as he was, saved both my leg and my life, and I spent 16 days of convalescence in the infirmary writing a thriller about oil boom skullduggery on a West Highland sea stack, which helped to take my mind off the discomfort. When my publishers later promoted the book, I modestly declared that I had banged it out in just over a fortnight, which prompted gleeful responses from critics such as: 'Dr MacInnes brags about writing this 'pile o' shite' in sixteen days—just imagine the outcome had he taken an extra day or two!' And the self-important: 'Hamish MacInnes says he wrote *Death Reel* in the spirit of Agatha Christie, one of his favourite authors. He has clearly never read an Agatha Christie story.' I carefully cut out these caustic appraisals and pinned them above my desk next to the weekly bestseller list—in which *Death Reel* appeared for several weeks.

Suffice to say, I recovered from the gangrene infection relatively unscathed, save for an angry scar on my shin and the withering book reviews.

While I had been recuperating, my comrade Dougal Haston had been involved with fictional foul play of a similar nature, as climbing advisor to Clint Eastwood during the filming of *The Eiger Sanction*, much of which was shot on the mountain's North Wall. I was fully occupied with the BBC's *Outside Broadcast* at the time, but I had recommended two of my instructors as assistants. When I was still limping around at home, I heard from Martin Boysen, who was working with Dougal, that one of the assistants, Dave Knowles, had been killed by rockfall on the West Flank. I was shocked, for I had known Dave since he and his twin brother had first come to Glencoe years before, and they had both been in our rescue team.

Two days later, the Swiss-American climber Norman Dyhrenfurth rang from Kleine Scheidegg, a hamlet and mountain pass between the Eiger and its neighbour, the Lauberhorn. 'Hamish, I wonder if you could help us out. Clint Eastwood is asking if you would be willing to come over immediately to take charge of the safety aspects of the film,' he said. It seemed that things had ground to a halt, and it was costing them £25,000 a day just to keep the unit on location.

'I can hardly walk, Norman,' I replied. 'I'm fresh out of hospital and recovering from a secondary infection. I'm not exactly a bundle of energy just now.'

'There is no need for you to walk or climb anywhere, Hamish. We'll supply helicopters for your use. Have a think about it and give me a ring.'

Norman managed to persuade me that I could juggle my BBC commitments and that he and his team would fit in around my schedule, so the next day, I flew to Zurich and caught the last train up to Kleine Scheidegg. Martin Boysen met me off the train, and I was soon introduced to Clint and his producer, who were keen to discuss the project and how it could be

An apprehensive Hamish and Clint before the epic stunt
© John Cleare

Hobbling Around on the Eiger

completed without further loss of life. I was relieved that both were 'spade men' who talked without frills. Clint drawled in his easy way, 'I'm sure glad you made it, Hamish. We'll go along with anything you say.'

Martin and the now late Dave had been standing in for Clint and others in various climbing shots on some of the trickier pitches that required negotiating technical rock and ice, and as well as advising on safety, I discovered that my know-how in rigging and setting up difficult shots would also be called upon.

For the first few days, we worked around the lower part of the mountain's Jungfraujoch railway tunnel, where we had access to the lower part of the face and an assortment of gullies, buttresses and rock walls for cutaway shots. Clint wanted to film on a subsidiary peak called the Rote Flüh and higher up at the so-called Death Bivouac, where German mountaineers Karl Mehringer and Max Sedlmeyer had frozen to death in 1935. Although the Rote Flüh gave us adequate protection from falling rocks, access to the bottom of it was not without the odd sniper-like missile, so I insisted that only Clint and climbers could go up to this point and that there should be no filming higher up on the wall. Happily, everyone agreed.

One sequence required Clint to dangle from a rope underneath an overhang with a bucketful of exposure, preferably near the centre of the wall. Never one to undersell a take, Clint was keen to use somewhere near the Gallery Window, a hole in the main wall where debris from the Jungfraujoch tunnel was chucked out during its construction. At this point, the wall falls away in a stomach-churning drop, but by using the tunnel for access we could avoid having to climb up there, so I agreed to have a look at it. The corridor from the tunnel to 'the door to nowhere' was an ice chamber. Above the entrance, the rock reared up in a vast overhang, and beyond this, avalanches and stones thundered down with monotonous regularity.

The next day, the main group was working on easy terrain on the Eiger glacier, so Canadian climber Chic Scott and I took the workers' train up to the Gallery Window. The train clanged ominously to a halt on the steep gradient and we stepped out with our ladders and drills; an unusual day's work was about to start. After a cup of coffee at 6:00 am, we opened the door to nowhere and clipped onto the ropes that had been fixed in place the previous day, moving in a matter of seconds from the claustrophobic icy tunnel out onto the vast, draughty wall. I had concocted a plan for engineering this particular shot, which would entail hoisting a steel canopy to the lip of the overhang high above the door to protect Clint from rockfall as he hung directly beneath it. I proposed making this steel 'umbrella' in the shape of an open-ended pyramid, but this required good anchors, so we positioned the ladders to reach the lip of the overhang and then spent the rest of the day drilling bolt hole anchors. The weather in the Alps was poor at the time, with piles of unstable snow on the higher peaks, and we were distracted by frequent spindrift avalanches raining down on us.

The following morning, I headed down to a small engineering shop in Interlaken, where I asked the shopkeeper if it would be possible for him to make a steel umbrella.

'Umbrella?' he repeated in English, thinking that I had used the wrong German word. 'There is a place, sir, that makes umbrellas in Bern, but not here in Interlaken.'

'Yes, but this is an umbrella for deflecting rocks. I want it for the Eiger North Wall.'

The shopkeeper exploded in a paroxysm of laughter and shook his way into the office like a blancmange. I could hear him spluttering to a colleague about a *verrückt* Englander who wanted a bombproof umbrella to climb the Eiger. Once his convulsions had subsided, I managed to convince him of the reality of the project, and we discussed the construction of the canopy at length and designed it together so that it could be assembled on location.

The next day, I returned to the overhang, and just as we were going out of the window, an especially large cluster of boulders hurtled by, ricocheting not far from the doorway. I realised that, even with the umbrella, the set-up was too dangerous, and I had to tell Clint that the window sequence would have to be abandoned. *The Eiger Sanction* seemed fraught with almost as many problems as the first ascent of the North Wall had been.

I suggested trying to get the footage we needed high up on the West Flank overhanging the North Face, but Dougal wasn't keen because Dave had been killed nearby and he thought the rock too dangerous. Although Dougal may have appeared to be a hard and inscrutable man, non-committal as a sphinx, deep down he was a sensitive sort. I probably knew him as well as anyone in later years, for we spent a lot of time together, and I was aware that a fatal motor accident in Glen Coe, for which he was responsible, still hung over him like a black cloud many years later. He never drove again after that, even though he travelled widely.

Reluctantly, Dougal agreed to come up and have a look at the West Flank position with me, and with a helicopter and a friendly pilot called Gunter at our disposal, we were flown up and landed by winch wire to a spot resembling the rounded top of a large submarine.

We inched our way to the edge on our stomachs and peered over the vertiginous drop. The wall slipped away beneath us for around 2,500 ft, so that we couldn't see it until the overhanging rock eased to vertical and swept down a considerable distance before running out into meadows. I flicked down a small stone, and we watched it get infinitely smaller until it disappeared.

'The rock does seem solid enough,' Dougal conceded, 'but how do you propose Clint should fall when he cuts the rope?'

'I'll extend a ladder out from where we're lying, like a diving board,' I explained matter-of-factly, 'so that the end is about 25 ft clear of the face, and then erect another one from here so that the bottom of it rests on the diving board ladder. The top of the vertical one will be connected to the end of the horizontal one and it will also be guyed back to the ridge behind us. We'll put in a couple of expansion bolts to hold the flank end of the diving board ladder in place on the rock face here behind us.' I gestured behind where we lay. 'It will work on the cantilever principle.'

'It sounds crazy to me,' he sighed, 'but it's your call. I agree, the place does seem okay.'

The contraption was ready by the next afternoon. When Clint and ace cameraman Mike Hoover landed, they looked somewhat alarmed when they saw the Heath Robinson-like structure we had cobbled together and realised they both had to perch on the very end of the horizontal ladder. Between them, they weighed not far off 400 lbs, and as they moved out over the drop, the ladder bent like a cheap plastic ruler. The plot involved Clint hanging from the end of a rope that had snagged on the overhang above the Gallery Window. In the script, two ropes were thrown to Clint from the window by rescuers, and these were the ropes on which Dougal and I now belayed Clint. In place of the snagged rope, we had one that hung directly from the end of the ladder, and Clint would have to cut this as he hung from it, simulating freeing himself so that he could swing down onto the face. Dougal and I lowered Clint 30 ft from the end of the ladder, and he tied on to the 'snagged' rope, which he was to cut as Mike lay spreadeagled above him on the end of the ladder with his heavy camera.

'Are you tied on yet, Clint?' I yelled.

'Yeah, I'm on. Wait till I get this knife out.' He rummaged in his pocket for the Swiss Army Knife.

Most people in Clint's position would have been spun out, but in his no-fuss way, he took it all in his stride like a true professional. It was highly risky for him to be holding a razor-sharp knife, especially once he had cut the rope, and he had to keep his cool and remember to drop it as soon as the rope parted. We also realised that the sudden departure of several hundred pounds of weight from the diving board would result in the ladder springing upwards. Mike steeled himself in anticipation.

After final safety checks and deep breaths all round, Clint yelled up, 'Hey, guys, is this safe?'

'It's safe enough,' I shouted, 'but I wouldn't do it.'

'Well, if it's safe, let's get the damn thing done. Ready, Mike?'

'Ready.' Mike replied, somewhat hoarsely.

'Here goes.'

The Swiss Army Knife slid through the Edelweiss climbing rope and Clint plummeted, swinging like a yo-yo beneath the overhang. After a few moments of utter silence, I called out, 'You okay, Clint?'

'Yeah,' came the nonchalant far-off reply. Clamping his jumars onto the safety ropes, he began hoisting himself back up to the ladders, where Mike, despite his sudden upward bounce, confirmed he had got the shot he needed after a single take. I wasn't sure if this statement was dictated by the quality of the shot or his reluctance to repeat the hair-raising scene.

The next day, we were back up again, this time to drop three dummies from the end of the ladder. These were supposed to be Clint's ill-fated companions, and their fall was spectacular, to say the least. Watching them spiral down was like seeing one's life racing away to its termination. Dougal said quietly, 'Makes you think.' We both knew the aftermath of a collision.

After we had dismantled the diving board and flown back to the hotel, I suggested to some of the guides that we should recover the dummies using the helicopters, but they didn't seem to think it was worth the risk, so I resolved to do the rescue job myself. I suppose it was an old anti-litter instinct I had after years of recovering bodies from the mountains back home. Anyway, I didn't want future generations of climbers starting up the North Wall to find these grisly mementoes of light entertainment so, with Martin Boysen as a spotter at the bottom of the Rote Flüh, I flew in with Gunter to the lower reaches of the face and began hunting. After a protracted search, we found all three dummies and prepared to winch them up. As I was lifted into the helicopter, the first 'body' cleared the deck. We rose another 20 ft before the second one was airborne and a further 70 ft before the last one was lifted. With all three dummies now dangling like a string of sausages from my harness, I felt as if I were being pulled apart in an aerial tug of war. We flew over Kleine Scheidegg just as a train from Lauterbrunnen was arriving and another from Jungfraujoch was due to depart. Word of our macabre air cargo reverberated through the trains and hordes of travellers streamed out for a look, assuming the dummies were unfortunate climbers being airlifted off the mountain. There is nothing like the prospect of human suffering to excite people; this, after all, is what the onlookers supposed climbing the Eiger was all about.

Later that day, we had to film a sequence where Clint pendulumed spectacularly across the Rote Flüh wall, running across the face as he clung on to the end of a rope. Mike was to shoot the first sequence parallel to Clint on the wall, but we also had to capture other aerial shots that could be edited in with Mike's, so I set off in the helicopter with a cameraman and a Westcam, a camera on a gyroscopic mount used to get rock-steady film footage from a helicopter in flight. The shot Clint wanted entailed coming up the valley toward Grindelwald and the Eiger, with the mountain appearing bigger as we progressed until the red face of the Rote Flüh, with Clint dangling in the middle of it, filled the frame.

That was the theory, but it was impossible to look through the viewfinder of the Westcam by normal means, as it was under the helicopter. Inside, the scene was displayed on a monitor, which only gave a black and white picture, and we couldn't locate Clint on the wall. Gunter flew the helicopter so close that I could have passed Clint a sandwich. We could frame him here, but not further out. Stumped, we circled for a while until I thought of a potential solution. 'Is it possible to reverse the footage during the edit, Clint?' I asked over the walkie-talkie. 'We can get you on the monitor when we're close by, but we just can't see you on an approach shot. If we pulled out the way we came in, could you flip the shot later?'

Clint considered this as he hung on his rope. 'Let's try it.' Although he was safe enough during all this, he was in a mind-blowing situation, and I admired his composure. The wall was so steep you would certainly lose your small change if it fell out of your pocket. Despite this, when Clint started to reverse-pendulum, he had the presence of mind to look in the opposite

A brave Clint trusts Hamish to lower him from the end of the ladder down the North Face © John Cleare

direction from where he was running in a great arc across the wall, so that when the film was edited, he would appear to be facing the right way. Even climbers familiar with such acrobatics wouldn't have relished running 'blind' in such a place.

Once we had completed the sequences with the actors, we needed a shot that would show the North Wall in all its savage grandeur. I suggested we take the helicopter up to 15,000 ft and make as rapid a descent as was safely possible, and Gunter replied that a drop of 4,000 ft a minute would be his limit. With a cameraman in tow, we soared upwards until the summit and the narrow snowfields of the notorious White Spider were framed on the monitor. Gunter gave us a two-second warning, and suddenly, we plummeted like a peregrine. I thought we would never slow down, but when we did, the machine started to oscillate and vibrate, the floor shuddering as if we were in a washing machine. Still we kept descending, and it seemed to me that the odds were against being able to brake at such a speed, but Gunter had calculated to the last millimetre. Suddenly, the mountain was spirited away in a fog, and the mellow contours of the valley of Grindelwald lay below us as we slowly made our way back to our landing spot at Kleine Scheidegg.

I like to think of the good times I had with Dougal Haston and not dwell on his last ski run close to his home in Leysin, where he was killed by an avalanche. He had stayed with me in Glencoe only two days beforehand.

In some ways, we had opposite tastes, Dougal and I. He liked Schoenberg, and I preferred opera. But we both liked chess and probably held the record for the highest-altitude game—on Everest.

Dougal and I both shared a need for solitude, and in a flapping tent or bivouac, we wouldn't say a word for hours. Dougal was a very special person, not just to me, but to everyone who knew him. No doubt he will be with his philosopher friend Robin Smith and a galaxy of rock stars who have also departed.

Dougal Haston

Thrashing through arrow grass
on the quest for treasure

24. NOT ALL THAT GLITTERS

Those of you who are obsessed with adventure stories will likely have heard of Atahualpa, the last emperor of the Inca, who was captured in 1532 and held for ransom by the Spaniard Francisco Pizarro and his fellow conquistadors as they sought to vanquish this ancient civilisation. Before his confinement, Atahualpa had been conned into meeting Pizarro at Cajamarca in Peru and had arrived in good faith with thousands of unarmed warriors. Pizarro, who had 80,000 fully armed soldiers, gave the war cry 'Santiago', and his troops duly massacred the unfortunate Inca.

The emperor, aware that his neck was on the line, promised to fill a room with gold and another two with silver in exchange for his freedom, but Pizarro grew impatient with the slow accumulation of ransom loot and had the emperor garrotted. This was probably a mistake, for there was a lot of the yellow stuff still en route.

An Inca general called Ruminahui, who was managing the heavy consignments from the north, heard of his boss's demise and ordered the main caravan back to Quito in Ecuador. To cut a long story short, Rumiñahui was later defeated by the heavily armed Spanish troops, and after Quito was razed to the ground, he hotfooted it to the small village of Pillaro with 12,000 guards and 750 tonnes of gold!

Out of the frying pan into the fire, the general was soon captured by another conquistador and tortured in a vain attempt to get him to spill the beans about the treasure's hideaway. Rumiñahui was ultimately burned at the stake in Quito's Plaza Grande, and the treasure was never recovered.

Next, let me introduce a man called Valverde, a hard-up Spanish mercenary who married a girl from the dusty town Latacunga some 50 years after Atahualpa's death. As a wedding present, her old man took the young Valverde to a cave in the Llanganates, a vast and rugged expanse of Ecuadorian wilderness, where a staggering amount of treasure was hidden.

Valverde rose up in the world after this financial boost, and on his death bed, he bequeathed the location of the cave to the King of Spain, who sent a royal warrant to the Corregidors of Latacunga to dispatch the gold back to the old country post-haste. They never found the repository, however, and lost some of their party along the way.

The trail went cold until the 1850s, when English botanist Richard Spruce, a self-taught scientist and collector for Kew Gardens, travelled to Ecuador in search of seeds from the cinchona tree, which were used to produce the antimalarial drug quinine. When he eventually returned to Britain, Spruce reported that he had uncovered Valverde's guide and a related map, made by a man named Atanasio Guzman.

In 1886, a treasure hunter called Barth Blake followed up Spruce's discovery and claimed to find 'the most beautiful goldsmith works you are not able to imagine'. Blake described a vast horde of life-size human figurines, birds and other animals, flowers, jewellery and 'golden vases full of emeralds'. Taking only what he could carry, Blake headed to New York, where he planned to raise funds for an expedition to recover his prize, but he disappeared overboard in mysterious circumstances. Many who have since attempted to retrace Blake's steps into the treacherous Llanganates have also paid with their lives.

There followed several expeditions to the place over the years, all of them unsuccessful. Men went mad; many got lost and perished. Eugene Brunner, a Swiss-German, spent 42 years searching for the treasure, and on one of his many abortive trips reported seeing the sun only once in 127 days. Other bizarre accounts include a husband and wife who were caught in a flash flood and had to scale a tree to survive. The wife died of pneumonia, and the husband spent the rest of his days in a mental institution. A fellow Scotsman, Captain Eric Erskine Loch, led an expedition into the region between 1935–37 and subsequently wrote a book on his exploits called *Fever, Famine and Gold*. One of his party was swept away in a river, and others succumbed to fever. The Captain eventually returned to his jungle home, lit two candles, drank a bottle of whisky, took out his service revolver and blew his brains out.

I read about all this chicanery with fascination as I sat in a tent in the far north of Scotland waiting for a weather window for a first ascent of the Great Stack of Handa. Despite the seemingly cursed nature of the quest, I resolved to find the stash myself. It would fund a lifetime's worth of adventures.

I knew that Joe Brown and Yvon Chouinard would be good fellows to accompany me, for our trio was a perfect match. We had spent a lot of time together in hostile environments and never argued, except in good-natured debate. When I suggested this 'working' holiday to my friends, they were enthusiastic.

'I've been thinking about where the treasure might be hidden, Joe,' I said. 'There's an incredible amount of loot involved—millions!'

'Okay,' said Joe. 'When do we go?'

'December.'

Yvon said he'd meet us in Miami and kindly agreed to bring a few packets of freeze-dried food and a stove.

Soon after we met up, we trawled through the descriptions and maps, which were as complex as a route plan for Fort Knox. We were headed for the Llanganates, for it was here that General Rumiñahui had reputedly hidden the gold. To the north, standing as a self-appointed sentinel at almost 20,000 ft, is Cotopaxi, one of the world's highest active volcanoes. The Andean people believed it to be a sacred place, a 'rain sender' that guaranteed the land's fertility. During a violent outburst in 1877, pyroclastic flows descended all sides of the mountain, melting the entire ice cap.

Quito was plunged into total darkness, and the city of Latacunga was levelled by mudslides. The base of the mountain has been devastated by earthquakes and buried in pumice and ash many times in its history, and its walls comprise alternating flows of dark trachytic lava and lighter-coloured ash.

Immediately south of Cotopaxi lie the Llanganates mountains, one of the most inhospitable and inaccessible regions on earth. In the early days, the area was more frequented than it is today, but it has always had a reputation as an evil place, thanks to its poor weather, swamps, dense jungle and fever-inducing diseases. As the trade winds from the east merge with the cold mountain air, fog and rain often shroud this soggy desolate altiplano for months on end. It is an elevated version of Rannoch Moor in the Scottish Highlands, but with the green swathe of the Upper Amazon Basin encroaching on its eastern flank.

Our immediate destination was Ambato, a town a few hours south of Quito, where the local driving style was a kind of dodgems-cum-Russian roulette. The journey began innocently enough, but glancing at the newspaper over the shoulder of the man in front of me, I read that 417 people had died on the roads in the previous 12 months, which didn't bode well. The bus was a cacophony of clucking and squealing as various forms of human and animal life jostled for space. It was illegal for passengers to stand while the vehicle was moving, so every time we passed a police post, the conductor would yell at everyone to lie down in the aisle. This was all undertaken in a spirit of great fun, and there was much hilarity.

It quickly became clear, however, that the journey would be akin to an ordeal with a drunk driver in rush hour traffic, as the cherubic face of our driver set in a wild-eyed grimace and he barged past rival buses, horn blaring. As we pelted our way along the steep narrow roads, the rain lashed off the mountains and visibility reduced to about 50 ft, but this didn't slow our hero down. Passenger insurance came in the form of regular donations into the conductor's cap, and the shrapnel would be deposited at the shrines of St Christopher—the patron saint of travellers—that punctuated each high pass. The passengers (bar three) seemed inured to the deadliness of the journey and would cheer like football fans when we vibrated past another vehicle on a hairpin bend. For several hours, I kept a nervous eye on the unhinged-looking driver in the rear-view mirror as his bloodshot eyes glazed over. There were further incidents involving a huge truck, which had slewed off the road and blocked it, and an encounter with another bus that had successfully squeezed past us on a blind summit, only to collide head-on with a tractor. When our own trusty steed finally skidded to a halt at Ambato, we staggered out, dazed and as traumatised as we could recall having been at any time during our long climbing careers.

To describe the Residence Ambato as filthy would be to do the place an injustice. The walls were cracked, the windows were broken, and unsavoury characters loitered outside our padlocked door. Some practical joker of a plumber had arranged the toilet to flush upward, and there was no bog roll. Under my bed—which seemed to be designed for guests with acute spinal disorders—lived a large rat that would eye me malevolently as it gnawed on whatever I'd been careless enough to leave lying around.

A few days later, we arrived in a remote village called San Jose. Dust kicked up by local cowboys rolled down the wide, mud-baked street, and old men languished under ramshackle verandas that a gentle Scottish zephyr would have reduced to matchwood. This, the highest village in the area, was the only place to find the local guides who we'd been told were essential for getting in and out of the Llanganates. We soon discounted that notion. Not only were they reluctant, they demanded exorbitant payment with bonuses we couldn't afford. When both Joe and I had climbed Roraima in Guyana a few years earlier, the local guides were true gentlemen who could move with

Arriving in Ambato

the stealth of a bushmaster and carry enormous loads faster than we could run. The locals of the high páramo of Ecuador, however, had an altogether different attitude. We felt dejected.

'Let's carry our own gear,' Yvon declared. 'We've got enough freeze-dried food, and we can all get in one tent.'

Joe and I were reluctant, for we had lingering memories of impenetrable bamboo, prickly pine, scorpions and spiders the size of dinner plates from our previous Amazonian sojourn to Roraima, but we agreed there was no alternative. After all, we had two air survey maps and a compass—what more did we need?

The next day, we took a hired truck along a winding dirt road to the end of the trail, passing a hacienda where fighting bulls were bred. Up ahead, the lake where the Inca had reputedly dumped the treasure centuries before shimmered in the heat, and beyond this lay the Llanganates, bleak and forbidding. We met a cowherd who told us that a trail snaked between two peaks, but that it was easy to lose it. We weren't sure if he was referring to the trail or our minds.

In this high-rise oven on the razor edges of the Cordillera de Jaramillo, the radiation was so intense that it burned the skin on the backs of our hands, and we had to cover our faces and necks with makeshift balaclavas. The temperature in the shadow was 105 degrees, and I succumbed to sunstroke, shaking all over and running a high temperature. The next morning, I was still as weak as a kitten and had to rest once again. We had chanced upon the best weather the region had seen in years, and despite our resemblance to pork crackling, Yvon muttered that we should count ourselves lucky.

Knowing that we had limited supplies and energy, we resolved to head for the highest peak in this wilderness, Cerro Hermoso (14,993ft), and then veer northwards to reach the general area shown on Valverde's map. However, when we reached the divide on the fringe of the Llanganates, we were confronted with stunted, sterile peaks covered in arrow grass 20 ft high and dense as a wire brush. There were no insects, and when we spotted a solitary bee, it seemed overjoyed to see another sign of life and buzzed around us as if we were old friends.

I had started the day depleted and soon felt exhausted. We crossed a stream, and out of a sense of duty rather than enthusiasm I prospected with my gold pan—AKA a plastic washing-up bowl—which brought to mind my forays at Long Beach in New Zealand many years previously. Later that afternoon, I collapsed and could go no further, so we made camp. Despite the extreme heat of the day, within an hour of the sun setting our teeth were chattering. A full moon soared triumphantly over Cerro Hermoso as a bitter frost descended and enveloped everything in surface hoar.

The next morning, a knife-edged ridge reminiscent of a cathedral roof led to the summit of Cerro Hermoso. On our left, the great carpet of Amazonia stretched out in the hazy-blue distance. For several days, we remained at an altitude of 14,000 ft but could find no route to take us north toward the area where the gold was likely to be stashed. Thrashing through the arrow grass, we drew close to the savage slopes of Cerro Hermoso in the hope that the valley leading toward Rio Napo, a tributary of the Amazon, might offer a golden shortcut.

At the base of the mountain, we found an old camp of thatched huts with ancient maps and bundles of dynamite lying around. The camp squatted at the brink of a deep, silvery lake, and the high cliffs rose above us in a great cirque. It was a geologist's paradise, with enormous bands of gneiss and iron and a summit of black shale. We found traces of gold here and workable quantities of copper. On the margin of the lake was an old prospector's hut, and we surmised that it had probably been used by Brunner and Blake.

Round the campfire that evening, we weighed up our options. Continuing from here was hopeless; there was no way we were going to find the cave, and we would have needed a large, well-equipped team to go in via the original route description. We were also out of grub and knew the weather wouldn't hold for much longer. Joe, who had been suffering from dysentery since the beginning of the trip, said, 'We've had the luck of the righteous. Which we're not.'

There was nothing for it; we'd have to head back along the rollercoaster ridge to the fleshpots of Ambato. After a comedy of errors and a dispute over a compass bearing that sent us off in the direction of Venezuela, we arrived back at our verminous residence. Our lips were cracked and bleeding, and our clothes were ripped and blackened from the campfire smoke. The local hotelier smiled knowingly when we admitted we hadn't found the treasure, for he knew it was out there but was certain it wouldn't be found by three filthy gringos.

That night, we ate pineapple for tea and let the juice run blissfully down our faces. 'Well,' said Yvon, 'if we can't find the goddam Inca treasure, we can at least climb a mountain. From experience, you have to do everything as soon as possible in Ecuador before the lurgy catches up with you. Let's bag one of the big peaks before we're carted off home on stretchers.'

'Cotopaxi,' I said, 'is one of the highest volcanoes in the world. How would that do for a day's outing?'

Joe and Yvon were all for it, but it meant we'd have to return to Quito. We waited a whole day for a lift at a dusty road end, then gave up and hired a jeep to take us to the remote Ribas Refuge, which perches at an altitude of 15,500 ft on the northern flanks of the volcano. After a lung-bursting drive up to the refuge, we stumbled out, gasping for air. We had climbed almost 6,000 ft in 45 minutes. The hut guardian greeted us warmly and made us herbal tea that tasted like nectar.

Cotopaxi, first climbed in 1872 by the German scientist and traveller Wilhelm Reiss and Colombian partner Ángel Escobar, had been quietly smoking its peace pipe for almost 100 years and we hoped it wasn't about to let off steam now. At 3:00 am, with headlamps probing the gloom, we crept up its glaciated flanks, turning sinister-looking crevasses and ascending steep icy walls. The conditions were perfect, but our lungs weren't yet acclimatised and felt the strain. It was also bitterly cold, and by the time we approached the summit, the wind cut through us like the arrow grass of the Llanganates. The violet sky was littered with stars, and the great expanse of the Amazon was bathed in diffused light as we reached the rim of the vast crater, where an ominous-looking wisp of smoke eddied as if at the behest of an unseen deity. Far below us, dawn was marching across the rainforest, but we couldn't linger, for Joe was already showing signs of frostbite. We hotfooted it back down to Quito and returned the jeep a mere 24 hours after collecting it. It had been a fast but memorable trip. We bought more succulent pineapples for 10p and ate our fill as we contemplated our next scheme.

Like the dead, exhausted and mad before us, we didn't locate Valverde's cave on that trip, but we felt certain we'd find it, not on the precipitous slopes of Cerro Hermoso but down in the Amazon Basin. Three years and two expeditions later, despite hot clues that would have taxed the brain of Sherlock Holmes and exploits that Baden Powell would have applauded, we still hadn't found the gold. Many have ventured into the Llanganates since our quixotic forays, and as long as the legend persists, there will be men and women willing to risk their lives in the hope of unearthing a fortune. Those who do not succeed may find something of greater intrinsic value, for it is only through mental and physical hardship that one discovers one's true nature. For all but the most determined and experienced, however, it is probably better to contemplate such adventures from the comfort of one's fireside.

Cerro Hermoso

An unwelcome encounter
with a tarantula spider

25. AMONG MY SOUVENIRS

Recently, I have been thinking of the many 'souvenirs' I've taken back from my travels over the decades. Strangely, I've gone back for more, even as the horrors of rapacious leeches and other unmentionables remain etched in my memory. I can recall boots soggy with blood after encounters with these jungle Draculas, which squeezed through my boot eyelets to gorge themselves until they looked like a clutch of slimy black puddings. On one trip, I awoke in my tent with a large leech lodged in the back of my throat, which was subsequently removed by my companion with the tweezers of his Swiss Army Knife by the light of a headtorch. Later, on that same expedition, I returned the compliment by cutting out huge ticks from under his armpit, this time by the glow of a campfire and with a blunt table knife for a scalpel—by then our torches had run out of batteries and the Swiss Army Knife had been exchanged for some ghee and three scrawny chickens.

Back home, after a particularly nasty upper Amazon expedition, I was congratulating myself on escaping unscathed when I noticed a subcutaneous dark smudge at the side of my big toenail. Thinking it was probably a small splinter of bamboo, I didn't give it much thought until several days later, when it seemed to have moved. I picked up the phone, for my local GP was a close ally. Not only had he spent several years in the army serving in the Malaysian jungle, but he also had a healthy interest in strange fauna. The good doctor wielded his scalpel, and a flesh tunneller resembling a mini armadillo was eventually extracted. I don't think we ever discovered what it was.

Some expedition memories are nightmares in retrospect. Once, I staggered into a sunbaked village in central Nepal after toiling up an endless trail with an oversized rucksack. The village well was a divine oasis, and I guzzled the well water as if it were nectar. Wiping my chin and peering round with red-rimmed eyes, I wondered why there was no one about, for in those days a white man was still a novelty. Only later did I discover that the inhabitants of the village had been wiped out by cholera.

It is not a great idea, however, to read up on these voracious residents of the rainforest as one's imagination goes into overdrive. On one jungle expedition, my companion's sole reading material over several months was a handbook of tropical medicine. Each night without fail, I would hear moans drifting across from his hammock as he complained of some exotic malady or other, from 'Chagas disease' to 'nematodes'.

Another time, we were headed for a remote region of the rainforest which, according to reports, was infested by bushmasters: venomous pit vipers. To the best of our knowledge, no one had ever been in this area, but we prudently repaired to a mission station on the fringe of the territory and consulted with one of the doctors. He was most helpful and offered us a serum but pointed out that it was only fractionally less dangerous than the bite from the snake itself. 'Do you have an outboard motor with you?' he asked. We shook our heads. 'A pity, for we have discovered that if a shock is applied from the spark lead to the victim between the bite and the heart, it can have dramatic results.' We left without the anti-venom and deferred purchase of a second-hand outboard, for there were white water rapids with drops of up to 6,000 ft every few miles.

I have had a few legacies from the rainforest, including a 15-year fungal infection under a nail that took an ultra-dry stint in the Atacama Desert to eradicate. One expects frostbite at least once in a climbing career, but having been a regular victim of these tropical afflictions, I count myself lucky that I still have all my fingers and toes.

Other long-term guests were giant roundworms, which I picked up while in the Karakoram. Two years later, when they had put on considerable weight at my expense, I was a guest at a party. After I had consumed more free alcohol than was good for me, I was sick. Ugh! The sight of a tangle of roundworms compounded my nausea. This experience wasn't as bad as that of a friend of mine, who had a tapeworm 18 ft long removed from his innards, or the plight of one of our porters who collapsed at altitude and had to have a fist-sized ball of worms dislodged from his throat when he was resuscitated.

I was so preoccupied with creepy-crawlies on my first expedition to South American jungles that I bought nylon boiler suits for all the expedition members, even though we would be within one degree of the equator. Sometimes the tables were turned, and occasionally I took bugs back as souvenirs. One was a bird-eating spider with a nine-inch leg span, and another was a centipede about the same length. I dipped my newly acquired pets in clear casting resin, which generated considerable heat and resulted in the corpses being unintentionally cooked as well as preserved.

As I look through my expedition notes, I realise that I could write a book on these tropical hazards alone. If you go tripping off to some far-flung rainforest, consider yourself lucky that in Scotland all we have to worry about is the odd cleg, a tick or two and clouds of midges.

The Drongs © Joe Brown Picture Archive

26. THE DRONGS

The year was 1982 and the latitude 60 degrees north—the same as Cape Farewell in Greenland. The place was Hillswick in the Shetland Islands and the objective was the Drongs, a group of pinnacles standing to attention about half a mile offshore. These shapely spires are exposed to the full fury of southwesterly gales and are surrounded by treacherous submerged reefs. Despite the rock having a reputation as rotten, it is in fact superb granite that glows a deep russet red in the evening sun, or *simmer dim*, as it's known in Shetland.

The etymology of the word 'drong' probably dates back to pre-Viking times. In Danish, the name can mean a drone, redolent of the freak gales that whip round the pinnacles. The main Drong is known to locals as 'The Sail,' for its detached columnar pinnacles look very much like a mast with a granite blade like a sail.

The late Tom Weir had told me that the Hillswick area had the best climbing prospects in Shetland, sending me a bundle of photos to prove it. I had planned to visit the place but never quite managed to, for it can be tricky to pin down dates that coincide with optimal conditions.

Sensing that there were excellent routes to be bagged, I eventually made the journey north with my climbing pals Cynthia Williamson and Kenny Spence from Edinburgh for some exploration. I also gave Joe Brown and Don Whillans a ring and persuaded them to make the long trek to the farthest-flung landmass of the British Isles.

It is an unlikely place to find a mountaineer, but in the packed bar of the St Magnus Bay Hotel, Don, having arrived still bronzed from his latest Everest trip, was waiting for me to return from a sortie with Cynthia and Kenny to the Gordi Stack. This is a forbidding looking finger some 200 ft above the sea, whose dangers primarily involve being sprayed with the luminous, evil-smelling vomit of the native fulmar population.

An elderly fisherman by the name of Anderson approached Don as he slowly sipped his pint. 'Would you be one of the gentlemen wanting to go to the Drongs?' said the fisherman.

'Aye, well, it's my friend Hamish who asked for a boat,' replied Don, 'but he's away climbing a stack just now and he doesn't know I've arrived.'

'Well, the owner of the hotel has asked me to take him and his friends out to the Drongs,' said the fisherman. 'But the water's dangerous and the rock's terrible. Ye'll no' get up them.'

That was enough to quicken Don's interest, and he replied with the wisdom of someone well used to sizing up people, 'But you boatmen up here must be experts in big seas.'

'Well, we know the waters all right,' admitted the fisherman, reluctantly. 'But there are terribly whirly pools and heavy swells around the Drongs.'

'Anyhow,' said Don soothingly, playing another softening gambit. 'Have a drink—we can always go and just have a look at them.' Of course, he persuaded the boatman to take us out the following day, weather permitting.

By the time I arrived back at the hotel, Joe had arrived. Don, now well lubricated, greeted us warmly in the bar, and we spent the evening contemplating possible lines up the Drongs.

Early the following morning, Anderson was waiting on the beach in front of the hotel with his motorised boat, payment made with a bottle of rum. He looked with trepidation at the mound of ropes and equipment but passed no comment.

As he steered the boat through the seaweed, he said, 'There's a bit of a swell running.' An understatement. It was immediately obvious to us that the chances of any landing at the Drongs were slim.

We slowly made our way round the headland of Hillswick, passing by the elegant Gordi Stack, which looked like an island version of a Chamonix aiguille. On the shoreline to the north reared the heads of the Grochan, imposing red cliffs overlooking myriad sea stacks, all as yet unclimbed. Ahead lay the Drongs.

'Any chance of taking us right in?' I asked.

'Ye'll no' get up the Drongs,' he repeated. 'But, aye, I think so. But you can see for yourself that the sea is coming up fast. It may slacken when the tide turns.'

With unerring skill, he took us right below the main Drong. Here, we were in the lee of the swell, though the boat was still rising and falling over

Navigating the swell en route to the Drongs © Joe Brown Picture Archive

The Drongs

six or seven feet. To our right, like the second of two ugly sisters, the other gangly Drong rose gracelessly from its pedestal. The conversation on the boat grew more animated as we discussed possible routes, none of which looked easy. Using the oars, the fisherman guided us through the convoluted reefs along the overhanging west face of the main Drong, and all the while we were being tossed around by the swell.

'I wouldn't mind just seeing how they look,' I said to Joe, eager to get off the boat and onto some kind of dry land.

'Good idea,' he agreed. 'Can you take us back round to the lee side again, Mr Anderson, we'd like to step ashore and have a closer look to see how good the rock is.'

'Well, I'll try,' said the seadog. 'But I can't keep her here for long.'

With the skill of Charon, he eased the craft in, bow first at the only possible place, and Joe jumped off at the opportune moment. Two waves later, I followed.

In a trice, we were soloing up solid rock. 'Worse comes to worst,' Joe yelled optimistically over the crash of the surf, 'we can abseil right into the boat. There's plenty of overhanging rock.'

With patience that can only come from a lifetime of living by the rules of the sea, Anderson agreed to try to hold his boat, which bucked like a wild beast in the foam-flecked sea. Don had in the meantime 'stepped ashore', and we threw a rope to Kenny, who quickly tied the gear onto it.

With Joe and Don climbing together on unchartered territory, this felt like a historic day for Scottish climbing. Having first climbed together in 1951, the intervening years had been an active time for them independently, and they had made major ascents of some of the world's most difficult mountains. Now, the old team were back together. We just had to bag the Drongs!

Up the steep rock, hanging out from the face, Joe studied the problems ahead with perhaps the most experienced eyes of any rock climber in the world.

'How does it look?' asked Don, standing a few feet below with the peak of his customary white cap pulled down over his forehead.

'I think she'll go alright,' Joe replied simply.

Buoyed by Joe's assurance, I shouted, 'Hey, Mr Anderson, I don't think we'll take too long to climb it. Can you take the boat in again and we'll pull up our gear?'

We proceeded up the routes in pairs, Kenny and I privileged to be following the footholds of two of the great climbing masters.

Joe reached a steep section, which even from the boat we had known would be hard, but he expertly hammered in a couple of pegs, and in one elegant movement, he was up on a ledge.

With varying degrees of grace, we progressed diagonally up the east side of The Sail on superb rock to easier climbing and a scramble to the top, where a narrow cleft separates it from the 'mast'. Reaching the summit, I was relieved to find that only a single young fulmar lay in ambush, and it had used up most of its ammunition on Joe and Don, who were now cowering behind a large chockstone as an army of dive-bombing birds tried to puke on them.

The 150-foot abseil down the gap between mast and sail was a sensational pirouette toward a heaving sea. Back on the ledge at the base of the climb, we had a celebratory sandwich, and Don and Joe lit cigars.

'Well, she's only about 160 ft high,' said Don, exhaling a cloud of blue smoke triumphantly, 'but a great climb!'

'Yes, this is the life,' agreed Joe. 'I have my rod at the hotel. Do you fancy fish for tea, Hamish?' he said, for he counted fishing as his greatest passion next to climbing.

'Fabulous,' I enthused. A fitting end to our Viking-themed saga.

On the way to Hillswick, round the headland, Don was already contemplating buying a boat. 'Something about messing about in the sea and climbing appeals to me,' he mused.

Happy memories with
friends and their families
© Graeme Hunter Collection

27. A CABIN BY THE SEA

Writing guidebooks has taken me to places I wouldn't otherwise have ventured to, and over the years I have become intimately acquainted with Scotland and its islands. With its ragged coastline and rich patchwork of glens, mountains and forests, the country is a kaleidoscope of landscapes and cultures.

I had hitherto resisted the urge to buy some lonely bothy as a bolthole, for I knew that being tied to one place meant other intriguing corners of the land would be neglected, but eventually I succumbed to the wild, rugged hinterland of the North West Highlands, a place that has always held special appeal for me.

My friend John White told me about a vacant croft not far from his summer retreat on the shores of Loch Torridon, and he suggested that I contact the landowner, a Brigadier MacKenzie, whose family had owned the land since 1494. It transpired that the Brig knew of me from my mountain rescue work and was happy for me to take over the site, along with a substantial tract of land adjoining the edge of Loch Torridon. The croft itself was dilapidated with no electricity or running water, and the easiest access was by boat, but as I didn't intend to live there full time, these drawbacks didn't curb my enthusiasm.

This was just what I was looking for. Scenically, it is breathtaking, with a clutch of hill lochs and one of the most important outcrops of gneiss in the country on which several triple-starred classic climbs can be found. It was certainly remote, with only a few ruins mouldering in the heather—a reminder of another age and harder times.

This was the end of my search for my very own Shangri-La. Now only the paperwork remained and the place would be mine. However, things happen slowly in this part of the world. John told me that when he first obtained the lease on his cottage, he had an option to buy the place. After protracted negotiations, the transaction finally went through—15 years later! I was pleasantly surprised that the acquisition of my own wilderness retreat was completed in a matter of months despite the complications of ensuring the ground would no longer be subject to crofting regulations.

My first priority was to build something habitable. I resolved to put up a log cabin, as this would be unobtrusive and easier to transport by sea. The alternative was a tent, and I had already devoted a considerable part of my life to such shelters. Preferring a coastal site for both practical and aesthetic purposes, I eventually chose a sheltered bay that offered good access by boat and five-star views of the Little Minch and the north shore of Applecross. A stream gurgled cheerfully down a steep hillside to a boulder beach, ensuring a good water supply from one of the lochs above. It was an idyllic, if lonely-looking place, fashioned like a Roman amphitheatre specialising in aquatic events. To walk out to the road from here took about 45 minutes, and in times gone by the children who lived there had to tramp along a rough footpath past the Whites' place, climb to the second loch, then thread through a network of cliffs high above the natural harbour of Diabaig before descending to the village. Different days!

Diabaig must be one of the most scenic villages in Scotland. It is situated where a ribbon of single-track road, after surmounting the Pass of the Wind, finally plunges to the jetty and the Atlantic Ocean. Whitewashed cottages perch serenely on the steep slope. This unspoiled bay was an anchorage for the Vikings for hundreds of years.

As I began construction of my bothy, the seals seemed to appreciate my taste in classical and Celtic music as they sunned themselves on a nearby rock. Other swimmers included occasional basking sharks, schools of porpoises and a couple of curious otters exploring the stream for sea trout. Sometimes they came within touching distance and would size me up with the appraising looks of building inspectors. A particularly smelly family of wild goats stopped by daily, eating everything in sight. Billy had a superb sweep of horns and his matted beard was the size of my shovel, while his partner was petite, shy and ladylike. This family of five, including the kids, thrived on a varied fibrous diet just above the shoreline, which was no doubt helped along by the warmth of the Gulf Stream. Golden and sea eagles were regular visitors, keening their support for my endeavours, and a pair of peregrine falcons made their home on the rocks high above the bay. The Whites were keen naturalists, and they told me they had once left their lobster creel on the shore with the bait still in it. The following morning, they found a wildcat inside it.

I sussed out a mooring site nearby at Wester Alligin, a bay with a cluster of houses facing south. Access was by the narrow single-track road, an offshoot of the tarmac strip that runs out at Diabaig on the other side of the Pass of the Wind. With apprehension, I approached one of the crofts, where a weathered-looking man with a shock of white hair was engrossed in repairing a fence.

'Excuse me,' I addressed him haltingly.

'Aye?' he responded gruffly. 'What do you want?'

'I was wondering if I could anchor my boat here. I've building materials to ferry round to the bay on the other side of the Whites' place, at Eisean Dubh.' This was the name I had given to my bay—a Gaelic description of its centrepiece: a black-rocked waterfall.

'Why should I mind?' he said truculently, fixing me with a pale blue gaze, calm and unflinching.

'Well,' I replied, 'it's your pad, and I thought I'd better ask your permission...'

He shrugged and returned his attention to the fence.

So, now I had a mooring. Later, I became friendly with the gruff crofter—who was called Dougal—and found his bark to be worse than his bite, although I had the feeling that he thought me a lightweight as I wore a lifejacket and had a spare outboard for emergencies. With many of my climbing colleagues having come a cropper over the years, I had learned to take sensible precautions.

One day, Dougal came to help me load my dory with heavy steel tubes for my bothy project.

'I think it's a bit low in the water,' I observed, trying to sound casual. I was concerned that there were only a few centimetres of freeboard and the sea was rough that day.

'Not at all. You told me this boat can't sink,' he retorted with a gleam in his eye as he threw a couple more tubes aboard.

'Well, I don't think it will,' I agreed reluctantly, 'but I might get my feet wet!'

And so I did. By the time I was halfway round the rocky coast, the 'unsinkable' craft was filled with water. A pal who had come to visit saw me rounding the point on the final approach and wryly called out that I resembled Jesus walking on the Sea of Galilee. The boat was all but submerged, with me standing on the rear transom, effectively screening the top of the outboard.

A short time afterward, while still digging and moving boulders (a job that was later interrupted by an Amazonian expedition and took about a year to finish), I badly gashed a finger, leaving part of the bone exposed. Being alone and far from help, treated the wound myself. I didn't have any sutures in my first aid kit, so I did the next best thing and used a needle and thread to repair the laceration, something I had seen Himalayan porters do with gashes on their feet. When I eventually managed to see the local doctor, he was impressed with my embroidery, but it was several weeks before I could use my hand again.

Despite my solitude, there were regular social calls from the Whites, who were now in residence until late autumn. On a good day, they would row round, usually with some delicious home baking and the latest wildlife gossip. During one of their visits, we heard a plaintive bleat from the slope above. This was Blodwyn, a maverick sheep who had a mind of her own and the appetite of a horse. She had a bohemian look, with remnants of several years of unbelievably filthy fleeces dragging behind her, matted and intertwined with brambles and bracken like a macabre bridal train. Her one remaining horn gave her a lopsided look. Blodwyn had an unerring ability to sense when a crofter was in her territory, and she would secrete herself in a cliff-bound hollow out of the reach of eager collies. The Whites told me that she would often casually enter their cottage and steal potatoes or anything else that took her fancy, including food directly from the kitchen table.

I was making good progress with the cabin, but I still needed to transport building supplies from my base in Glencoe. My old pal Mo Anthoine, sympathetic to my plight, gave me the name of a milkman who was based in a nearby Highland outpost. Jackie the Milk, as he was known, operated the longest milk round in the British Isles, collecting his wares from Morayshire at the crack of dawn each day before driving back to the North West Highlands to deliver to far-flung places like Gairloch and Dundonnell, mostly on single-track roads. In need of a large vehicle to transport some of my building materials, I rang the milkman, and after formalities, asked him how big his truck was.

'Oh, don't worry about that, Hamish. We'll get it all on somehow. I'll take the big flat-top lorry.'

Looking at the pile of tiles, I didn't share Jackie's optimism, but he and his lorry duly arrived in Glencoe on a balmy spring morning as the last snows glowed pink on the summits. He had already driven 120 miles. Some of the rescue team were mustered, and two other friends, Mike Begg and Ian Sharp, made the mistake of stopping by just as the truck drew in and were promptly put to work.

Four hours later, Jackie's truck squatted alarmingly on its springs. I feared it wouldn't leave my back yard, let alone drag itself up the hills of Wester Ross. Jackie was contemplative and scratched his head.

'I don't think the old dear will make it the normal way, Hamish. I'll have to make a detour to avoid the steep hills round Loch Carron.'

'Are you sure?' I asked, worriedly.

'Aye, I think so, but I'll wait till dark. She's a bit overloaded, and I don't want to get booked.'

I realised that the hard work was just about to start, for the tiles had to be unloaded at Shieldaig beach, several sea miles from my site, and the timber cached until I could build a raft. In the meantime, I had moored an outsized ex-RNLI inflatable in the bay.

The agreement was that Jackie would rendezvous with us at Shieldaig at 8:00 am. I had arranged another press-gang and Mike and Ian were going to stay close by at a hotel.

That night, I camped on the edge of a tranquil lochan amongst ancient Caledonian pines. The moon suddenly drifted into view above the crags and cast its silvery reflection on the water. Two red deer hinds came down to drink a few metres from where I lay in my sleeping bag before bounding off through the trees, moonbeams catching their bobbing white tails.

A couple of ravens in the rocks above were harshly debating some important topic as I cooked my breakfast on the primus stove the next morning. It was another glorious day, and in the half-light of the spring dawn, the woods exuded a quiet ambience.

I ambled down to the sleepy village of Shieldaig as the sun was rising in time to see Mike and Ian arrive.

'Two reluctant tile movers reporting for duty,' grumbled Ian.

'Fall in,' I instructed. 'You'll be pleased to know that the reinforcements are on their way.' Charlie Rose, leader of the Torridon Mountain Rescue Team, had agreed to give me a hand, along with a friend of his. The people in this part of the world are like that: always willing to help out.

Suddenly, everything seemed to happen at once. Charlie and his pal turned up. Then, a squeal of brakes accompanied by rapid backfiring heralded Jackie the Milk's descent into the village. The truck veered sharply onto the single-track road that ran along the shore and shuddered to a halt. Jackie flung open the door, looking surprised to have arrived in one piece.

'It was a bit slow, but the old girl made it!' he cried.

We had the truck unloaded in three hours. All the timber was stacked at the side of the road beside a derelict jetty, ready for raft building, with the tiles at the top of the beach like lines of tombstones. Work in the Highlands progresses more enthusiastically with lubrication, so I had taken with me encouragement in the form of a bottle of Famous Grouse whisky, which inevitably proved more popular than the flasks of tea.

We slaved most of the next day, carefully placing timber of all shapes and sizes into the skeleton frame of the raft, inside which we had laid out a large tarpaulin. We had to move fast to make good use of the rapidly rising tide, which took the raft closer to the shore and shortened the distance we had to carry the timbers.

Eventually, the wood was enclosed with tarpaulin and bound with steel cables winched tight round the structure. We moored our new craft and collapsed in a heap on the shingle beach, admiring our handiwork. A ritual dram was called for. The maiden voyage would have to wait for another day.

The following Saturday, with ominous-looking clouds overhead and a swell out on the loch, I headed down to the Sheildaig jetty to meet two local fishermen, Kenny and Richard Livingstone, who had offered to help and were only free that day. I knew that we would have to take a risk with the weather and hoped that the raft wouldn't disintegrate. With these thoughts running through my mind, I perched on a pile of rope and, right on cue, I saw the brothers' boat, *Fran*, butting her way toward me. Ian, the third Livingstone brother, and a local hill shepherd had also come along to give a hand. We pulled the raft over to the jetty to re-tighten the binding cables and make final adjustments for the tow.

With everything shipshape, Kenny took up the slack on two climbing ropes that functioned as tow lines and we chuntered off, a dinghy obediently following on another lead. Despite our precautions, Kenny had to retrieve some planks that had come loose and were now adrift. Someone ungraciously described my raft as resembling a 'clootie dumpling'—a traditional Scottish pudding steamed in a cloth.

By the time we got to the bay, the steel frame of the raft was warped, and we had to wait for the tide to go out before we could start dismantling it. Although the high tide had taken this gigantic parcel almost up to the site, it was late afternoon by the time all its contents were manhandled into neat stacks and we retired to the site hut for refreshments. As I boiled water on the primus stove for a brew, I passed round drams of a rare single malt, The Angels' Share, a present from a friend in H.M. Revenue and Customs. The Livingstone brothers took water in their whisky, and I noticed that the usual enthusiasm for this nectar was subdued. It was only when I took a sip from my own cup that I realised that out-of-date helicopter fuel had dripped from the primus stove valve into the water bucket.

It was autumn by the time the logs I had ordered for the walls of my cabin arrived. The Livingstone brothers and I had decided that trying to transport these logs by raft would probably damage them, so we would load *Fran* with as many as possible, go round to the bay, anchor some 30m from the shore and haul each log ashore by rope. No sweat!

The first journey was fine, but by the second loading, *Fran* was bucking at the jetty and I was disconcerted to hear that one of the Diabaig locals who had helped us with the first load had declined to make a return trip.

The boat tipped alarmingly from side to side as we made our way round the base of the cliffs through the turbulent water. 'Just as well we're not towing a raft, Hamish,' Kenny said calmly. 'I think you would have lost a few logs.'

At least it was more sheltered when we reached the bay. Kenny stayed aboard while Richard, Ian and I rowed ashore in the dinghy, taking the tail end of the long rope with us. The other end was secured to *Fran*'s stern. Kenny had now dropped the anchor, and the boat was flexing its muscles as it faced into the strong southerly wind.

Kenny busied himself by throwing logs overboard single-handed, then clipping them onto the rope for their final journey. Some timbers were both long and heavy as we carried them up to the bothy site, and I felt my legs buckling under the strain, but Richard and Ian made light work of it. I was knee-deep in the water to prevent the square timbers from being smashed as they entered the channel when I sensed something was wrong. Looking up, I did a double take.

'Hell's teeth,' I shouted. '*Fran*'s moving.'

The wind had notched up a couple of octaves and the sea was now roiling, sending the boat toward the solid gneiss at the west side of the bay. Kenny sprang into action. In an instant, he cut the stern log line, clambered over the pile of logs in the well of the boat and abandoned the anchor. Rushing back to the wheelhouse, he steered the boat seawards, away from the rocks. By now, a maelstrom of spray had charged across the loch.

Kenny and Richard, who spent every working day together, had a profound understanding of the sea and their own capabilities. To them, this was a fairly minor incident and common during the winter months. There was a logical way to deal with it. No flap; no fuss. Now, the objective was for the three of us to get the dinghy out to *Fran* and climb on board. To take my mind off the prospect of making acquaintance with Davy Jones's Locker, I resorted to bailing with an old evaporated milk can, my eyes focused on the rising water in the dinghy.

During a second precarious circuit, Kenny, who had lashed the helm, threw a line across to us, which Ian grabbed and secured to our painter. We managed to clamber aboard *Fran* as the sea heaved and the dinghy was flung around like a rag doll. I heaved a sigh of relief as we cleared the headland to the north of the bay and headed toward the sanctuary of dry land and Kenny's croft house in Sheildaig.

Safely inside, we were greeted warmly by Mrs Livingstone, who brought us hot tea and homemade scones as we discarded our wet gear and sat down gratefully by the cosy Rayburn.

'You'll be pleased to know,' she said in her soft West Highland burr, 'it will be alright by late afternoon.' She continued buttering more scones, for the large pile was rapidly disappearing. 'It's dropping to severe gale.'

The next day was the Sabbath, so we didn't do any real work. Even today, in isolated pockets of Scotland, Sunday is still a day of rest, although it isn't observed as rigorously as it was in the past, when it was impossible to do anything. As a boy, I recall that I wasn't even allowed to whistle on a Sunday; however, for once, I was grateful to my ministerial ancestors for the break, for it meant I could stay at the site and sort out the chaos before Kenny and Richard, who had generously agreed to give up a day's fishing, arrived on Monday with *Fran*'s precious cargo.

Joe Brown arrived from North Wales on Sunday afternoon and immediately pitched camp on the only level spot between the piles. After our ritual brew, which I managed to make to his satisfaction for once, he telescoped his fishing rod and went over to the west side of the bay to see if he could wind in some supper. He returned in half an hour, empty-handed. 'I guess it's tinned spam for dinner,' he said with resignation.

After another brew, we contemplated the logs and scrutinised the plans for the cabin. 'This is going to be fun, Joe,' I said with enthusiasm. 'Everybody should build a log cabin once in their lifetime.'

'These logs are really well machined with their triple tongue and groove,' he said admiringly. 'Let's hope we don't balls it up. By the way,' he added darkly, 'talking about mistakes, how did you level up these foundations?' He pointed an accusing finger at the 16 concrete monoliths between which his tent now stood.

'I made a theodolite,' I said smugly. This is a surveying instrument for measuring horizontal and vertical angles.

'Well, they don't look level to me. We'd better check them before we put down the base logs.'

Joe, I should explain, was an experienced builder. Though a plumber by trade, he had done all sorts of construction work and what he didn't know about concrete, drains, joists and lintels could be written on the head of a six-inch nail.

'Have you ever heard of a water level?' he asked in superior tones.

'Of course,' I replied testily. It sounded like such a simple thing.

Joe, suspecting my ignorance, explained as if to a two-year-old, 'A water level is a flexible pipe containing water, free from airlocks, with calibrated transparent ends. It is used for establishing exact heights—like,' he pointed, 'those bloody piles!'

'Well, I bought a cheap lot of alkathene piping at one of the sales...' I offered sheepishly.

Joe sighed and shook his head as he inspected a length of the flimsy piping, but we proceeded to fill our water level from the stream. This appeared a simple enough job, at first. But we soon discovered it was nigh-on impossible to do without getting air in the tube. Using my small kettle to fill the hose and with our respective thumbs firmly on our end of the pipe, we chose our piles.

'Right.' Joe cleared his throat and adopted his best gaffer's voice. 'Now you stay there, Hamish, at that centre pile, and I'll go round the others in turn. Is that clear?' His tone suggested that he considered me to be an imbecile.

'Yes, sir.'

'Keep your finger on the end of the tube for the moment,' he cautioned as he pulled the tubing over to a corner pile and held the clear end of it perpendicular to the top edge of the concrete. 'Now, you eejit, you do the same.'

I copied his technique. Taking my finger off the end of the tube, I peered down it to see what had happened to the water and received an eyeful.

'Bloody hell!' I cried, reeling back.

At least that made him laugh, but a couple of minutes later, the same thing happened to him. Now it was my turn to bellow, and in so doing, I dropped the tubing, which fell into my welly boot and immediately filled it with water. This was Joe's cue to double up. Next, it was another airlock, then another. The whole operation was pure pantomime, more like Laurel and Hardy than Brown and MacInnes, expert mountaineers. At least I hadn't professed to know everything about a water level.

An hour or so later, with my stomach in knots from laughing, it was established beyond any reasonable doubt that my piles were two inches out. 'Well, Brown, you bastard, you were right for once,' I admitted grudgingly as Joe smirked in an 'I told you so' sort of way. 'I'll have to do some cosmetic surgery with Portland cement.'

At eight o'clock the next morning, *Fran* glided like a portly gondola into the now placid waters of the bay and Kenny dropped anchor a short distance from shore. What had been a trial by wind and water on Saturday was now a balmy sojourn in the sunshine.

By midday, the logs were stacked in their designated lots, and Kenny and Richard set off for half a day's fishing. It was typical of them to go to all this trouble to help me out, and it was the same with Joe and all the others who mucked in. In years gone by, it had been a Highland tradition for the whole community to build a new house for one of the clan or tribe. As part of the ceremony, the men would try to toss the final ridge pole or caber, but Eisean Dubh's was, unfortunately, too long and too heavy.

After a brief lunch, Joe and I contemplated the raw materials of the building. It was difficult to imagine that this pile of timber would soon be transformed into a cabin. We were looking forward to getting to grips with our Lego kit.

Brown was a hard taskmaster. There was no knocking off to watch the seals or other distractions, and I considered myself lucky if I was allowed to make the odd brew. Even then, it was a guilty gulp and back to hammering and heaving until the sun, glowing red, hovered over the western horizon like a beacon before dropping, as if making an emergency landing, on St Kilda in the distance.

I hadn't enjoyed myself so much since playing with my first Meccano set when I was a kid. Joe had to go back home to Llanberis in North Wales the next day, so we kept hard at it. By the time he took his weary leave, we had the walls completed and the roof trusses in place.

Shortly after Joe left, Mo Anthoine and his wife Jacky arrived to help out. Mo had bought a church near Achnasheen, close to where Jackie the Milk lived, and had converted the building into an ice axe factory. Mo probably had the most interesting life of any mountaineer I know. He had been down and out in India, roamed the Australian outback, and had driven to the Himalayas three times. Together with Joe, we had shared several Amazon trips, one accompanied by his wife, Jacky, who was also an accomplished climber. Her delicate, almost china-doll frailty belied a tough nature. Capable of hard climbs and hard work, she proved to be a good site labourer.

'Hiya, cock.' Mo's greeting echoed round the bay.

'Hello!' I straightened with relief. 'The Lord of the Flies has departed.' This was a reference to Joe, who had in the past been dubbed 'The Human Fly' by the popular press. 'He left me with a building blunder, though. Wait till I see the swine. Thanks to his wrong measurements, I've one end of the roof overhanging more than the other!'

Mo cast a critical eye over the structure. 'Not bad,' he conceded. 'But I'm surprised you let that bugger Brown anywhere near the place.'

I told him about the water level fiasco.

'I offered it to you about six months ago, you idiot,' berated Mo.

I thought that the water level had sounded familiar when Joe suggested it.

One thing I discovered about log cabin construction is that walls can compress as much as 50 mm, and you have to allow for this when installing doors and windows. Mo and Jacky had just left, and I was kneeling within the door frame on two floor joists when I heard an ominous creak before a heavy section of larch hit me on the base of the skull, propelling me between the joists and depositing me at the base of a pile. The next thing I saw was an extreme close-up of my cement handy work. I realised that I must have been knocked out for some time when I looked at the clock that rested on top of my toolbox. The Whites called by an hour or so later with some fresh bread, but I was too shamefaced to tell them of the incident. Later, after my tea, I fell unconscious on the kitchen floor.

Not long after this, I headed back home to Glencoe to stock up on provisions. One day, a distressed motorist came over to my house to report that he had hit a sheep on the nearby road. The black-faced ewe lay inert, a newborn lamb bleating alongside it in some distress. I tucked the struggling orphan under my arm and went back to the house. After several attempts, I succeeded in bottle-feeding the creature, for it was obviously hungry. I knew the owner of the unfortunate sheep was already feeding several lambs whose mothers had met with a similar fate, and when I next saw him, he suggested that I become a foster parent.

Daisy, as I named her, thrived and ate into my daily routine. She had a voracious appetite and followed me like a white shadow. I had to shoo her into the garden or the back porch, where, when she wasn't attacking her bottle like a jousting knight, she bleated her head off.

This additional family member created logistical problems. What would I do with Daisy when I had to head north to work on the cabin? The answer was simple: she followed me everywhere anyway, so she would come with me.

Daisy settled into the car journey north like a seasoned traveller, and was unperturbed by my habit of going as fast as possible between two points on four wheels. Her slightly damp fleece gave off a comforting odour, reminiscent of the woollen Dachstein mitts I used for winter climbing.

Parking at a remote layby, I took an alternative route to the cabin over a pass. With Daisy trotting happily beside me on a makeshift lead, I forded a stream between two lochans, and was soon looking down at the expanse of Loch Torridon. I had decided to take this clandestine route as I didn't want to be seen in Diabaig, my usual way in, with a sheep on a lead. Memories of livestock rustling could still be lingering.

Upon arrival at the cabin, I untied Daisy and she took up position on the veranda, philosophically surveying the ocean as she patiently chewed some indigestible fragments of vegetation. Over the next day or so, she took no interest in my cement mixing and sawing but diligently munched seaweed and appeared to be enjoying her holiday. I hadn't noticed that this new diet affected her bowel movements, and it was only when we were speeding home to Glencoe along single-track roads in the dark that the smell in the car seemed more pungent than usual. When I stopped, I discovered that the rear of the estate car was awash with green slimy gunge and Daisy's behind was the colour of kelp.

Sadly, Daisy's preoccupation with food was to be her downfall, for some months later, she was found dead by the roadside, not far from where her mother had met her fate, after overeating the fresh spring grass. I dug a grave for her a short distance from where she had been born and made a cross with some scrap aluminium alloy from an old stretcher runner on which I stamped her name.

Some time later, at the same spot, a buzzard was pranged by a passing car, and the driver came to my door holding the unconscious bird by the legs and neck. A wise precaution, for the predator was armed with vicious talons and an intimidating beak.

'Can you relieve me of this eagle, sir?' he entreated in a broad Glaswegian accent. 'It hit my windscreen.'

I took the offering reluctantly, muttering that my house seemed to have been designated the local veterinary clinic.

'It looks in a bad way,' I observed, peering into its hooded eyes. 'I'll try egg and brandy. I was once told that is a good pick-me-up for sick animals.'

'Buzz', my new lodger, was indeed revived by the cocktail and occupied a perch on a chair in the back porch. I splinted his broken leg and wing with a strip of plastic I cut from an ice cream container and caught some mice for him, but he preferred brandy and egg yolk. I tried to release him a couple of weeks later, but he still couldn't fly properly, so I took him back to his favourite chair and he carried on devouring his three meals a day.

One glorious morning, I threw Buzz up into the air. For a few moments, he weaved about like a drunk driver and then soared—inelegantly, for he still had his splints on. I saw him a couple of days later high above the house and a streamer from his bad leg glinted in the sunshine, the remnants of the transparent tape that I had used for a bandage. I felt a certain satisfaction knowing that I had nursed him back to health.

Meanwhile, back at Eisean Dubh, trouble was brewing. Council planners had gotten wind of my Robinson Crusoe retreat. I heard through the grapevine that official looking men—i.e., people in green wellies with clipboards—had been spotted wandering the hills and asking questions about my cabin. The locals were non-committal of course, for there was a long tradition going back hundreds of years of marauding excise men searching for illegal whisky stills in the area. In fact, I had found an old still on my land that hadn't been used for decades. Anyway, I was told that members of the planning department had set off in search of my bothy and had gotten lost. Others had followed without success. They had asked some locals to supply a boat for a maritime solution to the problem but had been told politely that there were none available. There was even word that they were considering conducting a night search in the assumption that I would have lights on which would guide them. Then, a colleague of mine who ran a helicopter business was approached to assist, but he too was 'busy'. I was flattered that I had so many loyal friends, but disturbed about the fuss over my wee cabin, which had been built with good intentions and had now become an issue in the local community.

Eventually, a member of the planning department, who had taken a rowing boat and then set off on foot, found the place. In due course, I received an official letter:

'The Divisional Planning Committee take a very dim view of unauthorised development and the matter will be brought up at the Committee Meeting of 1 December, with a view to taking enforcement action...'

Fortunately, the climbing fraternity is all-embracing. George Ritchie, with whom I had climbed over the years in both the Alps and Caucasus, agreed to help. He had recently retired as Deputy County Clerk for Midlothian and was well versed in the niceties of planning law. The press, too, rallied and ran regular leaders in my favour.

One day, I met an old fisherman at Diabaig who lived close to the jetty. He didn't recognise me, but he set off on a long-winded monologue that meandered through the First World War, broody hens and herring fishing, before segueing into the local planning saga.

'That planning war with the climber chap. It's jest bureaucratic nonsense!' He stamped his welly boot, adding, 'One o' those officials, dressed in new-fangled oilskins and wi' a plastic map hingin' roond his neck. Ye'd think he was feart o' falling off the edge of the loch! Mind you, I'm sure he got lost as well as the others, looking for that wee place, for he came back drookit and clarted in mud. Anyhow, I widnae take him in ma boat. Sometimes in life, ye must take a stand. I told him the engine was being overhauled.'

'So you didn't take them round?' I asked, realising that here, too, was an ally.

'No' on yer life!' he exploded. Spitting with impressive accuracy at a floating twig, he added, 'The man has done a' that rescue work!'

I told him I was the 'climber chap' he was referring to. He looked me up and down sceptically and said, 'Ye're too auld-looking to be MacInnes!'

On the day of the planning inspection, George Richie and I stood sentry-like on the shore at Diabaig as the Planning Committee arrived in a beat-up boat propelled by an equally rickety outboard motor, an ancient-looking mariner at the helm. Dropping our tools, we wiped our muddy hands in the heather and walked slowly down through the rocks to the edge of the slip like a scene from a western showdown. However, the negotiations progressed in a civilised fashion, and I kept my mouth shut in case I put my foot in it, leaving the negotiations to George. Expecting a shack, the officials were impressed with the bothy, and eventually agreed that I could apply for a change of use for the building so that I could legally sleep there. The meeting was concluded to everyone's satisfaction.

'Well,' I said to George as we climbed back up from the bay at sundown and headed for home. 'At least they can't put a restriction order on this superb view.' We had just crested a small pass, and we paused to admire the sublime sunset. The Cuillin mountains were etched red against the dusky sky and to the north and west lay the flotilla of the Outer Hebridean islands.

Joe Brown returned north once the building was more or less completed. Acting as plumber's labourer, I witnessed the transformation from basin and bucket to the comfort of bath and toilet. The space was really something, and on my next visit, I moved in. I now had a bottled gas cooker installed, which was a real luxury after the primus stove but came with its own risks. Once, when I was engrossed in some building task, I inadvertently left the gas supply valve on, as well as one of the burners on the stove. Absent-mindedly, I returned inside for a belated cuppa and struck a match, whereupon I was blown across the cabin and landed spread-eagled on the Douglas pine wall with an almighty thud. My beard, hair and pride were badly singed.

This misadventure brought to mind my good friend of many years, Chas, who also helped in the planning and building of my log cabin paradise and had an uncanny ability to attract problems with comedic value.

Chas had been house-sitting one evening for friends who lived in a large Victorian pile in an area of Glasgow that was more no man's land than a residential neighbourhood. (It was later bulldozed to ground zero.) The street was invariably in a state of gloom at night, for as soon as the lightbulbs were replaced, they were either smashed or stolen.

Nipping out to the local corner shop for groceries, Chas naively used only one of the four locks on the door, and returned with his loaf, butter, sausages and bacon to find the door ajar and the house in darkness. Sensing a human presence, he flicked on the hall light to reveal three thuggish-looking men. There was a pause, then all four exploded into action. Chas, still clutching his groceries, and the three burglars all jammed in the doorway. In the melee, the food was scattered over the stairwell and the three intruders bolted.

Eventually, two policemen arrived with a look of weary resignation; this probably happened a dozen times a day in that neighbourhood.

Triumphantly, Chas presented what he considered to be an important clue in the form of a flattened pack of butter with a perfectly preserved footprint embedded in it. The detectives were unimpressed.

'I dinnae think this will help with oor enquiries,' one of them observed dryly.

Back home in Glencoe, my Search and Rescue Helicopter pals still dropped in regularly for tea and biscuits. One day, I gestured to the lumpy sofa one of them was perched on and mentioned that I hoped to move it north to Eisean Dubh.

A few weeks later, I had a call from the helicopter squadron. 'Hi, Hamish. We've been thinking about your removal problem, and we may have a solution.'

'Go on...' I anticipated a humorous suggestion, such as a funeral pyre.

'As you know, at this time of year we're at the end of our fuel allocation for the aircraft.' He paused. 'Unofficially, we have to use this up, or it may be reduced in the future. We're keen to carry out some extended reconnaissance in Torridon, so we thought we could drop your furniture off en route. You know the size of the Wessex cabin, Hamish. It should take most of your chattels.'

Fantastic!

Some weeks later, I had the furniture assembled alongside the helipad at the house in Glencoe. It was a spectacular morning, with a low sun shimmering through the glen and just a hint of frost.

After a late breakfast, we packed everything into the large yellow canary. There was barely room for me to squeeze inside, and I had to sit on a rocking chair, which fortunately had a view out of the fuselage window. The Wessex buzzed like a heavily laden bumblebee northwards. From my lofty position, I decided that the ragged Highland coastline studded with jewel-like islands amid a glimmering sea was one of the most beautiful places on Earth.

By midday, we were circling the bay at Eisean Dubh. 'What now, boys?' I enquired over the intercom, realising that there could be a landing problem. Donald, the winchman, had the large fuselage door open and was studying the uninviting boulders below.

'I think we'll have to go up the hillside a bit to that first loch, Hamish. Let's have a look.' The big machine rose, flattening the heather with its

Not your average furniture removal van: Hamish onboard the helicopter

downwash. On the margin of the loch, the skipper landed the Wessex expertly and cut the engines. We were enveloped in silence.

I tried to work out how we were going to move everything from here, for there is a steep descent to the bay and it wasn't exactly conducive for manhandling furniture, with waist-high heather, bog myrtle, hidden boulders and holes, all on a slope of about 30 degrees. Then there was that millstone, my old settee. I was, however, instructed to relax and allow the newly appointed furniture removers to finish the job.

'We have an undertaking to complete this flitting for you, Hamish,' Donald declared as he hoisted the rocking chair onto his head and staggered off down the slope. The rest of the crew, in their heavy dry suits, approached the task as if they were attending a national disaster.

It must have taken a full hour to get the settee down, and it threatened to demolish the cabin at one point. By late afternoon, however, all the furniture was installed and the place was transformed. The crew were both sweating and exhausted after their efforts, and after a break on the veranda and several gallons of soft drinks, I locked up and we made our way back to the Wessex for the trip home.

The long haul of building Eisean Dubh was finally complete. From now on, I could enjoy the solitude and the sea with friends. It is a very special place.

Once the cabin was completed, I was inundated with visitors at Eisean Dubh, including a film crew who shot a sequence with two men in full Highland regalia jumping off a cliff for the Hollywood blockbuster Highlander.

'I'm a Jaguar man'

The summit of Ben Nevis

28. CHICKEN IN A BASKET

During my time filming *Outside Broadcast* for the BBC, I became good friends with the director, Mike Begg, and he was one of the many generous souls who helped me build my log cabin at Diabaig. Tall, laconic and devastatingly witty, underneath his tough exterior Mike was a warm-hearted iconoclast with a penchant for madcap schemes. He had an idea for a new feature for the programme and had persuaded Clive Gammon, a writer for *Sports Illustrated* magazine in New York, to cross the pond and take part in a wager with me to hot air balloon off the summit of Ben Nevis, the highest point in the British Isles.

The rules of the wager were simple enough: we would lift off from the summit of The Ben, one after the other. The winner would be the first to land, pack up the balloon, run to the nearest pub within a 50-mile radius and crack open a bottle of champagne. It would make for great telly.

Of course, air space is strictly controlled in Britain and you can't just hire a couple of balloons and float off the nearest mountain, so we needed bona fide pilots for the task. I'd spent a lot of time on The Ben and I knew we'd be negotiating cliffs, snow and most likely incessant gales and cloud cover—the place has an average rainfall of 171 inches. I didn't reveal this to Clive, however, who had visions of rolling fields, lazy days and wicker hampers replete with goodies, but had nevertheless arrived in Glencoe armed with a carton of tranquilisers.

Mike was a proponent of trying for himself whatever stunt was required for his latest broadcast, and over the years I had seen him swinging perilously under an overhang when there was some balls-up with ropes, or scrabbling up a greasy rock face after an all-night bender in a dank West Highland pub. During Mike's practice flight, his balloon had crashed into two fences and hit a ditch just shy of a high voltage power line. When we heard about this, Clive and I exchanged nervous glances, but neither of us wanted to be the first to back out. Sipping a malt whisky during our pre-flight sortie in the local pub, Mike said wistfully, 'Do you remember that earl who was fined last year for firing his shotgun at a balloonist who was disturbing his shooting party?'

After a recce to the summit of The Ben, the conditions were described as 'marginal'. But the helicopter pilot was lined up to take Rod Stewart on a fishing trip later that week, so the following day, Friday the 13th, was our only window.

The morning dawned bright and clear. A gentle zephyr wafted sulphur dioxide emissions from the nearby pulp mill. We arrived early at the landing site at the base of the mountain, and within an hour everyone was on the summit. Myriad peaks, lochs and seascapes surrounded us: a rare spectacle in a place usually smothered in thick cloud. I was almost looking forward to this challenge, but while I wasn't afraid of roaming around above the mountains, I did have a fear of landing in the sea. Clive, on the other hand, was worried about the cliffs and had bought a pair of 'high-altitude' boots for £15 from Woolworths in the hope that they might somehow secure his safe passage.

We were issued crash helmets and lifejackets to assuage our fears. I noted that the lifejackets were made by a company called, bizarrely, Frankenstein and Sons, and Clive's helmet was inscribed with the names of all its previous owners, each one carefully crossed out so that the ancient headgear resembled a small war memorial. What the hell had I got myself into? Neither of us had set foot in the basket of a balloon before and here we were, about to risk life and limb for the sake of light entertainment. Clive's hand shook as he lit another cigarette.

The press had arrived from Glasgow, weighed down with cameras and the cynical expressions of men accustomed to suicides. I was sure that nothing short of the contestants' blood soaking into the peaty ground of Lochaber would pique their interest.

After last-minute preparations, my pilot let off small helium wind-indicator balloons, which rose gracefully in the pleasant breeze like offerings to the Aeolian gods. Cameras rolled as the ungainly contraption sprang into life, shook and strained at its nylon leash. Gloves, Frankenstein lifejacket and helmet were donned, and I was aboard at last. The burners roared inches above my head, the nylon tape snapped, and the balloon was suddenly dragged across snow, rock and finally off the cliffs of The Ben toward Glen Nevis, 4,000 ft below. The cheers suddenly died away, and someone gave a small shriek as my balloon began to plummet as if two giant hands had slapped its sides. As I hurtled toward the abyss, I contemplated the feasibly of jumping upward at the moment of impact, but the thought of being cremated by the burners had even less appeal than slamming into the shoulder of the mountain.

'Give me a hand, Hamish!' yelled my pilot. He should have broken out the parachute before take-off for more lift, but instead, he had done this when we were airborne. We had lost so much air that the flameproof material of the tube leading above the burners had collapsed and they had stopped shovelling air into the balloon. After hasty alterations, the massive burners re-engaged and we began to ascend once more. The pilot's face was coated in a sheen of cold sweat. Even in my ignorance, I realised it had been a close call.

Getting ready for take-off

As we disappeared from view, Mike, never one to miss an opportunity for thrilling footage, sprinted across to one of the helicopters to see if our impending crash could be caught on camera, but the focus suddenly shifted to Clive's balloon as he and his pilot prepared for take-off. Clive had begun to climb gingerly into the basket when a gas leak ignited. Then the balloon broke one of its tethers, although, fortunately, this time there were two tapes instead of one. Clive hastily retrieved his singed leg and fled across the summit plateau as the pilot, whose flameproof flying suit afforded him some protection, grabbed a fire extinguisher and managed to douse the flames before they licked any closer to the large propane cylinders.

Despite the glut of film equipment and crew to hand, neither of these dramatic episodes were captured on camera, except for some footage of my balloon disappearing like Halley's Comet around the mountain. After my brush with death, my balloon drifted without event, and boredom set in as it became clear that there was no longer a wager to be won. We descended into Glen Nevis and landed with a thud. Reconvening later in the nearest pub, Clive and I called it a tie and agreed to split the winnings from our first and last hot air balloon flight.

29. JAGUARS IN GLEN COE

I had been asked to advise on a promotional film for British Aerospace to show what their Jaguar fighter jets were capable of. For the purposes of research, I contacted my friends in the RAF, with whom I had a close relationship through my involvement in search and rescue, and I was generously offered a supersonic flight over the North Sea in a rare two-seater Jaguar fighter. I was ignorant of the rigmarole I would have to go through beforehand: the fitting of the helmet took hours, and then there were the complications of the ejector seat and oxygen masks, although I was well versed in the latter from my Everest expeditions.

'Have you ever been upside down in an aircraft, Hamish?' asked the pilot once we were airborne.

Before I could reply, we were inverted, and the purpose of a g-suit quickly became apparent to me. Although this is used to avoid blackout, the pilot told me he didn't always bother with it unless he was engaged in violent, negative g-force manoeuvres during dogfights. I glanced nervously to see if he intended to deploy his g-suit now.

The British Aerospace crew had their own film unit, and after a lengthy discussion with them, I outlined a tentative plan: a slalom up Glen Coe at full throttle. Our venue seemed to fit the bill, although I recall that several kilograms of weight had to be removed from the craft to avoid collision with the 3,000-foot rhyolite wall of Aonach Dubh.

In mountain rescue, we use small hand strobes to pinpoint our positions, and I spent a day scrambling around placing five of these strobes at key positions to indicate the flight path. This was then inspected at a 'sedate' speed by one of the Jaguar pilots who deemed it feasible, so, with another rescue team member, I scuttled along the line of strobes and flicked them on.

The fixed cameras were to be remotely controlled by the film crew, and the jets had cockpit cams to record both g-force and air speed. After a final check to make sure everything was in place, we were ready to go. Above the hum of the radio channels, we heard a distant roar as three Jaguars thundered toward Glen Coe. I fled down the steep slope toward a surprised-looking herd of red deer and hunkered down on the wet grass with my hands clamped over my ears. The din increased to a crescendo as the jets passed immediately overhead and tore down the narrow glen. It really was the most alarming and surreal experience. Then, only the sound of the static of my walkie-talkie as a crisp voice stated with military efficiency: 'Thanks to all, we've done it.'

I didn't see the footage until several years later when I was browsing on Google. There was the complete film, all four minutes of it: cockpit cut-aways, the approach and the sharp left-hand turn. It was such remarkable footage that British Aerospace had won a major contract to provide Jaguars for the United Arab Emirates.

Hamish and the Jaguar

Glen Coe © Dave Cuthbertson

Filming the *Highlander* sword fight on top of the Cioch

30. KILTS, CLAYMORES AND CAMERAS

The Australian film director Russell Mulcahy was eager to find some dramatic locations for his forthcoming film, *Highlander*, and contacted me for advice. I had worked with top helicopter pilots and cameramen on the popular BBC production *Where Eagles Fly / Skye High*, and on a crisp autumn day, we had filmed a kilted piper playing on top of the vertiginous Cioch Buttress on Sròn na Cìche in the Skye Cuillin, a place renowned for its classic rock climbs on excellent gabbro. The whole place had been alive with climbers silhouetted against the sky and the skirl of the great pipes ricocheting around the cirque of Coire Lagan. We had raised the standard of aerial photography at the time, and it was my trump card. When *Highlander*'s director and lead actors Sean Connery and Christopher Lambert saw this footage, they knew it was just what they were looking for.

Our caravan of cast and crew first headed to Ardnamurchan on the West Coast of Scotland, for I had intimate knowledge of this wonderful coastline, and it had already been eyeballed from the air by the director. This spot is a Mecca for geologists, and its ring of gabbro hills is known as the Great Eucrite, a sort of full stop on a great seismic chain denoting a violent volcanic history. Crofts perch here and there amid the precious machair, and the place still has a wild and remote feel to it.

We were just about to start filming when I heard a shout and saw a stout figure barrelling toward us. This idyllic white beach was under the jurisdiction of a displaced Welshman who proved as stubborn as any native Highlander.

'You will not be coming over this sand with yer fancy buggies,' he declared, 'and even, I'm told, a bloody stag!'

This was a significant setback, for we were now committed to using the site. Eventually, after much debate, the irate Welshman conceded, 'Well, I see Mister MacInnes is with you. I'll put it in his hands. Whatever he recommends, I'll abide by it.'

Appointed chief arbitrator, I suggested only foot traffic to the beach through the protected machair, minimum crew and, most importantly, suitable compensation for the crofter. The proposal was duly accepted by all, and the now amenable Welshman produced binder twine and a bundle of stakes as the crew prepared their gear. Virtually the whole beach would be in shot, and out west, the small isles of Rùm, Canna and Eigg rising out of the turquoise sea provided a stunning backdrop. With the cast in their period drag, and the dogs, geese, goats and Highland cattle, we felt transported back to a bygone era.

The film *Highlander* chronicles an age-old war between immortal warriors, interweaving past and present day storylines. The director wanted to depict a violent switch from one century to another and asked if I had any ideas.

'Leave it with me,' I said. I had long standing connections with the military through my time in mountain rescue, and I arranged to make contact with the boss of an aircraft carrier currently engaged in a NATO exercise nearby.

When I spoke to the carrier chief over my mountain rescue radio, I casually asked if he could supply two of his supersonic rocket jets for the movie. There was barely a pause before he replied in a cultured naval accent, 'Okay, what's the score?'

'Can you buzz in with two of your supersonic Marine Harriers as low as possible over the heather in Glen Coe? It's to take Connor Macleod back to a new century.' Naturally!

'Hmm, well, I can only divert them for a few minutes, Hamish; we have a big manoeuvre under way.'

And just like that, it was arranged. I set off with a small camera crew for the rendezvous in Glen Etive. I gave the lead pilot a map reference and he said they were on their way. The cameraman crouched in position in anticipation and gave me a withering look as I suggested he brace himself.

A crackle on my radio accompanied the roar of the incoming aircraft. Having previously flown in an RAF Jaguar, I knew the thrill of being in the vicinity of such a supremely powerful machine. The ground vibrated as the Harriers approached at what seemed like head height, and the cameraman tumbled into the bog with the slipstream. With afterburners working overtime, the supersonic jets rose vertically, well above 3,000 ft, leaving ribbons of smoke in their wake.

The boss pilot's voice crackled over the radio. 'Did you get that?'

'Sorry, no. I think the cameraman just soiled himself. Can you do it again?'

'Right you are, but we've got two minutes.'

'Great,' I shouted into the mic.

The cameraman extricated himself from the mire and, now sodden with filthy bog water, sheepishly reorganised himself and his camera.

Another deafening roar, then success! We had the perfect shot.

The next day, we headed to the vertigo-inducing Cioch Buttress on Skye for the film's famous sword-fighting scene, which had been planned with Sean and Christopher down to the last detail. I had enlisted my old pal Paul Nunn, who was to accompany ace cameraman Tony Riley in a helicopter and help shuttle gear and cast up to the sloping ledge on top of the buttress. John Poland, a talented pilot with whom I had spent many bouncy flights, had taken the helicopter doors off to enable better access on this exposed platform.

A battle scene filmed in Glen Coe

Surrounded by a thousand feet of space, it was hairy, even for seasoned rescuers. Paul was fielding a large flight box containing an Arriflex camera onto the smooth gabbro shelf when it somehow became detached from the helicopter cargo hook and slid down Cioch Gully, where two unsuspecting climbers were making their way up the final pitch. The flight case narrowly missed decapitating them on its rapid descent, and in a panic, I rushed over to them as they topped out.

'Oh, we're so sorry if we've upset your film!' said one apologetically, seemingly oblivious of his brush with death.

Crisis narrowly averted, John offloaded his cargo and took off with Paul and Tony in tow, leaving me with Sean and Christopher. To mitigate the risk of one of them toppling over the edge, I had created short ankle loops from 2mm high-tensile steel aircraft wire, something that wasn't available in Britain at the time. The loops were painted matt black so they wouldn't show up on the wide screen, and on the bottom end I had attached alloy chocks, which could be jammed into cracks and act as anchors.

Despite these safety measures, it was still an intimidating place for non-climbers, especially when they were expected to wield large swords and leap around in a murderous fashion. The actors seemed sceptical about the integrity of the glorified shoelaces tethering them to the rock, but being consummate professionals, they took a deep breath, adjusted their plaids, and the surreal clash of Samurai swords began to echo around the crags.

The helicopter footage shots of the Cioch sword fight became famous among *Highlander* buffs worldwide, along with my photograph with a beam of sunlight highlighting the action—divine rather than digital intervention, I hasten to add.

Later, Sean Connery invited me to the opening of the new Scottish Parliament building, and we walked in procession down the Royal Mile as the crowds chanted, 'Big Tam, Big Tam'—his Auld Reekie moniker. We stayed in touch, and he enjoyed the dramatic setting of my house in Glencoe when he later came to visit me.

The cliff jump, filmed near
Hamish's cabin by the sea

Buachaille Etive Mòr, scene
of the Y-fronts rescue
© Dave Cuthbertson

31. Y-FRONTS RESCUE

Sometimes, the most memorable rescues are not the gruesome, visceral ones. The mind seems to have the ability to filter, or at least diffuse, memories of horrific sights and hours spent struggling up avalanche-prone slopes or running a gauntlet of falling rocks to look for buried, broken bodies. Only a few call-outs are fun, and the Y-fronts rescue, with its element of farce, is one that has stayed with me and that I recall with fond nostalgia.

I had enjoyed a glass of home-brewed silver birch wine before turning in one evening, which slowed my response a little when the telephone shattered my peaceful slumber at around 3:00 am. I knew before I picked up the receiver that it meant trouble. I was leader of the Glencoe Mountain Rescue Team at the time and well-used to receiving phone calls at any time of day or night, so the desk sergeant in Fort William didn't bother to acknowledge the ungodly hour as he told me that a group of climbers in Glen Etive had reported one of their party missing.

After a long hot day on the local crags, the climbers had allayed their thirst with a few pints of ale at the nearby Clachaig Inn before returning to their tents. One of the party, a 25-year-old novice climber called Dave, had stepped outside his tent to relieve himself in the early hours, dressed only in his underpants. When Dave didn't return, his companion looked out sleepily but couldn't see any sign of him. Eventually, she woke the others and they began to search the general area, to no avail. This far north, it doesn't really get dark in summer and Dave should have been fairly easy to spot, but they realised that it would be easy to miss someone lying amongst the heather or rocks, so they drove up to the Kingshouse Hotel on the fringe of Rannoch Moor and contacted the police. Hence, my wake-up call.

When we arrived at the layby where the climbers' van was now parked, the River Etive glistened in the moonlight and the heavens were aglow with myriad stars, as they often are when a large area of high pressure anchors itself over the Highlands. I have rarely seen such stunning clarity outside desert regions.

The friends were at a loss to explain Dave's disappearance, so we began a detailed search of the vicinity. We surmised that the missing man wouldn't get far without boots or clothing, for the pre-dawn air had a cold bite to it and the terrain isn't conducive to walking barefoot, other than on the main highway.

Above, to the west, the massive hulk of Buachaille Etive Mòr dominated the lightening sky, and on a hillock a short distance away, I could see the outline of a stag, like a cardboard cut-out, watching the proceedings intently. After a fruitless sweep of the area, we prepared for a thorough search of the river, speculating that the missing climber could have fallen into one of the deep, deceptively tranquil-looking pools, which had the beguiling appearance of quicksilver in the half-light of dawn.

We didn't think that he would have taken to the A82, as there was no civilisation to speak of for about 12 miles, and he hadn't turned up at the Kingshouse Hotel. None of the police or our team had spotted an underpants-clad apparition en route to Glen Etive, and it seemed unlikely that anyone would have stopped to pick up a near-naked man in the middle of the night. We all agreed, for the moment, that we would concentrate on the river, and as several team members were professional divers, they went off to collect their dry suits and air bottles.

By now, it was light, and the sun's heat was already intense as it drifted up over the edge of Rannoch Moor. The River Etive had a hypnotic effect as it meandered lazily through rocky pools that had been gouged out by the great ice cap, thousands of feet thick, that had covered Rannoch Moor aeons before. The divers could have spotted a one-pence piece on the bottom, such was the clarity.

Back-up rescue teams from various corners of the country, including SARDA, an RAF Sea King and a Wessex helicopter, were now arriving. With over 70 rescuers already assembled, we had set up a base and divided the area into search blocks, taking in the whole of the Buachaille Etive Mòr massif.

Within an hour or so, the helicopters, working on a grid search, had covered the large expanse of the east side of the mountain, but there were dozens of gulches and crannies where someone could remain undetected. However, being such a brilliant day, the hills were alive with the crunch of boots. A climbing party had reported seeing a solitary figure high above them early that morning as they made their way up Coire na Tulaich, the tourist highway to the summit of Stob Dearg, the first and most dominant peak of the massif. They confirmed that the man didn't appear to have much clothing on, but they hadn't thought this especially odd for, even on the north side of the mountain, it was already scorching hot.

If this was indeed Dave, it seemed remarkable, for to gain access to Coire na Tulaich from where the van was parked in Glen Etive required a hike along the A82. His alternative would have been to cut round the rugged base of the mountain and then, without footwear, climb the long escalator of the coire with its flint-like scree. This would have tested the soles of a fire walker, and it seemed a far-fetched possibility when Dave had a perfectly good pair of boots back at the van.

By now, there were over 100 rescuers on the hillside, most of them scantily clad and thereby resembling the elusive Dave, like some kind of lookalike contest. I had been pondering how Dave could have managed to traverse around Buachaille Etive Mòr then ascend Coire na Tulaich barefoot. According to the latest radio report relayed from the summit of the Buachaille, he had been spotted on top of the mountain at dawn!

I decided to call an old friend and expert in sports medicine, Donald MacLeod.

'Could there be a psychiatric explanation for his strange behaviour, Donald?' I asked.

'Yes, in certain circumstances someone with a specific mental condition, under medication and having consumed alcohol, could be more or less immune to physical pain and quite capable of taking an unusual hike.'

Although this theorising didn't help us much, it did put another slant on the dilemma.

At 1:45 pm, a man fitting Dave's description was spotted heading south to the second peak of The Buachaille, Stob na Doire. Members of the Glencoe Team who had ascended the long drag toward the summit ridge had fanned out across the eastern wall of the mountain, checking every depression and boulder field. Bob Hamilton spied a couple dressed in black motorcycle leathers, an even more bizarre sight in a heatwave than someone sporting only Y-fronts. Bob usually had a charmingly polite way of asking questions, but he somehow managed to frame his enquiry as: 'Are you wearing underpants?'

One of the men responded as if this was a perfectly common question to be asked on top of a mountain: 'If it's underpants you are after, there's a chap up above wearing only Y-fronts.'

Shortly afterwards, team member Ronnie Rogers, dressed only in white shorts, a rucksack and climbing boots, clocked Dave about half a mile ahead on the summit ridge, and he set off in hot pursuit. Ronnie's fleeting figure was then spotted by another member of our team, Peter Weir, who, from a distance, mistook Ronnie's running shorts for Dave's Y-fronts and also started running along the wide easy crest. (At this point Dave was out of Peter's sight, as he had dropped into a dip in the ridge.) David Cooper, a local businessman who helped the team from time to time in search operations, also joined in the pursuit, which now resembled a Keystone Cops sketch.

Ronnie, swiftly followed by Peter, David, and now Bob, eventually caught up with Dave and noted with relief that he appeared to be uninjured. Miraculously, even his feet seemed to be fine. Ronnie, ever polite, asked what he was doing.

'Having a shower—give me a hand!' came Dave's retort.

'Where did you spend the night?' asked the incredulous Ronnie.

'Oh, I had a terrible time,' cried Dave. 'Monstrous cats were going round all night; some of them had huge heads!'

Peter pointed out that Dave's naked back was an angry sunburnt red.

'Oh, yes. I slept in the snow last night as my back was burning,' said Dave.

A helicopter was fired up. The Sea King landed on the ridge close by and picked up Dave and some of the rescuers. On the way down to base, Dave, who had been given a headset by the winchman, told the crew, 'This is the best trip I've ever had!'

When the Sea King landed, Dave was checked over, but there was no sign of serious injury other than sunburn. I gave him the loan of a jacket and a pair of overtrousers for his flight to the Belford Hospital in Fort William, where he was treated for sunstroke and released later that day.

Hamish makes the jump

32. ACROSS THE DIVIDE

Over the centuries, much has been written about the 1692 Massacre of Glencoe, when 38 members of the MacDonald clan were slaughtered by soldiers under Archibald Campbell, the Earl of Argyll, for allegedly failing to pledge allegiance to the new monarch, William III of Scotland. The soldiers themselves had been hosted amicably by the MacDonalds for over a week prior to the killings, and the treachery of the attack is as infamous as its brutality. Dozens more MacDonalds, including women and children, would later perish in freezing conditions after their houses were torched by Campbell's men.

When the massacre began to unfold early that February morning at Achnacon, Maclain, Chief of the MacDonald Clan, was slain while still in his bed. Legend has it that his wounded son, Alasdair, requested that he be allowed to die out of doors and was summarily dragged out of his house to be executed by the King's men. Alasdair was a powerful man, and when he was pushed against the wall by the firing squad, he drew up his tartan cloak and threw it over the gathered redcoats' muskets. In the ensuing melee, Alasdair ran down to the river and escaped by making the jump of his life across the Achnacon Waterfall.

How much of this tale is true is moot. But, some 300 years after those tragic events, I decided to attempt the jump, just to see if it was possible. Since I'm a non-swimmer, it was no doubt a dangerous and foolhardy caper. The rapids at this spot are notorious, and beneath the waters are hidden hydraulics that can suck you into the undertow to almost certain death.

Anyhow, I calculated the risk, took a leap of faith, and lived to tell the tale.

I recently revisited my old house, Achnacon, after many decades—mostly to see the waterfall that had I jumped all those years ago. Even now I remain duly impressed, for it is a fair distance: some four metres across with a greasy, sloping landing no bigger than a paving stone the only alternative to the rapids below.

Tigh a' Voulin

33. JOURNEY'S END

After countless expeditions to far-flung corners of the earth with my pals, I had finally put some roots down in the far north of Scotland, and I felt a sense of contentment at the idea of settling there. When my homemade cabin was in the final stages of completion, I returned to my base in Glencoe and took on the mundane task of killing weeds. With a backpack and long spraying lance, I moved in arcs across the gravel like a latter-day peasant with a scythe. I have no recollection of what happened after that, but much later, I was found unconscious and face down outside the basement door. With much still to be done before I could finalise my move north, I waited until I was compos mentis again, and with true Calvinistic spirit, I went back to work.

My good friend Jimmy Ness, fellow mountaineer and chairman of the Lochaber Mountain Rescue Team, had been worried about my 20-hour days labouring on the house and my sporadic meals. He was also concerned about my safety while working alone on the roof and would drive from Fort William regularly to check on my safety precautions. Although he conceded my rope work was bombproof, Jim noticed that I had been behaving erratically ever since my weedkilling incident, and eventually he managed to persuade me to visit the Belford Hospital, where I was diagnosed with a urinary infection.

I was no stranger to hospitals, through my time in mountain rescue and after my extended stay in Edinburgh Royal Infirmary, when I had contracted gangrene after puncturing my leg on a rock whilst exploring the local sea cliffs. My post-weedkilling sortie to the Belford, however, was a different ball game altogether, although I experienced similar feelings of helplessness while lying prone in the hospital bed. I can remember only fragments of that unfortunate time and must rely on my hospital records and the recollections of my friends, particularly Sir Michael Palin, and other good Samaritans. There is no doubt that I was in a dire mental state, partly from the effects of the urinary infection but probably from the herbicide as well. This dismal period of my life lasted an interminable five years, during which time I suffered total memory loss and was virtually given up for dead. My older sister, Chrissie, was particularly upset when I was sent to New Craigs, an austere securely locked-down psychiatric institution in a remote part of Scotland.

Assessed as being a danger to the other residents—something I resented deeply after a lifetime dedicated to mountain rescue—I was sedated and put in a straightjacket. I felt as if I were destined for the scrap heap. In fact, although I was a bit tottery, my physical strength was still fairly intact, for even in my confinement I did daily press-ups. I had serious misgivings about my diagnosis and subsequent treatment, but I should emphasise that I found the nurses at both Belford Hospital and New Craigs wonderful.

Soon after my arrival, I was informed that I would be dining with other deranged internees to promote understanding and allow me to bond with my fellow inmates. The clinical setting of the dining room was at odds with the chaotic ambience of the place as the residents awaited their dinner. There was a lull in the pandemonium when the meal trolley arrived, then all hell broke loose, with spoons used as medieval catapults to send food flying everywhere, mostly in my direction. I had the feeling that they regarded me as an alien, which I certainly felt like. Then they began chanting my name, seemingly under the impression that I was some sort of messiah. After that unfortunate episode, I slunk away to the sanctuary of my room and made it clear to the staff that I would not be dining communally again. Thereafter, I had my meals in solitude.

Being sectioned is hard to comprehend, although at least at my lodgings at New Craigs I had a spacious private room and regular visitors. My grandniece, Jill Leighton, painted me a tranquil mountain loch scene in vivid colours, and this large canvas took pride of place on my wall. The painting had a mystic quality, and it transported me away from the present and gave me some reminder of who I really was.

I also had visits from some demented patients, harmless and in search of the treats my friends brought for me. One lady, possibly a retired athlete, would fleet silently through my unlocked door then sprint across the room to my snacks bowl. Grabbing a handful of goodies, she would shovel the lot into her mouth and beat a hasty retreat, now heedless of stealth tactics. I squirrelled what was left of my treats in a more secretive spot and was reminded of having to find ingenious caches for expedition food, away from prying beaks.

Sometimes in the evenings, when the cacophony subsided a little, one of the inmates, an elegant lady who had been a famous opera singer, would trill, in her still fine operatic voice, the sextet from *Lucia di Lammermoor*. It was one of my favourite operas, and I wondered if, as she glided by in her richly embroidered Chinese dressing gown, she imagined herself in her heyday on the stage at La Scala.

I was fortunate enough to survive all this, but I emerged from hospital a waif, weighing only eight-and-a-half stones. Some time later, I retrieved my hospital records and didn't recognise the person described therein. I felt as if I were reading an account of a stranger. My recovery, which seemed to startle everyone, can be attributed to the written, photographic and cinematic records I have kept of all my adventures and the many friends and colleagues I have had the good fortune to explore the world with. I immersed myself in these memories, and the pieces came back to me like ragged scraps of a map: exploits with the Creagh Dhu Club, youthful wide-eyed jaunts to the Alps, epics in the Himalayas and the Soviet Union, first ascents and countless rescues, with people of outstanding talent, character and integrity, and a few four-legged friends. Despite my advanced years, I can now boast of having almost total memory recall, dating back to when I was a young boy. I have lived in better times, but I am thankful to have been here before the advent of the digital age, when life seemed simpler and somehow more tangible. I am grateful for fast cars before speed limits and untrodden parts of the world with good friends to accompany me.

It has always been a long-standing ambition of mine to produce a magnum opus of a stature comparable to those late friends of mine, Tom Longstaff and Tom Patey. Alas! At the lowest point in my life, I was told by the doctors that I would never type again, yet here I am, adding the final touches to this weighy tome. Throughout these tales of knife-edge precipices, avalanches, the purgatory of high altitude, bug-ridden rainforests and hazardous movies is what might be called the 'character-building stuff' of life.

Horseshoeing 80-odd years into a single book has not been an easy task, as there seems so much to recount. Better late than never, I suppose, but it seems unfortunate that it has taken me so long.

Hamish MacInnes, 1930–2020

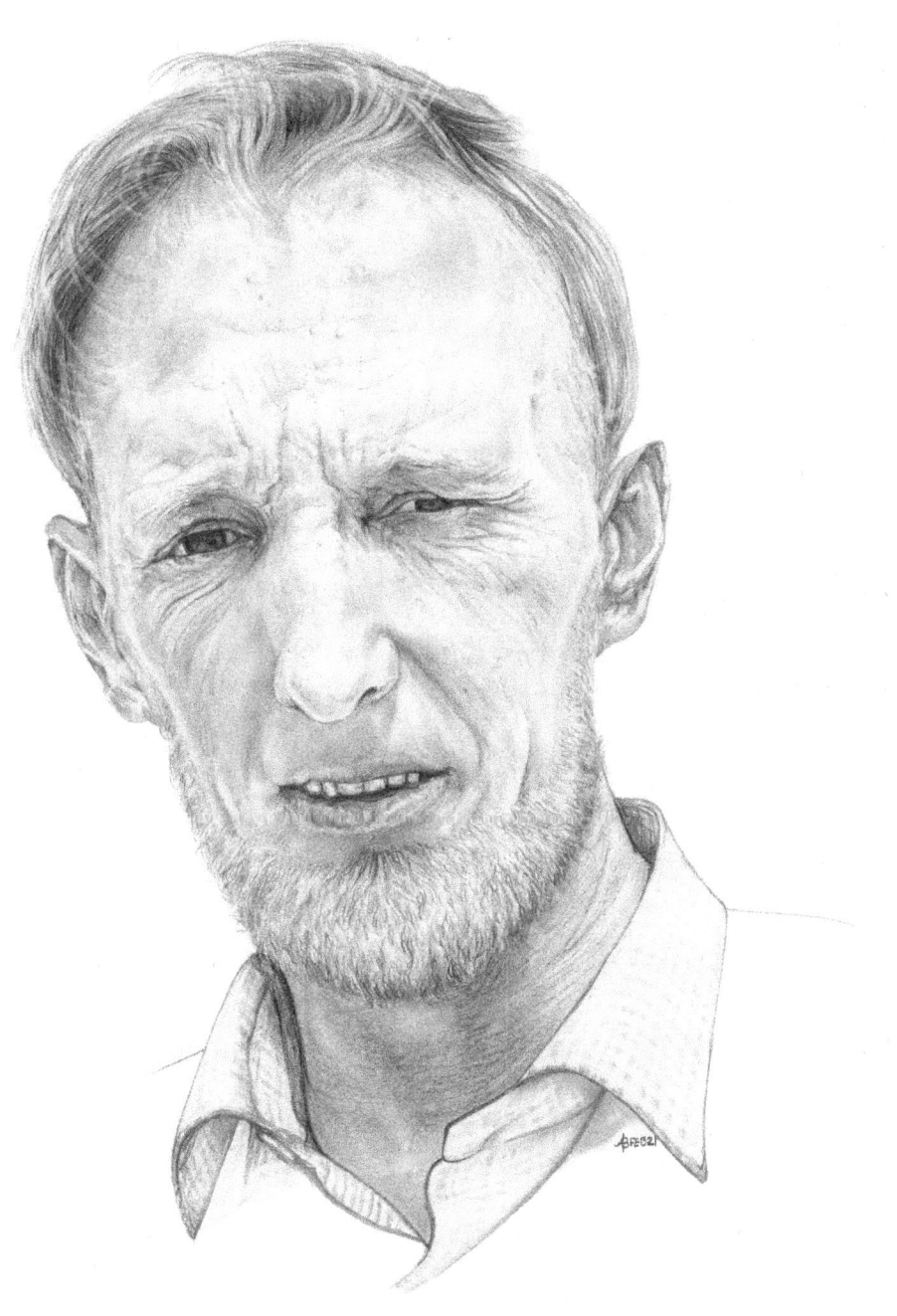

EDITOR'S NOTE

Despite never having met Hamish, I came to think of him as an old friend as I compiled these memoirs and sought to bring them to life.

Condensing such an illustrious history into a few chapters has been one of the biggest challenges I've faced as an editor. Few people cram as much into a lifetime as Hamish did, and trying to distil that into something digestible has not been easy. My initial tentative approach quickly evolved into something a good deal more ruthless as I sifted through several decades' worth of text and images, trying to decide which would best represent Hamish's many achievements and his multi-faceted personality. I reminded myself that a practical, unsentimental attitude would have chimed with Hamish's own. The result is therefore not a definitive history but a chronology of selected tales, both unseen and retold, that evoke the spirit of a remarkable man.

One of Hamish's defining traits as a writer was his ability to render perfectly in a couple of pithy sentences the hair-raising circumstances he often found himself in, and his recollections of harrowing events are often followed by comic asides. I've wondered if this was a deliberate attempt to thwart sentimentalism or just a reflection of his restless mind and perverse sense of humour. A little of both, perhaps, but it is an unusual quality that catches the reader unawares and one that has been crucial to capture to ensure that these manuscripts remain authentically 'Hamish'.

Working on such a large project has been all-consuming, and it is deeply satisfying to see the efforts of everyone who has been involved finally realised. This is, however, tempered by the regret that Hamish didn't live to see his memoirs published.

It would be impossible to name every individual who has contributed directly or indirectly to the stories in this book. That said, a handful of people helped document and breathe colour into these tales, and therefore deserve a special mention. Thanks go to Sir Chris Bonington and Sir Michael Palin for their heartfelt forewords; Graeme Hunter for his support checking facts, contacting people and pulling material together; Kenny Spence, Terry Gifford, Chris Lyons, John Cleare, Walter Elliot and the Patey family for supplementary prose; Alistair Borrett for original artwork; and Effie Tod, Sir Chris Bonington, Zoe Brown, John Cleare, Colin Monteath, Derek Sime, Dave Cuthbertson and Hamish Frost for additional photography that helped bring Hamish's stories to life.

PUBLISHER'S NOTE

As we bring *The Fox of Glencoe* back into print in this second edition, we'd like to acknowledge the generosity that continues to flow from Hamish MacInnes's life and work. The MacInnes Alpine Trust, established after his death, chose to pass its remaining funds to the Scottish Mountaineering Trust, which shares Hamish's desire to foster safe, lifelong engagement with the mountain environment. This often means something practical: pathways cared for, skills shared, rescue and safety supported, and opportunities created for those taking their first steps into the outdoors, or who would benefit from help to do so. We're grateful to both trusts for ensuring that this story continues.

All profits from Scottish Mountaineering Press books go to help fund the Scottish Mountaineering Trust, a Scottish charity that provides grants to projects and organisations that promote recreation, knowledge and safety in the mountains, especially the mountains of Scotland.

www.thesmt.org.uk